The Platypus Papers

Fifty years of powerless pilotage

Michael Bird

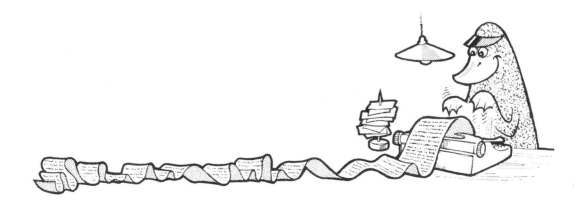

First Published in Great Britain in 2000 by
Platypus Publications
5 Glentham Gardens London SW13 9JN

ISBN 0953 8177 09

Edited by Michael Bird & Marion Barritt
Editorial consultancy by Barry Ketley
Design & layout by Sue Bushell
Illustrations by Peter Fuller
Cover design by Wendy Durham

Printed in Great Britain by
Hillman Printers (Frome) Ltd, Somerset

Distribution & Marketing (except in North America) by
Hikoki Publications Ltd
16 Newport Rd, Aldershot Surrey, GU12 4PB
tel: 01252 319 935
fax: 01252 655 593
e-mail: hikoki@dircon.co.uk
www.hikoki.dircon.co.uk/

Distribution & Marketing in North America by
Marion Barritt
1301 Windsor Court, Gardnerville, NV 89410, USA
tel: 1 775 782 7353
fax: 1 775 782 7353
e-mail: mbarritt@powernet.net

Editors' note
A large proportion of the cartoons no longer exist as originals, and have had to be scanned in from old copies of *Sailplane & Gliding*. We apologise for the fact that the customary pin-sharp quality of Peter Fuller's illustrations is therefore lacking in some instances.

To Alexander and Sophie

Acknowledgements

In addition to all the people named on the title page who have helped in bringing this book out, I must also give special thanks, in strict alphabetical order of surnames, to: Roger Quiller Barrett; Gillian and Bryce Bryce-Smith; Bill Craig; Ted Hull; Jane Reed; Dave Starer; Helen (Evans) and Nick Wall; and Gillian and Justin Wills.

One of their chief contributions was to help me decide what to keep in or throw out from a 40-year pile of writings. However they also supplied deep insights into the likely preferences of the readers of the book, as well as ancient photographs and even more ancient memories, and modern solutions to seemingly insoluble modern technological problems. I am eternally grateful to them all.

Platypus

Contents

Introduction by George Moffat

Lives there a reader of Sailplane & Gliding, *arguably the world's finest gliding magazine, who doesn't turn first to "Tailfeathers" – soaring according to Platypus, otherwise known as Mike Bird? In his column, month after month, Plat manages to cover the entire spectrum of the soaring world, always in forceful and satirically humorous terms. It's enough to make a fellow soaring writer green with envy.*

I first met Mike several years ago at one of the huge American soaring conventions where he turned out to be the superb main speaker, no mean feat when the after-dinner audience has been benumbed by endless awards presentations. On knowing him better it gradually turned out that he had another talent or two up has sleeve. Outstanding classical piano playing, for one. Not to mention a long and distinguished career in the publishing business. Titles like Editor, Publisher, Managing Director and even Proprietor abound, though he insists the last is on a very small scale. Oh yes, he does a bit of gliding, too. Some 4,000 hours' worth, with two back-to-back 1,000 km Diploma flights and lots of successful contest and record flying on several continents. Did I also mention vast depths of knowledge on a Renaissance man's gamut of subjects?

Leafing through a stack of Sailplane & Gliding *yields pieces showing the widest range of interests:*

The terror-inducing effects of Dick Johnson's flight tests on German glider designers. "Please God, let him stick it to someone else..."

The stirring cry of "Let's hear it for the leeches!" on the grounds that competitions would be down to five ships or less without them. Always the realist, our Plat.

The day he lost his virginity. I don't just mean aeronautically, either.

Wonderful and envy-making accounts of flying in exotic places, New Zealand, the USA, the European Continent. "The rain in Spain sprays mainly on my plane. Again."

The need to buy fine wines, grand pianos and new gliders to combat inflation.

The lack of any very deep nostalgia for the Good Old days of Gliding.

All these flattering things having been said, I'm sad to have to report that old Platypus is a bit of a fraud. You know his trademark cartoon alter ego, a bumbling, somewhat pot-bellied figure with a broad, innocent, duck-like bill, as drawn by Peter Fuller? Only the eyes are a give-away, with a crafty look at some passing female or one of fiendish glee if there's a chance to do the dirty on some competitor. Well, I happened to be flying with old Plat in a contest in Florida in spring 1999, and I am able to report that once the starting-line is crossed a Jekyll-Hyde transformation takes place. The broad bill narrows, the round eyes glint with steel and Lo! we have Plat the barracuda, terror of the skies! And jolly hard to get away from too.

What we have here is a man for all seasons who chronicles the soaring world with grace and wit. We are lucky to have him, and luckier still to have this book, bringing together the best of Plat.

Foreword by Platypus

These little pieces are based on articles I have written over nearly 40 years, most of them for Sailplane & Gliding. "Based on" seems pretty loose, but I have not been able to resist the temptation to tidy up stuff that was hurriedly hand-written, sometimes in airport departure lounges during fortuitous operational delays, and mailed to the editor at the very last minute. Indeed, some weird things I seem to have uttered years ago, before I got my first Apple in 1981 and started processing words, are simply mis-readings by the distracted editor of my artistic scrawl, which appeared in the magazine without correction, the author being by then several continents away. Naturally I have a right, nay a duty, to improve on the original.

In the hope that enthusiasts from other countries – and indeed people who are not glider pilots at all – might read and enjoy this book, I have explained things that all British pilots would take for granted. For instance, I shall decode incantations such as CBSIFTCB, the prayer before take-off, the careless omission of which is savagely punished by the Gods. I also needed to shed some light on names and events that have been forgotten by the old, or never heard of by the young. To meet that requirement has entailed some additions and amendments.

However I promise that where years ago I made some kinds of forecast, or issued clarion calls for change, which now seem way ahead of their time and uncannily prescient, I have not faked or fudged the record. Would I do such a thing? After all, it would be so easy for any of you to check.

In the magazine, whatever is said in one month's column doesn't have to take any responsibility for what was said in another month's. Each one stands alone. The apparent mood swings may be of interest to the clinical psychologist writing a thesis, but they often don't mean anything more than that, for example, it seemed fun on one occasion to play with the idea of a utopian future for our sport, then on another occasion to imagine a future that looks more like something out of Bladerunner *or* Alien 2.

Consistency is therefore one thing you should not look for in this book. I find I have contradicted myself all the time. I find that I said I would never again fly in the Alps, then just when everybody else felt it was safe to go to the Alps I was suddenly back there again. Well, as George's countryman Walt Whitman said, "Do I contradict myself? Very well, I contradict myself. I contain multitudes."

The period to which these pieces collectively refer covers most of the active history of British sporting gliding, especially if you take out the six wartime years when soaring was forbidden. There is a danger of this book being seen as a historical document, to be pored over by academics in hundreds of years time. However to treat this soufflé as a meticulous chronicle would be a grave error. These pages are my prejudices. If you are a serious archivist you had better read this in comfortable chair with the book in the left hand and a bag of salt in the right. Others, less pedantic and censorious, might prefer a glass of malt to a bag of salt: it is for the laid-back malt-whisky drinkers that this volume is compiled.

Platypus: a chronology

An old friend has suggested that a list of key dates in my life will help the reader put the following pieces into some sort of context. Here it is, heavily expurgated.

1934	Born Stoke-on-Trent, Staffordshire
1949	Gliding A Badge, Castle Bromwich
1954-7	Magdalen College, Oxford till 1957: gave up Logic & took up Politics as a better preparation for the real world
1958	Joined London Gliding Club, Dunstable
1958	Bought quarter share of Slingsby Kite 1 with Ted Hull and partners
1959	Completed Silver 'C' in open-cockpit Prefect, Dunstable-Membury 85kms
1960	First competition (Dunstable Regionals) with Geoff Kerr in Olympia
1960	Bought fifth share in aero-towable Cadet, restored by Peter Fletcher
1960	Editor of London Gliding Club Gazette till 1963: "Platypus" *nom de plume* invented
1960	Bought fifth share in K-7 with Peter Hearne and partners
1961	First time in Nationals, Lasham, League Two K-7 with Mike Riddell, R Q Barrett, M Broad
1961	New Skylark 3 with Mike Riddell
1961	Skylark 3 3rd in Northerns at Camphill
1962	First (and only one ever!) contest win, Northern Regionals in Skylark 3
1962	UK 100km goal speed record, Camphill-Ingoldmells at 116 kph in Skylark 3
1962	Firth-Vickers team trophy with Mike Riddell, Skylark 3, Nationals League Two
1963	First time in Nationals League One (Lasham) with the big boys in Skylark 3: sank without trace
1963	Married Janie Miller, two children: Alexander (1964) and Sophie (1967)
1965	Editor of World Championships daily newsletter, South Cerney, UK
1966	Bought new Dart 17R with Ted Hull and partners
1967	300km out-&-return for first leg of Gold Badge and Goal Diamond
1968	Became Director Odhams Magazines, then Publisher, Ideal Home magazine
1969	Gold 'C' height in cloud during Nationals, completed Gold Badge in Dart 17R
1970	Dinged (Dung?) Dart 17R in cricket field: first Plat-crash worthy of the name
1971	First soaring in USA: Black Forest Gliderport, Colorado, Schweizer 1-23
1972	First soaring on Continent: Zell-am-Zee, Austria, K-6e
1972	New Schempp-Hirth Standard Cirrus with Carr Withall and partners
1973	Janie and Michael divorced
1973	Bought new Slingsby Kestrel 19 with Carr Withall and partners
1974	Married Veronica Snobel (Mrs Platypus)
1974	First foreign contest: Huit Jours d'Angers in Kestrel 19
1974	Bought Kestrel 19, grand piano and 800 bottles of French wine; piano survives
1974	Bought the late Ray Stafford-Allen's Capstan
1975	Flew in Hahnweide contest in Schwabian Alps (Germany) in Kestrel 19: came 2nd two days, blew last day
1976	First 500km in Kestrel from Dunstable
1976	First Mrs Platypus pieces appeared in *Sailplane & Gliding*
1977	Only day win in 40 years, in Open Class Nationals, got delusions of adequacy, see next entry
1977	Wrote off Kestrel in landing (20%) and road wreck (80%) on last day of Nationals
1978	Bought half share of Nimbus 2 (refurbished by John Delafield) with Clive Hawes
1980	Diamond height, Nimbus 2
1980	Bought fifth share in Caproni Calif side-by-side two-seater with Tony Gibbs et al
1982	Became Managing Director Thomson Consumer Magazines (Family Circle etc)
1983	Bought into ASW-20L syndicate: Carr Withall et al
1985	Wrote first book: "The Time-Effective Manager"
1986	Veronica (Mrs Platypus) died of cancer
1986	Bought ASW-22 from Hans-Werner Grosse; became big wings addict. More TINSFOS!
1987	First trip to Australia: flew with Hans-Werner Grosse in his ASH-25 Tocumwal, New South Wales
1987	Second trip to Australia: flew with Hans-Werner Grosse in ASH-25, Alice Springs, Northern Territories on record attempts
1988	Bought new ASH-25.
1989	Navigator in ASH-25 at Lasham, when Robin May wins Open Class for second time (out of four wins in total)
1990	Entered semi-retired phase: began serious aviating
1991	British two-seat triangle 500km record at 131kph (with Reg Gardner) in ASH-25 Benalla, Australia, then 300 km out and return with G Dale
1991	World Championships – P2 at Uvalde with Robin May in ASH-25
1992	Third in UK Open Nationals with Ed Downham as co-pilot
1993	UK 750km Diploma in ASW-22 (same day as Robin May in ASH-25)
1993	First contest in USA: Minden, DG-300
1994	Fourth in Overseas Nationals at Leszno, Poland, with Marion Barritt in ASH-25
1994	John Good's "crew" at Hilton Ranch: flew Pegase, LS4, Grob 103, DG-300
1995	FAI 1,000km Diploma (twice in four days) from Minden, Nevada in ASH-25
1995	Fourth in (handicapped) Seniors Championships, Seminole Lake, Florida, with Marion Barritt as co-pilot in ASH-25
1997	First trip to New Zealand: flew Justin Wills's ASW-17
1997	With Barry Ketley, launched Hikoki Publications (military aviation history): 15 titles published up to March 2000
1998	Second trip to New Zealand: flew Justin Wills' ASW-17 (see Timaru Creek story)
1998	Bought "Zulu-Niner" Janus C, based Minden, Nevada with Tim Hirst and partners
1998	Safari: Nevada, Utah, Arizona in Z9 with Marion Barritt and Sam Whiteside
1998	Obtained Single-Engined power plane licence in Cessna 152 at NIFTI, Minden
1999	Ballast in Gavin Wills' Duo Discus in New Zealand Nationals
1999	For first time, Plat featured on front cover of *Sailplane & Gliding* (Oct-Nov).
1999	Second High Country Soaring safari from Minden: Nevada, Utah in Z9

Low hops and high hopes

One very good reason for reading history is make us stop complaining about the present. I am fiercely against sentimentality and rose-tinted reminiscence about the past. Our young days were great – in patches anyway – because we were young, that's all. For instance, the stuff I have heard about the joys of solo glider training and, indeed, its efficiency as a training tool, from people who should know better, just leaves me speechless.

Boys in blue (1999)

I got my 'A' badge with solo training in the ATC at Royal Air Force aerodrome Castle Bromwich in 1949. I only mention this very modest attainment in order to establish my right to talk grandiosely on the cover of this book of my 50 years as a glider driver. Somewhat to my disappointment, I discovered we weren't going to be bungied. I had devoured Robert Kronfeld's *Gliding & Soaring* and Terence Horsley's *Soaring Flight* ravenously since I was twelve. Castle Bromwich was dead flat – it's now blocks of flats, sad to say – and we were winched into the air. It was not the Wasserkuppe or Dunstable, where I was convinced they still did the real thing.

Another one of the gang was Keith Mansell, who was in the same year as me at school, and who is now the Treasurer of the British Gliding Association. Keith heroically owned up last year in *Sailplane & Gliding*, glittering organ of the BGA (and henceforth to be referred to in this volume as *S&G*), to having broken one Cadet. I am sure someone else broke another Cadet during that course. Not *cadets;* boys from King Edward's School, Birmingham were more resilient than anything that Fred Slingsby's best craftsmen could put together.

You could say that already we were learning the useful lesson that gliding, especially when taught this way, meant frustration and lots of waiting around. The next year the authorities banned children of our age from solo gliding, and raised the age limit from 14 – which remains the qualifying age in most other countries – to 16, so there must in that year have been accidents at other fields that damaged more than just airframes.

Yes, the ground-slides, low hops, high hops and eventually free flight, were exhilarating fun, but they didn't teach me to become a proper glider pilot, and it took a whole spring and summer of training at Dunstable nine years later to unpick the bad habits I'd acquired.

I sat on a massive sandbag which did double duty, simultaneously raising the cockpit load level with the minimum weight and raising my nose level with the cockpit combing, so I could see out. So far as I can recall there was nothing, apart from the friction of brown sackcloth against blue serge trousers, to prevent the sandbag sliding forward in a dive and jamming the stick in the full elevator-down position. Maybe I was saved by having built, trimmed, flown, broken and rebuilt so many model gliders in the previous five years that I knew what stalls and dives did to flying machines, had great respect for them, and managed to keep the nose more or less in the right place.

It is significant, I think, that Philip Wills did not learn to glide by doing groundslides, but owned a Monospar twin and other powered aircraft before he saw the light and dispensed with engines. However I do think this was not approved of at first, and he had to do some spectacular soaring to gain forgiveness for not having come up the hard way.

The groundslide and bungy method had one enormous advantage in Germany of the 1930's. It kept thousands of unemployed youngsters off the streets and out in *der frische luft* learning *der flugdisciplin* and all the other things they were to put into practice so very effectively a few years later. If our Prime Minister starts sending us free rubber ropes you'd better start digging that bunker.

Sheer bloody luxury (1986)

I'm sorry, but it's time for a limp down memory lane again. It was going to be a jog down memory lane, but for the third occasion in a row I've injured myself skiing and can barely walk: the thought of putting myself out of action for what could be a large chunk of the gliding season is too appalling to contemplate, so it's goodbye, snowy slopes, forever. (Did I just hear an audible sigh of relief from the snowy slopes and all who slide on them – and the Norwich Union insurance company?) May 12, 1958, is the 30th anniversary of my arrival as an *anfanger* at the London Gliding Club. There is supposed to be a commemorative plaque somewhere, but I've never seen it, so it must be in the ladies' loo.

Like a lot of young members at that time – and quite a few older ones – I first came up to the club on Green Line buses that meandered endlessly through leafy lanes to serve every village between Muswell Hill in north London and Dunstable. When the bus drivers went on strike I hitch-hiked or begged lifts with rich members who had wheels. The following year, for £3 a week I shared a flat next door to Harrods with a gliding crowd, one of whom had a car, so we pooled petrol costs and went up to the club every Friday evening regardless of rain, hail, snow, earthquake or landslide, and came back to London every Sunday evening. This was a rigid routine, which was only broken if Christmas Day fell on a weekend.

In 1959 I bought a quarter share in a 1930's Slingsby Kite 1 for £50; in 1960 a fifth of a Schleicher K-7 two-seater for £200. The bank manager lent me £100, cheerfully pocketing my life insurance policy as collateral. Finally,

with Mike Riddell as my partner, I acquired half of a brand new, state-of-the-art Slingsby Skylark 3f in 1961 for £675. It was in that year that I decided I could afford to learn to drive, and eventually in summer of 1962, more than four years after joining Dunstable, I got round to buying my first car. This was a 1958 Volkswagen Beetle, purchased primarily, if not exclusively, for towing gliders around the field and retrieving. It was a matter of getting one's priorities right, and no one thought it the slightest bit eccentric to own a top-of-the-range glider but no car. I can't imagine that order of priorities being applied nowadays. People turn up in shiny BMW's and complain they can't afford to glide.

On every single weekend day in 1958 there was ferocious early morning competition to get on the list for the T-21, so as to have a remote chance of getting more than the basic ration of three launches and creep a mite closer to going solo. The same dawn battle, coming close to blows, took place amongst the arrogant solo pilots on the Tutor – Mr Three Hours despised or at least patronised Mr Two Hours, just as snootily as Grunau pilots did the Tutor pilots. My fingers typed *Totur* in a Freudian slip just now. Torture well describes the ordeal of trying to soar from a series of 500-ft winch launches in the hope of finally getting 10 hours in one's logbook, so as to escape on to the high-performance Grunau Baby. To think about the appalling Tutor still makes me angry today because of the frustration and high drop-out rate it produced.

In the squalor of the bunkhouse nobody used an alarm clock, since that would have alerted everyone else and started a stampede, giving an advantage of two launches to the chap nearest the exit. However even one pair of eyelids cautiously opening would resound like a pistol shot, and the doorway would sud-

Did very basic repairs.

denly be jammed with bodies fighting to get to the bar where the list was kept. It was a Darwinian struggle for survival amongst a group motivated to the point of mania. Most people only got two weeks' holiday then, so there was no hope of escaping from the weekend treadmill to speed the date of going solo. It took a whole season and exactly 69 launches for me to go solo, and I wasn't a great deal worse than the average trainee.

I'd like to say all this poverty-stricken struggle was character-forming for everyone who joined, but I'm not at all sure about that. The desertion rate was massive, especially as the flying got worse, rather than better, after we went solo, the Tutor being vastly inferior to the T-21 as a soaring machine. (T-21s have done 100km triangles and height records; Tutors haven't, so far as I know.) However the fact that those that were prepared to stick it out lived every leisure hour at the club, not being able to afford time or money to be in any alternative place or indulge in any other pastimes, created a quite different climate from that which we have any right to expect today. We uprooted hedges to enlarge the field, we drove winches and did basic repairs on club gliders and equipment. Very basic in my case: laminating skids was my high point, after which they hurriedly removed the tools. When we were pooped at the end of the day we went to the members' kitchen and made our own meals. On the strength of having lived some months in North America I was voted the hamburger king, and my fellow members would not allow even women to interfere when Platypus was tackling the chopped steak.

The story of how I was formally stripped of my chef's hat, after blowing up the member's

kitchen with a vast superheated can of steak and kidney pudding sitting on a red-hot stove while I was oblivious at 3,000ft in the Kite, will have to wait till another day. By way of penance, I spent hours picking hundreds of metal fragments and specks of rock-hard, impacted steak out of the walls and ceiling with a wire brush. Even now I am shocked when I think somebody might easily have walked in at the *moment critique*. Thinking of nothing at all but gliding can be dangerous.

Works and Bricks Committee dug holes.

The fact that the members' kitchen is no more – not as a result of the pudding disaster – reflects people's ability in 1988 to pay for professionals to do everything for them, whether it is hamburgers or winch launches. And if you want home cooking – or any other domestic comforts – London today is only 45 minutes away by a motorway that didn't exist in 1958. We all have our own cars. The moment things look a bit boring we can take off – not into the air, but for the other pleasures that beckon.

A friend has pointed out to me that those awful discomforts were tolerated in the 1950's partly because all of the male recruits to the club had done National Service for two years, or had even fought in the War, and living in a cold hut with damp blankets and other people's smelly socks was something we were used to. (They say the reason British officers seem to have had such a whale of a time as prisoners in Colditz[1] is that the notorious prison was just like a typical English private school, except that Colditz had better food and nicer guards.)

The women's living conditions were even worse than the men's, especially in wintertime. Because of the relatively small numbers of female members, the women's blankets

---

[1] A replica of "The Colditz Cock" two-man escape glider actually flew in February 2000. If the prisoners who built it had been American it would of course have been called "The Colditz Rooster".

and beds might lie unused for weeks in a freezing hut. One January morning I was sent to knock up – sorry, arouse – sorry, awaken a lady winch-driver. In the half-light I could just discern a few sleeping forms in the women's dormitory, all under a dense pile of damp blankets. Above each form rose a cloud of steam, a ghostly pillar of white vapour drifting right up to the ceiling. It reminded me of Alfred Stieglitz's famous photograph of sweating horses at a New York tramcar terminus in the snow. Not what you can call a defining erotic moment in a young lad's life.

So there is not a lot of use in bewailing the loss of *esprit de corps*, sterling virtues, moral qualities etc in the modern generation; such considerations are irrelevant. The context in which we live is simply different, that's all. Leisure is a vast multi-national money-making industry, highly competitive and very professional. What was the alternative to gliding courses in the 1950s? Bicycle tours or Butlins holiday camp, not much else.

That the ten years after World War Two were austerity years is borne out by the account in Gliding (which shortly afterwards merged with Sailplane to give us our present magazine) of the 1951 UK Nationals. Only ten pilots had enough money to afford to fly a glider on their own: all the rest had to share gliders. How many team efforts do we see nowadays, even in Regionals? In terms of sheer hardware, at any rate, we are far, far better off.

To pre-empt a hail of mail from Tutor owners, I shall admit that if you can be aero-towed to 2,000ft then all sorts of possibilities open up. But that was not an option to early solo pilots in 1958.

The bringing down of Platypus (1986)

It is the doomed attempt in 1950-something to throw one more circle in the club Prefect downwind of the site that leads Platypus to a desperate, heart-pounding scramble back through the Tradesman's Entrance. There are no bad landings, only bad approaches. This one is terrible: no plan, just a wretched slipping and drifting, with not enough speed to round out parallel to the rough steep slope of the first bit of London Gliding Club soil that presents itself to the sweating tradesman.

"Tradesman's Entrance" is a very 1930s expression. In those days such signs were posted on the back gate, where a path led up through the kitchen garden to the cook's door of any typical bourgeois residence in the Home Counties. In the war, however, butchers and grocers made a point of coming instead to the front door, if they came at all, where they were treated like royalty by the lady of the house in hopes of getting a little something over the meagre rations of the period. Nowadays there aren't any cooks or maids, tradesmen don't deliver and the sign-makers, never short of something to extol or prohibit, have gone over to printing savage threats against smokers.

The fact that a hollow in the rolling Bedfordshire farmland adjacent to our field is called The Tradesman's Entrance would give away to a non-gliding social historian both the date of the London Club's origin and the type of comfortable citizen who could afford to glide. To have to arrive through this declivity, low and grovellingly slow, is proof of a cocked-up approach, poor airmanship and altogether the mark of a cad. By doing so you show yourself up as a member of the servant class, earning scorn and demotion.

Awful cracking noises as the skid decides it has just been turned into a ploughshare and prefers to chew earth rather than remain part of a rich man's toy. Daylight appears sudden-

There are no bad landings, only bad approaches.

ly through the cockpit floor. The other Prefect pilots give vent to their feelings. Whatever happened to the stiff upper lip? What sort of people are they letting in these days? he asks himself. He is grounded and dejectedly takes the bus to London, bereft of ways to amuse himself, so totally does soaring possess him.

Back in Chelsea he rings up girls with whom he had shared innocent passion when an undergraduate (what they now call a student). The mother of the first tells Platypus, with evident satisfaction, that Katie is getting married

Platypus takes the bus to London.

tomorrow, so there. Plat's call must have made her day. The next one is on the phone like a shot, however, and Plat explains how busy he has been with one thing and another. He has been busy with just one thing, if he is truthful. He asks her, despite the fact that she lives right over the other side of London, if she will come across. Which she does.

And that is how Platypus lost his virginity. (Look that up in the dictionary, too, you young people.) Mrs Platypus, whom sadly I did not meet till many years later, has given me permission to write all this on the tolerant grounds that I am no longer a serious hazard except as a pilot, and this is pretty well ancient history.

So when in her splendid piece in *S&G*, August 1976 (which he conceitedly and absentmindedly keeps taking credit for) she says to Platypus, "Gliding is a substitute for sex" and he retorts, "Nonsense, sex is a substitute for Gliding!" he is not throwing off an Oscar Wilde witticism. He is only stating what every glider pilot's wife knows to be the plain and sober truth.

Nostalgia and other diseases: an address to the Vintage Glider Club (1991)

Back in 1971 I worked for the world's greatest advertising agency. One day the boss asked all his bright young executives to write essays about the social and marketing trends of the future. I did not win the prize, though I felt then that I should have done, modesty always having been one of my weak points. I certainly feel now that I should have won it. I wrote that since everyone believed that things were steadily getting worse, the greatest trend of all would be nostalgia. "The past has a tremendous future," I wrote. If only I'd had the courage of my convictions and filled a barn with 1960s cars and stuff that people were paying the dustmen to cart away, like Victorian fireplaces, I'd be a millionaire now. Everyone is wild about classic bikes, old 78 rpm records – and who'd have predicted 20 years ago that in 1991 the citizens of Leningrad would rename it St Petersburg?

The trouble is that the nostalgia boom has encouraged pedants and authenticity bores; nit-pickers who are forever writing letters like this to the Daily Telegraph:

Sir,

Was I the only television viewer to be dismayed by scenes in last night's play, set in the year 1933, in which a naked couple make violent love on a train to Penzance? Does the BBC not realise that the Great Western Railway did not use locomotives of the 4-6-2 wheel layout on the Cornish peninsular? Moreover, the upholstery on which the two young men were exercising themselves bore the GWR monogram in black, though it is well known that it was woven in green until 1936, in which year it was changed to black as a mark of respect for the late King George V. It is this sort of sloppiness that has brought this once great country to the brink of decadence.

Yours Disgustedly,

Brig-Gen (retd) Q. Huffington-Bellows, OBE, Tunbridge Wells

This craze for authenticity is spreading everywhere. You can't perform Mozart on a Steinway nowadays; it has to be a 200-year-old *fortepiano* or a faithful copy, played in the original hall. They should go the whole hog:

the performers ought to wear wigs infested with lice, mice and other vermin, while expiring of tuberculosis, and the audience should talk loudly, eat oranges, spit on the floor, ogle the bosoms of each other's mistresses, and duel with swords in the interval.

Across the water, enthusiasts of the American Revolution make exact copies of 18th century muskets, and take special pride in using the same tools and methods as the gunmakers of 200 years ago, as well as grinding their own powder and casting their own shot. If one of them, dressed in 1776 uniform, should grind too vigorously or shoot himself in the foot, I trust that the well-regulated militia will not send for a helicopter full of paramedics, but will summon the local barber, with a blunt saw and a pint of gin – to anaesthetise himself, not the patient – and a bucket of hot tar to dress the stump. Accuracy in these matters of fine historical detail is all part of the fun.

Some years ago the legendary Walter Neumark, one of the most creative minds in our sport, made a meticulously exact copy of the glider in which Percy Pilcher killed himself in 1899. No, don't laugh. Walter not only adhered as faithfully as possible to the design, he took his Hawk replica to the original location of Pilcher's last flight, and re-enacted the method of winching himself up. The subsequent crash would therefore have been a totally authentic replay of Percy's fatal plunge, except that with the help of the electric telephone and motorised ambulance Walter got to the hospital quicker. And survived to fly again.

Some of the great cross-country flights done in vintage gliders today are achieved with the help of aerotows, and there is no doubt it makes all the difference. Is that authentic? Of course it is. There is a spectacular piece of film taken by Dudley Hiscox in the 1930's showing an Avro 504K towing a glider from the foot of the hill straight at the camera, which was fixed in the Dunstable clubhouse. What you can't see but can only imagine is the members, in their plus-fours and wing-collars, all diving under the tables as the two aircraft fill the screen and, in the last second, stagger over the dining room. Any attempt to replicate that today should take account of the 20ft or so of 1990's radio aerial on the 1936 roof.

The modern competition pilot is a totally different creature. What a contrast! The 1991 World Championships was an education to me, as a backseat observer in an ASH-25. The French team in particular – who conducted themselves with great gravity in the air and great levity on the ground – flew identical pairs of gliders as if tied together with invisible string, and talked incessantly to each other and their manager, giving their respective positions accurate to ten metres. It went something like this:

"Ou etes-vous, Jean-Claude?"

"Pas de problème, mon nez is right up votre derrière, Pierre!"

"Formidable! Je thought je had a confortable feeling."

And so on all day. The general rejoicing when, in spite of flying brilliantly in many weeks of practice, the French failed to win anything at all, was quite unseemly but very understandable. De la Rochefoucauld would have had a maxim to describe it. There is a theory that someone from another team cut a hole in the razor-wire that kept the Frenchmen in (or the Texas women out, whichever way you like to look at it) with a consequent loss of the drive and focus that a winning team requires.

Competition pilots seem to suffer from the four least attractive of the seven deadly sins – envy, avarice, anger and pride. (They are very intolerant of the more attractive deadly sins like sloth and gluttony, and take a pretty dim view of lust, at least during a contest, as being a distraction.)

The true contest pilot's aesthetic sense is zero. If you ask him as he hauls himself out of the cockpit, after a 600-km triangle in eight-knot thermals over dazzling scenery, "Did you enjoy the flight?" he merely snarls, "How do I know till I've seen the score-sheet?" Then he comes back from the scoreboard with a seraphic smile on his face. His nearest rival has landed at a sewage farm near the first turnpoint. It was indeed a beautiful day after all!

Whatever their other virtues, such as skill, courage and endurance, competition pilots don't display much love. They don't love the task-setter or the Met man. They certainly don't love each other. They don't love their crew, not even their wives and children, they just tolerate them for the duration of the contest. They don't love their gliders: the aircraft are just something to be strapped on your back, to be discarded as soon as something better comes along. That's why they don't give their gliders names any more than you would give your trousers a name.

What I had not noticed until a few minutes before speaking to the VGC was that it is called the Vintage *Glider* Club, not *Gliding* Club. They do love their aircraft. The most important instruction in music is not *allegro* or *appassionato* but *con amore* – with love. Only if you can play *con amore* are you an artist. If there are any artists left in gliding most of them will be found in the vintage movement. Long may they flourish!

I know one is supposed to flatter one's audience, but did I really say that? What a load of sentimental old codswallop! Everybody knows I much prefer to zoom along a cloudstreet with a bunch of other hooligans at 120 kts with the vario screaming its head off. (Yep, I've got every smarmy word right here on tape. Ed.)

Never again! (1983)

To clubs thinking of ways to raise extra funds, this speech at a club dinner comes as a warning:

It may just be old age seeping into my bones, Mr Chairman, but I feel that life at Dunstable was so much more eventful when I was starting, 20-25 years ago. To give you an idea of what I mean, I would like to take the liberty of reading to you a confidential letter purporting to be from the then CFI of the club to the chairman around 1963. It was leaked to me by a former member of the committee who wishes to remain anonymous – not so much a Mole as a, er, Platypus. Whether the letter itself is authentic or not, the actual events described certainly did happen, being etched indelibly on the memories of many of you here tonight. The writer was clearly recovering from an end of season breakdown, since the letter is addressed from – THE UNSTABLE BEDS REST HOME FOR NERVOUS DISORDERS, Dunstable, Beds.

"Dear Chairman, Thank you for the grapes. I shall soon be fit to return to work in good time for the new season, but only on one condition – that we do NOT have an air display next year.

I fully realise the urgent need, expressed by the committee, for such essentials as a heated indoor swimming pool, sauna, solarium and a new girl behind the bar. I am also aware that last season's courses were a financial disaster entirely because of the weather: the total absence of rain, fog and high winds resulted in a ruinously high number of launches with consequent wear and tear on gliders, tugs, winches, cables, tractors, etc.

With luck next season's weather will revert to normal and the members will be more profitably confined to the swimming pool, sauna, solarium – and the new girl behind the bar. But there must be no air display. Let me refresh your memory – if that is necessary – about the last one.

The day was supposed to begin quietly with the arrival of visiting power pilots from all over the country and a few gentle joyrides in the T-21 for members of the public. The visiting pilots fell (in some cases literally) into three categories: those who could not take-off properly; those who could not land properly, and those who could not quite manage the bit in between. In the second category a Piper Tri-Pacer, after sniffing nervously around the circuit a couple of times, landed on Hangar Ridge, trickled down into the gully and there stove in its nose wheel and prop. The public might have thought this was all normal, or at least a planned part of the entertainment, except that Geoff Kerr on the public address interrupted his immaculate commentary with an undeleted expletive which raised more comment than the flying.

In the first category, a Cessna took off with a small boy as passenger and made a neat furrow with one of its wheels in the roof of a Jaguar parked in an enclosure packed with hundreds of people and cars. The Cessna got airborne OK, but it was found impossible to open or shut the Jaguar's doors, so it was a write-off. Which is nothing to what would have been written off had the passenger been an adult. Amazingly the Jaguar owner was delighted: he obviously hoped to get a brand new one. 'Just wait till I tell the insurers how it happened!'

In the last category, Godfrey Harwood arrived with a motorised Tutor, probably the most inefficient aeroplane ever built since the Spruce Goose. He proceeded to do aerobatics, of a sort, in an aircraft that was marginal even in level flight. The distinguished chairman of the BGA Technical Committee described it well. The Motor Tutor 'ran out of height, speed, power and control simultaneously' and plunged into the side of the hill which was covered with spectators. There was no fire, and the cut and shaken pilot was rushed to the Luton and Dunstable Hospital. His wife Rika, it is said, rushed in shortly afterwards, shouting 'Don't worry darling, I've found your false teeth under the wreckage'. 'What do you mean,' he says, 'I've got all my teeth right here!' The only way we will ever discover how false teeth came to be discarded on the Downs is by asking the club member who is always watching the goings-on on the Hill through a telescope[2].

The Technical Committee chairman actually was in no position to criticise this performance, since while joyriding he managed in landing to bounce the T-21's wheel on the wings of two parked Blaniks in one pass, creasing them as badly as the aforementioned car. Like the Jaguar, the metal wings were not repairable. After this the numbers of joyriders fell off somewhat. Since joyrides were the prizes in a raffle, the club did quite well out of this sudden loss of nerve on the part of the winners. Our T-21 was unmarked and the two Blaniks belonged to other clubs, so again God – or somebody – was on our side.

The spectators were having a grand time. The parachutist ended up on the clubhouse roof with a broken leg[3], and in the middle of what was supposed to be a solo aerobatic display in the Jaskolka, Ralph Chesters looked down through the top of his canopy to see the Luton Flying Club pass through the middle of his loop as they strafed the field, the timetable having got into some disarray. Ladi Marmol, the émigré Czech pilot, roared under the Whipsnade power wires while Derek Piggott's plane just scraped over. The crowd went wild. I don't anybody was using radio to co-ordinate things; it was all loud-hailers and waving of arms in the early 1960s. John Hands, the marshal, was going round like Gregory Peck in _Twelve o'clock High_ muttering about living on borrowed time.

Finally, there were those pestiferous hot-air balloons. Thank God they will just be a short-lived fad. First the unmanned Montgolfier replica broke loose from its tether in an east wind and, belching smoke and flame, skimmed over the Tiger Moths which were refuelling at the pumps: it crashed 20 yards from the clubhouse amongst a mass of cars and people. The crowd attacked the balloon as though it was Moby Dick, and had to be beaten off by the balloon's distraught owners.

To lose one balloon is a misfortune. To lose two, as Lady Bracknell might have said, was bloody careless. But that is what happened. A schoolmaster, who with the help of his class had built a huge envelope out of clear plastic bags and Sellotape, planned to do a brief flight on a tether using a hand-held blow-lamp as a heat source. Of course the lousy tether breaks again, I suspect not without encouragement, and off he goes – without his blow-lamp.

From the spectators' point of view (they were getting real value for money) it was a brave sight: the tiny figure crouched in an open steel tube frame dangling under what looked like a gigantic prophylactic drifting translucently across the setting sun towards Totternhoe. As he got low in the valley and the sun finally set, someone said, "I hope he knows about the power wires," though what good that knowledge would have done him is beyond me, since he had no rip panel, no trail-rope, no burner, nothing. Anyway, hardly were these words uttered when we saw a big blue flash – and all the lights went out for miles around, ruining a planned dinner at the Golf Club that evening and endangering the tropical fish at Whipsnade Zoo. The pilot – if that is the right description for a completely passive piece of ballast – was unscathed. Indeed, in the whole display no one was maimed or killed, and our Club fleet was intact. The end of a perfect day, we all said. But please, Mr Chairman, Never Again!"

It's throwing up time again or, hit & myth (1985)

Rhoda Partridge, in a recent _Sailplane & Gliding_, "wants to write about some of the crazy happenings that gliding throws up." I think she really means she wants to write about some of the crazy people that gliding throws up. (They don't normally stay thrown up for long – indeed the really crazy people get thrown out, or even carried out.) However, it is splendid to hear that Rhoda is active, though semi-retired

---

[2] The false-teeth story is now said to be apocryphal. But then so is most history.

[3] The parachutist was Mike Reilly, who drowned in the English Channel after making a jump for the film "The War Lover" starring Steve McQueen.

from gliding. It is a good idea to retire first before writing about gliding's weirdos and crazies. Why didn't I think of that? I'd spend less time examining the ship for sawn-through elevator cables and glue in the vario.

Anyway, Ms Partridge gives us an example of the sort of thing she is looking for – an Olympia 463 pilot flies from the Mynd to Yarmouth and the crew arrives with trailer ages later to find another Oly already in the box. Well, when I heard it first the Oly 463 hadn't even been built (there's a snide put-down for you!). It was an Olympia 2 or 2B and the damn thing had just made it to the bottom of the ridge at the Mynd, a million miles away from the North Sea. It does go to show, however, the way myths encrust and embellish a good story – and why not indeed? I've never known a good true story that couldn't do with a bit of improvement.

Someone else can rush in and correct me, but I believe the intelligentsia on that retrieve were from Cambridge University, the home of lost gliders (as distinct from Oxford, the home of lost causes) and the source of more crazy stories than anywhere. All of them are true, too, though again the fisherman's long arms may have to stretch a bit to accommodate them as time matures them (the stories, not the pilots – they never mature). I believe that the glider-already-in-the-box story, having over the course of the years exhausted the scope of our small island, went into the export business and has now been expanded into an epic retrieve across the entire continental USA.

Should Rhoda run out of myths (and it could be interesting for a historian of her stature to find when the original event occurred – if ever – and how many different forms it took on its long journey into legend) then I'll promise to make up a dozen or so to order, provided the price is right.

Talking of crazy people being thrown out, there was this fellow at Dunstable who'd heard chaps boasting about "hangar-flying" which I take to be flying the glider back in the evening to a point where it can be very conveniently hauled into the hangar. It's an expression I never use since I never ever attempt anything like that. It's far too much like tempting providence. Anyhow, this bloke forgot which knob was dive-brake and which was cable-release, so flew the K-8 not up to, but *into* the hangar, with

the release-hook chattering away urgently but uselessly. He was still more or less in full flight as he hurtled into the dark interior. Mercifully he caught his wing-tip on the bar – leaving a vivid green paint-mark high enough up on the building to prove he was airborne at the time – and was twirled into the hangar sideways and

"The really crazy people get thrown out."

backwards. This slowed him down somewhat and probably saved his neck, at least until JJ, the Chief Flying Instructor, got to him...

The following year a great soaring pilot, grounded for many years by sinus problems, returned to the sport, and told me the definitive story of the Olympia in the trailer. For the pilot was Charles Wingfield, who had no idea how much his little adventure had been embellished over the years. Read on.

The wrong box: truth revealed (1986)

Now there comes from the horse's mouth the authoritative version of what happened when an Olympia trailer set out on a retrieve from the Long Mynd with another derigged Olympia already in it. It was Charles Wingfield who was the pilot in 1949 and who has written to me with a full account. Having whistled up to 11,650ft in a cu-nim, Charles got lost in cloud. "When I eventually got my bearings, I was compelled to land at the house of a friend, $1\frac{1}{3}$ miles short and 700ft lower." And it was the Cambridge mob who came on the chaotic retrieve, he says, though Frank Irving's statement that an Imperial College man was at the wheel does not necessarily conflict. This was quite a party, not one of today's Spartan one-man or one-woman retrieves. "Cambridge University Gliding Club arrived very quickly to collect, so we all had a few drinks... Sometime later in the hay field someone mentioned a key for the lock. 'What lock?' They had to go back to the club (eight miles by road each way) for the key, so it took even longer than it should to discover the surplus Olympia in the trailer."

The Cambridge mob on chaotic retrieve.

Thus the whole business was even more disorganised than today's legend suggests, apart from the small matter of distance. No doubt it is from this event that we derive the sacred principles a) check the trailer all over and count the fittings before leaving the site and b) no drinks for anyone till the whole thing is derigged and stowed and safely on the road behind the car, pointing towards home.

Incidentally Charles, now back in gliding after nearly 30 years absence for medical reasons, landed in the same field again, about three years ago. His last shot: "The moral is that there is no need to embroider a good story, but if you insist Wally Kahn might oblige." Come on, Wally, send us either some embroidery or a writ.

Wally it was who drove the retrieve car.

Impressions of Doc (1979)

When the BGA celebrated their 50th anniversary in 1979, I wrote this tribute to the man who had edited our magazine as long as anyone could remember and retired in 1971. Doc Slater was coming up to his 85th birthday and was to live another eight years. I seem to remember that his rendition of Eine Kleine Nachstsmusik on a penny whistle at his 90th birthday party was slightly less crisp than at his 80th, but otherwise he seemed ageless. Doc was so delighted with my sincere offering. When he died in 1987 Gillian Bryce-Smith used it again as an obituary.

In the summer of 1961, when cumulus still seemed to bloom effortlessly all day and when any worthwhile flight ended in moonlit retrieves along winding roads before motorways were invented, we rumbled in through the gates of the Derby & Lancs Club close to midnight. In the little square of light which was the courtyard of the farm, an impromptu concert was in progress. A young Camphill member, wrapped around a cello, was making a brave and pretty successful attempt at sight-reading a hand-written score. The bar piano resounded and shook under the attack of ten large outspread fingers. Light glinted on massively thick spectacles through disordered strands of waving white hair. It is not my first memory of Doc, but it is my most vivid.

I was delighted to discover that Doc's enthusiasms were the same as my own – gliding, photography, model aeroplanes, astronomy and always music. What they have in common is that they are all beautiful, but that beauty can only be enjoyed as a reward for concentration, continual practice and patient analysis of one's mistakes. Only a fool says, "But that's work!" I define work as wishing you were somewhere else. Total absorption in doing something which, if successful, is beautiful and satisfying is never work.

In a 16-millimetre film that is not merely a magnificent piece of almost cinecamera work but a priceless historical document, Dudley Hiskox recorded the visits of early British gliding enthusiasts to German gliding sites in 1931. In addition to elegant new soaring machines, we see a tall young man, serious and light-hearted at one and the same time, launching tiny paper gliders of unorthodox aerodynamic form down the slopes of the Wasserkuppe. Yes – across half a century one recognises Doc Slater, and the audience gives an affectionate cheer for the most loved figure in our movement today.

Doc's Box Brownie – succeeded by a Leica in 1935 (which I remember him using at least 25 years later) – took hundreds of irreplaceable pictures of every aspect of British gliding: the pilots, the designers, the machines, the workshops, the instruments, the wreckage, but above all hills and clouds and great expanses of ever-changing sky. People today have forgotten how to use a yellow filter and black and white film. Doc's skies remind us what gliding is about: the freedom and the mystery and the never-being-the-same of the sky.

What makes *Sailplane & Glider* in the 1930's an exceptional magazine still worth reading today (and not just for nostalgia's sake) is Doc's intense curiosity and truly scientific interest in every aspect of gliding weather. The articles "Queer soaring at Dunstable" (a title unlikely to be used nowadays) are a classic of devoted observation and analysis. Doc's articles make it clear that it is simply not the case that standing waves were a mystery in the 1930s. Predicting and using them was difficult, but the principles were well understood.

Doc's easy-going and amiable temperament has not prevented him from expressing furious scorn for a fair number of knaves or fools. Leaving individuals aside – though there are some whose names, long since forgotten, still provoke scathing references to BGA battles of years ago – the categories who felt the lash in the pages of *Sailplane & Glider* in the 1930s would have to include:

– *most power pilots, especially when they leapt gaily into a glider and shortly afterwards stepped or crawled ruefully out of the remains. Doc would really make their ears burn.*

– *popular newspaper journalists, whose ignorant banalities and inept sensationalism on the subject of gliding were pilloried with a mixture of loathing and glee.*

– *people who wanted to exploit and misuse gliding, whether as a "youth movement" or as a source of notoriety, money or power.*

Doc is a true Victorian: not one of the stuffy, repressed 19th century figures which the 20th century wrongly imagines the Victorians to be, but lively, creative *doers* with their strong belief in Reason, Science and Progress, in the spirit of Brunel and Darwin. He despises the pseudo-science of the pulp writers of the UFO, Bermuda Triangle and Visitors from Space school, and the astrology and superstition into which so many of the present generation have retreated.

The man who in the same day could compose a piece for piano, voice and any of 12 different wind instruments (all of which he could play), perform a tracheotomy to save the life of a child, design a flying wing that would do aerobatics under and over the hospital beds of his young patients, edit a magazine, formulate a new meteorological theory,

Doc's favourite picture.

observe an occultation of the moon, has only one serious deficiency – he doesn't know the meaning of the expression too often heard among today's young, "I'm bored."

Jack the Knife, or trailers that went with a swing (1996)

Histories of sailplane design and soaring are fairly common, but let me put it to you, has anybody written a history of glider trailers and the art of towing? You may think it an unworthy subject for serious interest. Trailer spotting and the collecting of such memorabilia as vintage Austrian tow hitches sounds like a hobby for pimply nerds in anoraks and geezers in cardigans, I know. But I'm sure there's some genuinely fascinating stuff to be mined here.

After all, when the top German pilots were daily flying 500km and more from the Wasserkuppe in the 1930s, the distances trailed during the big contests would have run into tens of thousands of kilometres. Of course the roads would have had little traffic, but with all-night dashes to get back to the Wasserkuppe for the next day's task there must have been some heroic driving. The crews battled continuously against sleep (despite training all winter on non-stop performances of Wagner's Ring) and coped with temperamental road-holding, imperfect headlights and the mysteries of trailer stability when hurtling through mountainous hairpins in the dark; no doubt there were some epic crashes. I wonder, is there a plaque, somewhere in the Schwabian Alps or the Teutoberger Wald, commemorating the world's first recorded jack-knife of a car and glider trailer? Somebody must have done it first, but who, and where?

Doubtless we imagine that German glider crews all drove those spectacular open Mercedes staff cars such as Rommel had. I don't think a glider trailer would have dared to fold up alongside one of those glossy vehicles. But the early Volkswagen would have been easier to take unawares.

What about America? No, I doubt it. In the 1930s American cars were steadily getting huger, and the combined weight of a low wing -loading glider and its (usually open) trailer was probably quite small, so I doubt if history's first account of a car's front end trying forcibly to mate with a glider trailer's rear end comes from the western USA.

Of course the British in the 1930s had tiny, feeble cars (exacerbated by stupid taxes that rewarded the most inefficient engines) and glider pilots naturally complemented such inadequate tow vehicles with large, high sided trailers of very low strength-to-weight ratio. Furthermore our roads, though not alpine, were undulating and winding and infested by irresponsible cyclists and motor cyclists (see the opening sequences of Lawrence of Arabia) so maybe we can lay claim to the first glider trailer jack-knife.

It's a matter of national pride to nail this one down for Britain. We in this island have pioneered notable engineering disasters way ahead of the competition, from the Tay Bridge and the Titanic to the R101, though the Russians did beat us to it with Chernobyl, I have to admit. We slipped up there. Another indication that we are falling behind.

I went on my first retrieve in a Land Rover in the 1950s, towing a Rice trailer with enormous wind-embracing sides – all the better for advertising Ovaltine, I suppose. I don't know who Mr Rice was, but if he is alive I hope his lawyers do not see this book. This monstrosi-

Trailer waves a final goodbye.

ty, typical of the day, constructed from soft, heavy fibreboard that got even softer and heavier when it rained, had tongue and groove flooring that offered no useful stiffness whatever. Horrible, horrible in every way – except you could stand up in the damn things, if you are looking for mitigating graces. The retrieve was unendingly noisy as the hitch clinked and clanked, being a simple bracket taking a crude half inch steel pin, not a snug-fitting ball. I suppose such pins rattled their way non-stop across continents before World War II.

In the late 1950s; the light monocoque plywood trailer was pioneered (I claim this originated at Dunstable, but am not prepared to do battle for the honour) and the first speeding ticket for a Morris Minor and fully-laden glider trailer became a practical possibility without the accompanying near certainty of a catastrophic fold-up on the next bend.

I'd better not go on, but you can see the amount of reminiscence this topic can evoke. Please send in any solid archive data you may have. What about the history of trailer suspensions, lights, stabilisers and override brakes, and brakes that automatically operate if the trailer waves a final goodbye to the car?

"Brakes, indeed!" mutters some grizzled veteran into his whisky and soda. "The damn cars didn't have 'em, let alone the trailers!"

And the future of trailers – why can't we have trailers which are also self-rigging devices? In fact why isn't the trailer designed integrally with the glider?

No, of course those wretched motor gliders and their misguided enthusiasts will absolutely not make trailers redundant. They'll still need something to cart the bits home in. ■

Over the hills and far away

It will be very sad if we ever lose the sense of wonder at the fact that we can go for a stroll in the sky without an engine. The people who have that sense of disbelief are ordinary members of the public who ask questions like, "If you're going to fly a hundred miles in one go without a motor, how high do you have to be towed?" We should not despise such incredulity but should share it. We are so lucky to have been born into century when we had both the technical means and the freedom to do this miraculous trick, which in any earlier age would have been considered pure magic. Magic is just what it is.

Howididntdoit or foiled again (1968)

I have longed for years to write a Philip-Wills-style "howidunit" describing a brilliantly-organised 300-km Diamond out-and-return. In fact the prospect of writing this epic was far more entrancing than the idea of the flight itself. I saw myself painting a dazzling word-picture of heroic struggle crowned with success when, from the last exhausted thermal of the day, I slip across the club boundary going downwind at nought feet, to the cheers of amazed fellow members...

For me, however, literary success has been easier to come by than the brilliantly-organised 300-kms. So I have written articles in *Sailplane & Gliding* insolently telling real pundits how to write howidunits, and even a presumptuous article on planning the great feat, called Howwe'regonnadoit. Now I sing of heroic struggle crowned with absolutely nothing, except for a few salutary lessons, that is.)

The first task of the day is the battle of wits with the weatherman. This goes best if he has been on duty all night. "Today's forecast?" he says blearily. "Well, same as yesterday really." Rapier-keen I shoot back, "Same as yesterday's forecast, or same as yesterday's weather?" A pregnant pause at the other end of the line while he ponders whether saying, "Carry oxygen and a map of Scotland" or, "Rain all day" would punish my sarcasm more effectively. Finally he comes up with a real teaser designed to maximise panic. A belt of rain would move from east to west at about 10 knots reaching Dunstable at 3 o'clock – and it would probably be 11.30 before I could get to the club and organise myself into the air.

I decide on Dunstable to Ludlow and back, about 308 km. A swift dash downwind to the turning point and a battle upwind in the strongest part of the day might bring me to the edge of the murk, say 15 miles from home, around tea time – then a bold glide-out. The Dart 17R was capable of it even if I was not.

Downwind first is a good rule when flying self-imposed tasks, particularly if the weather is expected to deteriorate. You burn your boats quickly instead of hanging about with one foot in the club, and you can enjoy several hours' good soaring before being washed out of the sky.[4]

Now all I have to do is simply:
Rig three other chaps' gliders.
Rig own glider – Hey, come back, you three !
Smoke barograph.
Wind barograph.
Inscribe barograph baseline.
Seal barograph.
Start barograph ticking.
Load Camera.
Now, photograph the official observer by the tail. First *catch* your observer by the tail; have they gone into hiding or what?
Get barograph signed by official observer.
Find map.
Put barograph in the glider, idiot!
Inscribe line on map – blast! No Chinagraph pencil for glossy Fablon-covered map. Have to do without a line.
Declaration form! Heavens, any well organised (ie Lasham) pundit has declaration forms strapped to his knee and an official observer on a chain. I use a scruffy bit of paper with Ludlow Town scrawled in blood or charcoal or something.

---

[4] The idea of deliberately setting off downwind in a wooden glider with little or no chance of getting home, on a weekday and with no crew organised, now makes me shudder. But it was the 1960's, and getting home was so rare as to be positively eccentric.

Right, now, out to that far distant knoll at the end of a bit of string. (I hate that long, slow tow-out to the north-east run.) Sorry, no. Help another pilot out there first. Come back, all set. Heck, where's my telephone money. Run and get the money, then Ye Gods! The parachute! Rush to the parachute rack – not there. Not in glider or trailer. A process of ruthless deduction establishes that it must be strapped to the behind of a lady member who is – aaarghhh! as they say in the strip cartoons – circling manfully so to speak, under fat cumulus. To add insult to injury Mike Till flies past in the Tiger Moth bellowing and circling his finger over his head, meaning, "Come on, you idlers, the air's lovely!"

Exactly the same thing happened the last time I got the Dart out. That time I brought another lady down to earth with a bit of black magic, now I repeat it – a sort of rain dance with eyeballs rolling skywards and added curses. It works again and the dear girl winds round and down only slightly later than the tug. As she rolls to a halt the owner of the parachute flings himself upon her and a fierce tussle ensues. "You might let me get out of the glider first," she shrieks. She has a point there; it makes it a lot easier to tear the parachute off her back. An ugly episode, even if I was only asserting my rights.

Three more gliders have now arrived in front of me at the aero-tow point. Oh well, now it's past 12 o'clock and the whole thing looks daft, but eventually I rumble away and up and forget all my worries as the thermals bump me around on the tow.

After the earthbound drama the flying is fairly prosaic. As the day builds up I discard modest thermals; strong ones are gleefully circled in to the accompaniment, as usual, of raucous bathroom-style singing. A very noisy regional competition is in progress. I turn the radio off, better to hear the vario sweetly sing top C to my C flat. Ludlow is lost, found again, photographed and left behind.

Galloping back upwind I see high in the eastern sky a grey line spreading. The forecaster was right. Calling Dunstable I learn that it had clouded over at 3 o'clock and now at 4 o'clock it was raining there. About 5 o'clock I meet the murk near Bicester, 25 miles out; a smooth toboggan-ride in dead air brings me to a large field with 600 ft. to burn, just outside Aylesbury, about ten miles from home. Little

do I know that around the car radio a debate has been raging – should my partners let me know that stretching the glide a mile or two could give me Gold C distance? Sensibly the temptation is not put in my way; I am blissfully unaware since with no line or distance marks on the map I have no clue how far I have gone. I land safely, but have I made it?

Drama once more, back on the ground. There is just a chance I had done it! The beautiful barograph trace is carefully removed, carefully signed by an official observer, carefully lowered into a dish of clear dope – and gently floats off in a little sooty puddle, leaving the foil clean as a whistle. My boggling eyes discern the advertising message "Ilchester Cheese with Beer" mocking at me through the fixing fluid. A partner who shall be nameless has used cheese-foil as an *ersatz* for proper barograph foil, and I am the first to discover that the coating must have been soluble in cellulose dope. I could cry; I do cry. Some wag suggests that the trace should have been fixed in beer, like the cheese; I decide to fix myself in beer instead.

Then I am told that Ludlow Town is not a proper declaration anyway. Much too vague. Should be a railway station, a public lavatory or some other unique landmark.

I also learn that being off the line loses you distance in a failed out-and-return attempt. If you declare Hartlepool in a straight line and land at Plymouth that's all right for your Gold, but not on tasks with legs. Sorry, but there it is. Oh yes, and I was one witness missing on the landing certificate. Knowing me they should he grateful for a landing certificate at all, with or without signatures. I stumble off and get fixed some more.

After all the fuss it was an immense relief to be told, days later, that I had done just 299.5 km., so the whole gruesome business of the mis-declared turning point, the vanishing barograph trace (the official observer's energetic signature in ball-point is embossed on a shining roll of Ilchester Cheese foil, which I suppose I could frame or put in my log book), the distance off the line that I hadn't drawn on the map, and the missing witness did not have to be explained in triplicate to the BGA, the FAI, the CIA and the House of Lords. The Flying Committee gave me a conditional discharge with costs and I was bound over to be of good behaviour for the rest of the season.

Happy ending: shortly after, while tilling the weed-plagued Islington mulch at 11 o'clock on a Sunday, I am called by my partners. Bloated with hours, they generously offer to give up a perfect day and insist I fly. Everything – barograph, camera, parachute, paperwork – will be taken care of. After wrestling with my conscience she agrees to let me go and my Beetle roars up the M1 to arrive at the launch point at 12.15 for an instant launch. I trickle up to Lincoln and back and sure enough, "...from the last, exhausted thermal of the day, etc, etc."

The moral here for the incurably incompetent is – if a job's worth doing, someone else had better do it for you. But you may have to wait ten years before they take sufficient pity on you.

The shorter the nastier (1983)

The disputes about who has inflicted the worst retrieves on his friends are usually won by Platypus, because the other disputants suddenly remember that they were the ones who retrieved him. It occurs to me that my worst retrieves have been within sight of the club, while the smoothest have been those that fetched up 200 miles away. The reason is obvious when you stop to think. You don't land 100 or more miles away without knowing in advance that you are going on a long flight (unless you are JJ) so like a Wise Virgin in the Bible you get all the junk out of the trailer, check that all the lights work, count the fittings, fill the car up with petrol, entrust the keys to someone who is willing to retrieve and tell them where you are going, like well, north-ish.

Unscheduled outlandings are quite different.

It is early March 1960. While soaring the Dunstable east wind wave I overestimate my skill and the penetration of an Olympia 2. I descend through a feeble lenticular and, falling out of the bottom of it just 400ft above ground, I "choose" a field, which is to say the field chooses me. No damage, no problem. But it's winter-time, and it's dusk before anyone arrives from the club – all of three miles away. Never mind, I say, hot toddy in the bar for all of the retrievers (one) when we get back in half-an-hour. I speak too soon. Clearly

Certificate of Airworthiness time, eleven months ago, was the last time the Olympia was rigged. The damned main-pin just won't shift. A desperate phone request from the farmhouse to the club for a three-pound hammer eventually produces one large hammer, accompanied by some more Olympia pilots wondering what the hell Platypus is planning to do to their favourite ship. (Their *only* ship.) Eventually a mighty blow expels the main-pin like a 37-millimetre cannon shell: it ricochets off the fin and whistles away into the mud. It is pitch dark by now and sleeting. It takes some while to find the main-pin.

Eventually all the bits are back in the trailer. Now, off we go, chaps. Oh no, we don't. The little A35's wheels spin in the mud, as it sinks up to the axles. Unhitch the car. All lift together and push the car out of the mud. But that walking in and out of the trailer with wing-roots etc has bogged the trailer down to the axles, too. It doesn't budge. After an age we give up. It is late Sunday night and there is no one left at the clubhouse. So we sheepishly knock on the farmer's door. We get him out of bed so that he can bring his tractor to tow the trailer to the road. He is amazingly restrained in his comments. Probably because he is still asleep. There is no tow-hitch that fits the trailer, so the tractor drags it along with great chains. We sit in the back of the trailer with our feet dangling in the dirt trying to stabilise it, though it still makes a bow-wave through the mud.

Eventually we get back to the darkened clubhouse, filthy and exhausted. It is a few minutes to midnight, the bar has been closed for hours and it is still sleeting.

When it comes to retrieves, small isn't beautiful.

Coldest, wettest, muddiest & most labour-intensive retrieve (1975)

This next narrative also proves the point that short retrieves are the worst. We are spoilt in 2000 by having mobile phones and practical footwear. Nevertheless, horrific retrieves will continue to furnish stories for old glider pilots to frighten their grand-children with so long as the sport endures.

After being compelled, by a sudden Easter blizzard which was full of lift but also full of other gliders, to escape into clear air but hearty sink, I put my brand-new Kestrel 19 down in a nice big cow-pasture only about two air miles from the club. Fifteen minutes later, when I had negotiated, in bare feet, the 200yds of knee-deep mud (made by the cows on their daily journey from the field to the farm buildings to be fed and milked) which represented the only exit from the field, I telephoned for the trailer, ten men and a pair of wellington boots. My wife and seven chaps arrived in no time, but spare wellington boots were simply not to be had at the London Gliding Club, since the site was also a quagmire.

I was barefoot because the suction of the mud not only pulled each shoe off but effectively buried them under a foot of icy water topped with a thick layer of slush. It was better to go barefoot, except the stones and thorns and the snow were sheer torture, and the shoes had to be replaced from time to time in order to forestall frostbite. Imagine, it was the very end of winter rather than the beginning of spring, and I was flying a glider in ordinary city shoes that had once done reasonably smart duty at the office.

Towing the Kestrel to a relatively convenient spot and derigging it was merely purgatory. Hell consisted of carrying the separate pieces in the approximate direction of the trailer. One ingenious thought was to pass the wings across a hawthorn hedge and a deep ditch full of freezing water and snow, into a less muddy field so as to circumnavigate the cow track. Like most cures it was as bad as the disease.

A dozen times I lost my shoes while carrying the bits and had to abandon them until a place could be found to rest the precious glass-fibre – then we would go back and poke about in the water-filled holes that marked our progress and retrieve the vanished footwear. A vile, miserable affair; I can't think why some of them thought it was funny. I can only put it down to hysterics brought on by physical and nervous exhaustion.

As the fuselage was hauled along the cow track, the undercarriage bay filled up with mud. The wheel became a gigantic ball.

Discussion as to whether it would be better to slide the thing along on its belly with the wheel up was now academic, since the fuselage was at this stage filled with so much mud that it would soon occupy every crevice from the cockpit to the fin. As the muscular team heaved upwards, Isaac Newton (every action producing an equal and opposite reaction) forced them *downwards* into the mud so that, at those rare moments when the fuselage was momentarily clear of the quagmire, the crew were even more firmly immobilised by it. Wise virgins all, they at least had stout boots which didn't come off. Laurie Ryan, however, has a tin leg which was sucked into the mud; this had to be retrieved and re-attached. An interesting mixture of rain, hail and snow blew horizontally across the grisly scene.

About two hours after arriving, the trailer was eventually loaded and the grubby bits stowed. The Kestrel had travelled the last 200 yards at roughly one yard every 30 seconds.

A royal retrieve (1982)

If I set aside the humiliation, disgrace, loss of 900 points, chagrin and fury at seeing the cumulus blossoming the moment my wheel kissed the stubble (a rather brutal kiss which b.gg.r.d the wheel brake, as R. Jones Esq delicately observed) then my most enjoyable outlanding of recent years was on Charles and Diana's Wedding Day.

The farmer showed the usual abysmal ignorance of gliding. "Those flat-topped cu can be a bit deceptive early in the day, can't they? You weren't very well-centred; the cores were obviously shifting upwind, etc. etc." You know, the usual sort of thing.

I accepted a lift into the village, about ten miles from Stonehenge. One pub, one church, one telephone. A one-horse town, I guessed. Between the church and the village green a small group of people were waiting. Along a wooded lane there eventually came a procession of children in fancy dress, all looking dreadfully self-conscious, led by a bearded man in a top hat and a white smock with bells tied under his knees, banging a massive drum. And the one horse, whose young rider promptly fell off. After what seemed to a thirsty stranger like an age, beer and cider barrels appeared,

cooks with a barbecue almost as hot as that miraculous sun after the long wet summer, Morris dancers, musicians and finally, in the middle of it all, my crew and trailer. It's the first time my son has crewed for me and he now thinks crewing's terrific.

I have not yet explained to him that a real retrieve entails arriving in a ploughed field at midnight, in pouring rain, the pilot or glider untraceable, all pubs and garages and restaurants closed (especially the type that advertises itself as 24 Hour Service. Some friends of mine tried one such at 3am: Indignant, sleepy face appears at window. "What the hell?!" "Aren't you a 24 hour service?" "Yes we are, but not at this bloody time of night!" Slam.)

No, I'm not going to get nostalgic about old-style downwind ballooning – in which the average achieved still-air speed of the glider was about half the windspeed – or about the all-night retrieves that ensued. I can only say that in those days crewing was crewing, just as being a merchant seaman today is a skilled job but it doesn't quite compare with reefing sails on a schooner in an icy force 8 gale. It's just different now. Thank Heavens.

"Don't come in the bar in those filthy shoes!" bellowed Jeffries (whose fault it all was for throwing us into the air anyway). Obligingly I stepped out of my shoes and squelched across the parquet in bare feet with the mud and ice water dribbling between my toes, to collapse at the nearest beer-pump.

The thin red wobbly line (1984)

It's a long time since I happily soared the 300 ft high ridge at Dunstable at well below hilltop height all afternoon in the hope of the weather perking up. Since then I have grown less bold (= more sane) but the experience does come in useful from time to time, even in contests. I certainly make a point of marking the wind-facing slopes before any cross-country. In fact I have more or less given up the use of rulers in preparing my maps. Mainly it's because I've mislaid the ruler anyway, but I genuinely pre-

Platypus's maps look as though drawn while drunk.

fer to draw a meandering line through, or near to (a) areas of high, dry ground, (b) other gliding clubs, where either the thermals will be well marked or the bar well stocked (I didn't claim this was a method for winning contests) and (c) unambiguous landmarks that will steer me towards the turning point – rivers, railways etc. Platypus's maps are easily recognisable, therefore, appearing quite mistakenly to have been drawn while drunk.

What you don't know can't hurt you, can it? (1986)

I once had a share in a Capstan, and it was the most enjoyable machine for friendly local soaring ever invented. On a good day it could do creditable cross-countries too, but only in

Wilbur was Wright (1988)

In the 1950s a wise old bird under the nom de plume of Uncle Wilbur used to write a column in the London Gliding Club Gazette, giving digestible instructive titbits to the fledglings. One of his simplest and best bits of soaring advice, which has stuck in my mind for 30 years (most things stick in my mind for all of 30 seconds) was, "If you're going to circle, then circle, dammit, don't wander in vast arcs!"

"Why waste space", you snarl impatiently, "telling us what might have been news to Lilienthal but is now obvious to everyone?" Well, I see scores of beautiful modern gliders, with crisp 1980's controls, wandering in vast arcs all over the country and failing to go up. The pilots clearly expect to black out at 15° and to pull the wings off at 20°. You might just climb at 20° in the late afternoon near cloudbase, but it won't get you out of trouble if you're low down at high noon – the thermals then are mean and narrow.

It occurs to me that many pilots have no idea what angle of bank they are flying at. If you can't afford a fancy swivelling compass like a Bohli, which you can line up with the horizon after setting it for 30°, 45° or whatever you fancy, then try some bits of cardboard or wire on top of the instrument panel, or put wax pencil marks inside the canopy. Let's get that wingtip down and start moving the scenery round!

PS. Apologies for the Orville pun at the top of this little piece. I believe Uncle Wilbur was Godfrey Lee, sometime Chairman of London Gliding Club and a senior aerodynamicist at Handley Page.

Most things stick in my mind for all of 30 seconds.

light winds, since its penetration was pretty miserable – about 8:1 at 70kt if you were daft enough to push the stick forward and about 24:1 at best glide angle, I can safely say now that I have sold my share.

The first flight a relation (a stepson-in-law, if you can work that out) of mine ever did in any glider was with me in this Capstan. I was determined to give him a taste of cross-country soaring, and set out boldly eastwards for the Cambridgeshire Fens. To cut a saga down to manageable length, we were returning by way of Bedford and ran under three plausible clouds, each of them all talk and no action, pretentious windbags which refused to suck. I began to have doubts about my infallibility, which doubts I concealed from my passenger in light banter about the lovely, and progressively more detailed, scenery.

At 500ft over the M1, about three miles from the club, I ran into zero sink which tempted me onwards, spurning the few remaining safe landing fields. Outside the club

Outside the club bar betting money was changing hands.

bar betting money was changing hands on our chances of making it home. My passenger chatted happily on, not noticing how his pilot had suddenly gone very quiet. The only way to cross the Tring Road telephone wires was to dive sharply and pull up over them. Then, sustained by pure ground-effect, we chased our shadow over the undulating contours of the last two fields, and faced only the great boundary hedge, the last obstacle to our triumphant arrival before a cheering throng.

But then for some unaccountable reason a momentary spasm of common sense seized me: I glanced at the airspeed indicator, which read 38kt. My apparently high ground-speed at nought feet was largely due to a tailwind: we were clearly in no shape for anything better than a spectacular fully-stalled pancake on the other side of the hedge or into the thicket itself. So I rubbed the skid (lovely things for

stopping gliders, skids) into the harrowed soil and slithered to a halt a few yards short of the brambles. My passenger hopped lightly out, said he had hugely enjoyed this typical glider flight and hoped he would have many others like it in future, then strolled off to the bar via a hole in the hedge (doubtless made by a more determined pilot than me). I staggered after him, when I had got my breath back and some strength in the knees.

Of course, I do sometimes wonder what would have happened if it had been a competition...

MacCready's magic ring (1982)

If I read another solemn article about speeds-to-fly and all the gadgetry and trigonometry that is essential to the understanding and exploitation of that subject, I swear I'll explode. Relief can only be obtained by writing such an article and getting my own back on the pundits of OSTIV (the official technical body in world soaring).

The first thing that gets me about the OSTIV papers on speeds-to-fly (with which the walls of a whole asylum could easily be papered) is not the mathematics; nor is it the diagrams of plumbing and electronics. No, it is the little drawings of what always look like a row of perfect, creamy-white, flat-bottomed meringues. These are meant to represent a side view of the sky on a typical summer's day. This should immediately arouse one's suspicions if one is British, with a healthy distrust of all theorising: any such pictures can only be drawn by foreigners. These foreign geezers then put the edge of a newly sharpened saw (something I've never seen either) under the meringues, thereby transporting the British reader into the realms of utter fantasy, since this is meant to represent – wait for it – a typical cross-country flight.

I'll let a minute or so pass for you to get your breath back after rolling around on the floor hurting yourself on the furniture...

If one is to anglicise MacCready, some radical changes to those meringues and saw-teeth are needed. First of all the meringues should be stomped on, melted, blackened, chewed by the cat, and in some cases blown up to dangerous proportions. Next the saw-teeth must be replaced by something looking like a skein of wool after that cat has had it. In Britain, to be fair, there is nearly always one perfect cumulus – 25 miles away – but when you get to it, it has invariably been stomped on, melted, blackened, chewed etc, etc. That's another point: these foreign skies are always the same in the OSTIV papers. The clouds never seem to go through Shakespeare's Seven Ages of Man from infancy to senility, but are always mature and healthy. British cumuli usually go from infancy to senility quite abruptly without any normal adulthood in between (a bit like Platypus? Ed.)

Another gripe about the line of meringues is that it misrepresents the choice before the pilot who is assumed to be flying down some aerial tram-lines diverting neither to left nor right.

The sideways-on treatment – the meringues joined by tram-lines mounted on saw-teeth – simplifies things splendidly because it assumes that pilots x, y and z, who follow different speeds-to-fly strategies (bold, timid, etc) will all

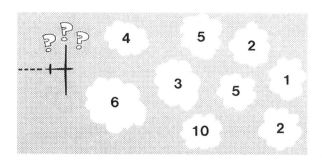

encounter the same thermals. But in practice they don't go through the same air at all, the timid diverting, the bold pressing straight on. The theory assumes the air is two-dimensional when it is three-dimensional. I am not saying that the theories are invalidated because of this, I am just deeply suspicious, that's all. I also feel that in the three-dimensional real sky the pilot has a lot more to worry about than the setting of his MacCready ring. It is the least of his problems.

Like Alexander the Great slashing through the Gordian Knot at a stroke, I'll boil down the Platypus theory of speeds-to-fly to a simple statement of principle. You can call it the *Minimum Acceptable Instantaneous Rate of Climb* or MAIROC for short.

Always set your speed-to-fly ring to the rate-of-climb that you would be happy to accept RIGHT NOW.

This may sound odd if applied to the typical situation when you are traversing a vast expanse of dead air, travelling hopefully towards a far distant area of potential lift. *But that is the whole point.* You say to yourself, as you toboggan smoothly through these Doldrums, "If at this very moment I were to encounter a thermal, what strength would it have to be for me (for *me*, not some other pilot with far greater skills than me) to stop and circle in it?"

Top pilots expect stronger thermals than mediocre pilots like me because they habitually find stronger thermals than I do and so they are entitled to set their ring to a higher rate of climb than I do. (Of course the top pilots can't tell us how to find these stronger thermals: generally they don't know how they do it.)

Of course as you traverse this great expanse of air between thermals all sorts of things change, in particular the appearance of the sky ahead. So your Instantaneously Acceptable Thermal also changes, maybe improving to 3kt or dropping to 1kt, so that your ring-setting changes, and you speed up or slow down accordingly.

Seen from the side therefore your glide path is not a straight line at all – even if the air through which you have travelled is in a flat calm devoid of lift or sink – because of your changing expectations. That is perfectly right and reasonable since we live in a world of uncertainties. It is a bit like the market for gold – pure speculation.

I suspect that this does not in any way contradict one word of Helmut Reichmann's classic book or the OSTIV papers, but I feel it expresses it in a much simpler form. For one thing it doesn't ask you to calculate laboriously the average strength of past thermals (old theory) or to guess the strength of the thermal ahead or the strength of the lowest part of the thermal where you are likely to enter it (Reichmann) but simply asks you to express your general state of confidence about the sky ahead. That embraces in one number all your worries about sink, the possible disappearance of the cloud you are hoping to use, the distance of the next thermal, etc, in one simple, highly subjective question, "What rate of climb would I accept *right now*?"

One interesting thing about this approach is that it confirms the Reichmann view that you should hardly ever fly with the ring set to zero, *ie* for absolute Max glide. Ask yourself, if you were crossing a big gap, under *what* conditions would you circle in zero sink? (That is, under what conditions would MAIROC be zero and the ring set to zero?) The only imaginable case would be if you were sure that you could not reach lift at all in present conditions and decided to hang around killing time, circling in any zero sink you could find, hoping that conditions ahead might improve. In that special case you have given up racing and are simply hanging on, hoping to survive. If your MAIROC was 1kt, however, then you should set the ring to 1kt. You would fly about 15kt faster than Max glide but with a glide angle only about one or two per cent worse.

MAIROC also works if you are unwilling to go into cloud and are flying straight and level under a street, climbing at say 2kt. At 500ft below cloudbase you probably would not want to stop for anything less than 6kt. OK, set the ring to six. At cloudbase itself MAIROC might rise to 10kt. Just remember to change it back later!

Remember: Don't calculate the past, don't try to predict the future. Just ask WHAT WOULD I ACCEPT *RIGHT NOW?* You know it makes sense.

The lostness of the long-distance pilot (1988)

Personally I feel that nobody under the age of 40 or with less than 50,000 kms cross-country flying in their logbook should be allowed to have a GPS.

Doubtless a previous generation of curmudgeons would have said something similar about variometers. The ability to navigate in the air is fast becoming a lost art, like the ocean-going skills of the South Sea Island canoeists who years ago travelled thousands of miles under the stars. However some great pilots never had that ability. I pay tribute to the navigationally-challenged JJ.

I have a very old friend (well, ancient, really) who would have been National Champion umpteen times if he had not got one small flaw. He can't navigate. He just presses on, getting more and more lost, through rain and hail and clamp and the occasional 1/2 kt thermal under a 1,200ft cloudbase until he reaches the sea – say, the Irish Sea or the English Channel or the German Ocean – then he turns round and comes back.

How he ever *gets* back, considering he doesn't know where he's been in the first place, is one of life's mysteries. I suppose some places nearer to home, like Oxford or Cambridge or Upper Heyford, trigger off some vague recall in his brain, since he has been over them a thousand times before. This does not always work, though. Some of his biggest so-called "flattened triangles" are the result of having overshot the club on the way back from one coast and he doesn't realise till he rebounds off the opposite coast and eventually rolls, like a snooker ball, into the right pocket more or less by chance.

If it were not for his photographs of what turn out to be the Menai Bridge, the Portland Bill lighthouse or Sir Walter Scott's Memorial

---

Spellbound (1994)

Incidentally, you can always tell the truly brilliant pilots when they rush into print: they have the most creative spelling. Moi, I scorn spellcheckers on the computer because although I am a crummy pilot I can spell like a whiz. Yes, say the computer people, but even Charles Dickens can hit the wrong key on his word-processor. So I have just put this column through my Mac's spell-checker and it throws out lots of words, "Not in Dictionary: soarers. Try soars, sharers, Sierras." I like that. I've shared soaring in the Sierras with soarers. You won't believe this next one. "Not in Dictionary: Sailplane. Try Sail plane (two words)." Who are

these lexicographical clowns, I ask? Then it rejects winglets: "Try wingless." No, thanks! Then "Benalla? – try banal or Bengal." Apologies to John Willy – sorry, not allowed: I can have Willie, or wild (not really) or wily (that's better) – and to the Victorian soarers.

Worse is to come "Gliding" is replaced by "Gelding." Ouch! For the "Kuppe" (as the Wasserkuppe is affectionately known, they suggest "Kipper", for "Brits" it suggests "Brats" or "Brutes" (hard to choose, really), instead of "Ovaltine" it prefers "Ovulating" (Yecchh!) and worst of all, in place of "Plat" recommends "Splat."

one would suspect that he had made up the whole thing, or at least had hazily imagined an Odyssey that can't possibly have happened.

Even with a 1987 nav-computer which should tell him pretty accurately how far he has gone since his last fix, he manages to come out with grandiose, vague statements like, "Over the river Trent" or "Over the M1 motorway", which cover a margin of error of a good 100km. If you ask him for his position he utters a tense, teeth-clenched, "Hang on..." as if you have crassly interrupted his concentration when he is barely staying airborne at 500ft. He is in fact at 5,000ft, happy as a sandboy (whatever that is) but utterly lost – again.

Seven deadly sins: gluttony (1990)

This should be a nice short one, since glider pilots are about as interested in gluttony as they are in lust, which is to say not a lot.

For years I used never to eat or drink while flying. On one nine hour flight in 1975 I lost eight pounds without benefit of pee-bags. Then I learnt that getting dehydrated was bad for you, so I started taking pure Dunstable Downs water, straight from the chalk, in a plastic bottle, but no food.

Then I was corrupted.

It was the two-seatering that started the rot. When you are on your own, the urge to eat or drink is minimal. But company changes every thing. One of my passengers insists on taking vacuum flasks ("What d'you want? Hot coffee or tea?") and a variety of freshly cut sandwiches.

At first I tried to ignore this, believing that a serious pilot had higher things to worry about.

But the aroma of bacon sandwiches in a confined space is hard to resist. Has some one been wiring up a waffle iron to those massive batteries behind the back seat? No wonder the artificial horizon has been toppling lately; if we spin in at least the condemned men will have had a hearty breakfast. Others specialise

---

The "sucker thermal" (1982)

Some of my friends' grizzling about British weather is really quite unwarranted: I usually find, for example, that there are two good thermals on any soaring day. That's two more than you expected, I bet.

The first is the one you get shortly after being launched. This one whisks you straight up to 4,000ft at 5kt. No time to waste! Mightily encouraged, you set your MacCready Ring to 5kt (fool) and hurtle away into the middle distance, ignoring all the little two and three kt thermals you pass through – until eventually you are down to 700ft, quivering with a mixture of rage and anxiety, trying to centre on a miserable half knot. If you survive this the best you get for the rest of the day will be less than half the strength of that first thermal of the day, which I would call the "sucker thermal." By the way, cloudbase also comes down to 2,500ft as you scratch and scrape down the track. For other people cloudbase always goes up as the day goes on; for me it just as often tries to rub my nose on the deck.

There is, however, one more really good thermal during the day. If you succeed in struggling around your triangle until eventually you believe that you can just make it, and if you do manage to get a little 1kt thermal that grudgingly lifts you to the height where, praying to St Willy, you believe you can crawl in at a sweaty 55kt with nothing to spare to cross the finishing line – you can bet your boots that when the finishing line is safely in sight a mile ahead and you know, with immense relief, that you will have a hundred extra feet to burn off as you finish, that is when you get the second great thermal of the day, an incorrigible five-knotter, quite useless at this point of the proceedings to man, beast or glider pilot.

Well, if you can't take a joke, you shouldn't have joined, as the sergeant said.

in Kit Kat, Twix bars and other sticky confections. In warm weather chocolate melts horribly and dribbles all over the maps, not to mention the luxurious upholstery. One considerate co-pilot of mine used to wait till we were at 5,000ft, then unwrap the Kit Kat very carefully in the cool draught from the ventilator. Then only after it was reasonably solidified was it fit to be passed to the Pilot-in-Charge. The co-pilot's reward for all this trouble was to get to fly the ASH-25 for a while. After a minute or so a loud belch from the

front seat would signal that the senior pilot was ready to take over once more.

Hunger is not the only reason for the compulsion to stuff one's face. A 17-stone Billy Bunterish character that I flew down to Cornwall in a K-7 sucked boiled sweets constantly, in between observing gloomily that we always seemed to be getting lower. Nonsense, I said, the ground is just getting higher, as we slid over Dartmoor and watched the ground drop away again. I think it was worry that made him eat, and my flying simply accelerated an innate tendency towards pessimism.

Years ago (1963, when the Beatles first came to power, and satire became the new craze) I invented for the entertainment pages of this organ a ruthless glider pilot called James Bend, whose adventures were so popular that I was asked to give the readers more in 1964. Sorry, I said, but this whole 007 James Bond nonsense will be played out by then, and satires on yesterday's cult always fall quite flat. How wrong I was!

But I remember that our hero Bend celebrated a height record with champagne and a Havana cigar while airborne: then I asked the readers to turn to a far distant page, in the infuriating way that American magazines have. The page number in question did not exist, of course. "What happened?" a thousand

eager subscribers clamoured to know. Well, one of them clamoured to know, if we are precise. The rest just assumed the printer had lost part of the copy as usual. I had no idea what happened to Mr Bend. But it now occurs to me that at 40,000ft or so a champagne cork, bottled at 400ft, would come out with magnum force and destroy the canopy. Lighting up a cigar in the presence of pure oxygen would be even more dangerous. So the story might well have ended with our somewhat scorched adventurer swinging down on his parachute, pondering whether it wasn't better to stick to lust after all.

Forget lunch, launch! (1991)

A few times I have got my act together just about in time for an early launch, and I have been continually astonished how soon in the day the good soaring weather can start. On so many days thermals are bubbling at 10 o'clock (0900 GMT) and I realise I could already have been 40km or more down the first leg of some vast task. Some days are perfectly usable a good three hours before the typical competition pilot crosses the start line.

Years ago I arrived overhead a famous club more than 250km out from home in an ASW-20 on a Sunday lunch-time – about 1.30pm – and people were saying on the radio that they'd just discovered it was a rather nice day and maybe they ought to aviate a bit. On the ground, high performance gliders could be seen preparing for their first, leisurely launch of the day. They would have discovered that it had been fantastic since 9.30am if only they'd got off their backsides. (To be fair, I'm sure the same leisurely carry-on was taking place back home.) It wouldn't matter so much if were not the same people that whinge about the horrendous cost per hour of gliding, the rarity of good days, the difficulty of getting utilisation etc, etc.

If you want a worthwhile resolution for the New Year, it is this: get up early; get the equipage and all the assorted junk out on the launch point and get your behind, and all that is strapped to it, into the empyrean at the earliest opportunity. If you are a slow pilot like me, the only way you will ever cover the ground is to use all the soaring hours that God sends. A few more touches of the blindingly obvious:

- It helps to pair-fly with friends; tiptoe along at a little over max glide speed, and stay in touch by radio and eyeball.

- Remember that when cloudbase is low the thermals are closer together, so it isn't so difficult as it looks. The lift at breakfast time is not strong but is almost continuous. That is how Hans-Werner Grosse used to do 1,000km flights in his ASW-17 years ago.

- Try to set a task such that there is a friendly airfield on track in the first 20 or 30km; then you can be reassured that if you do burn your boats too early you can get a relight and not waste the whole day in some meadow glaring up at the clouds and cursing Platypus. Take a good book along, though, just in case.

Killing retrieve time.

- If you really have launched prematurely, and the tug pulls you through dead air all the way to 2,000ft, carry on to 3,200ft over the site, announce Start in a clear, confident voice and glide out on track, praying. You are giving the thermals 20 minutes in which to wake up. (You are also impressing the hell out of your friends, who are listening to the radio still in their pyjamas and eating toast and marmalade. The lower the performance glider you do this in, the more impressed they will be, especially if they have shares in it.) If you get nothing by the time you get down to 2,000ft, you either press on or turn back as the mood takes you. I take no responsibility from here on.

In the greatest flight ever done in this country, 808km from Lasham to Durham and back in that other *wunder-jahr,* 1976, Chris Garton was 30km along track in his Kestrel 19 and down below 1,000ft, with no usable airfield in range, before he got his first thermal. That's the way to write a big flight not just into the logbook, but into the record book.

You will note that the sailplanes referred to in the foregoing piece are all available at reasonable prices these days, being to greater or lesser degree obsolete, but capable of terrific performance. So it is not a question of this being advice for Nimbus 3 owners which all others can ignore. It is a question of attitude. Lastly, if flying for seven hours and more does not appeal, then land at lunchtime and throw your partners into the air.

In 1999 Plat started the Dunstable Big Distance Group which uses the Internet to swap information about weather, ideal tasks and pair-flying opportunities.

Rules are like records: to be broken (1994)

On this freezing Saturday morning in January, unable to afford the time to go to Australia, there is nothing for me to do but fantasise about forthcoming big flights in the northern hemisphere in the spring of 1994. First I started browsing through the Times World Atlas, with the help of carefully measured lengths of string. Did you know, a straight distance 1,000km flight from the heart of England will take you to the Czech Republic?

Then I dived eagerly into the FAI Sporting Code, which I have never read before. I am of course, as W C Fields said in his old age when he was caught reading the Bible, looking for loopholes. My, that volume is an absolute cornucopia of laughs – not the Bible, silly, the FAI Sporting Code – a real bumper fun book. For instance the definitions, of which there are eight pages, are fascinating. Take this one:

"1.3.1. A Glider Flight: A flight by a glider starting at the take-off and terminating with the landing."

Phew! I wonder how long they sweated over that in smoke-filled rooms. Actually there is some sort of method here. After all they could easily have said, "...terminating with a cartwheel into a pile of rocks, the pieces to be distributed over at least three counties, states, *départements*, provinces or other administrative districts." But in their calm deliberations the committee refused to panic, and chose otherwise. A landing it has to be.

However, the way I read the small print, if you insist on cartwheeling into a wilderness, distributing bits over several local governmental regions, it still counts as a landing – BUT you must survive 48 hours to collect your badge, diploma, contest trophy or record. Well, that's not quite accurate either. If you step out of the wreckage with a huge sigh of relief and tread on a rattlesnake (or more likely expire from dehydration, if you forgot the wise advice of Dr Walt Cannon) then your sad departure to the everlasting gaggle within 48 hours does not disqualify you from getting your badge etc. It is the crash itself that has to do you in, not rattlers or thirst

Such a nasty word, *crash*. The FAI prefers *accident*. Ah! If you deliberately fly the machine into a spruce forest it doesn't count as an accident, then. The FAI rule-makers forgot that. (Gosh, I missed my vocation. I should have been a lawyer, haranguing juries in my wig. What a pleader the world has lost!)

A flight also fails to count as properly completed if anybody bales out. I'm always having to remind my passengers of that rule as they fumble nervously for the canopy release. "You might want to live," I say sternly, "but I want my record, so just stay put." If they continue fumbling for the canopy release, I start wondering out loud about which of the two parachutes was involved in the great pee-bag disaster last month, and about its not having been repacked yet.

Again, the FAI very fairly stipulates that a flight is not complete if the glider is not complete – that is, if anything important falls off or is jettisoned, like a wing or tail. This is to discourage people from continuing as if nothing had happened after a collision, and a very

Continuing as if nothing had happened.

> ## The 45-degree club (1994)
> *A chap I know once had a splendid day flying out of a wave site in dead of winter. He covered 500km over a glorious variety of countryside with not a sniff of a vulgar thermal from dawn to dusk. At the bar his flight was discussed along with the others as pilots compared notes on the day. The phone rang: a club member who had not flown that day was calling from home to ask how good the flying had been. The man who answered the phone, who had just been talking to my acquaintance, said, "Well, Mabel Higgs got to 15,000 and Basil Snooks got to 18,000, nothing much else," and put the phone down. The 500km was not interesting enough to mention because it was carried out below 12,500ft.*
> *It takes all sorts, I suppose.*

good rule it is too. It is so humiliating when other pilots fly better than you do with only half a glider. I took a dim view of it in the 1960s when Tony Deane-Drummond climbed past me in cloud and went miles further than me with a vast chunk of one wing missing after having collided with another high-ranking officer in an earlier cloud-climb.

Having enjoyed the simple definitions so much I naturally anticipated pruriently the trickier definitions: those applying to women pilots, for instance. I was disappointed. The committee utterly balked at defining a woman. All they say is:

"3.2.1.3. Feminine Records. Records obtained when all the persons aboard are of the feminine gender may be classified separately as well as in the general classification."

That expression *feminine gender* means *female sex*, but the committee doesn't like to talk dirty. To this Platypedant, glider pilots don't have gender, only words do. When trying to speak foreign languages the bane of an Englishman's life is gender. Thus we must remember that in French a fuselage (coque) is feminine and a rudder-bar masculine – don't ask me why. And German nouns and adjectives have three genders: masculine, feminine and neuter. In Russian even the wretched verbs, as well as the nouns and adjectives, have three genders. But to stop people babbling about *gender* when describing the sex of human beings is a losing battle. I guess the silly habit is here to stay. No doubt the job of a chicken-sexer, mildly challenging and even amusing for the first five minutes, will be reclassified as a fowl-genderer, but it won't make the chore any less tedious.

Many years ago a male glider pilot underwent a sex change and became a female glider pilot, then started swiping records that had

Compromises have to be made.

"Sorry, I thought you asked me to find a good place to LUNCH!" (1986)

For 1986 our old friend, the distinguished ex-chairman of the BGA, has picked a site reasonably near the middle of the Hexagon. (This is what French journalists like to call their country. Rivalling Fleet Street in leaving no metaphor unmixed, they blithely use expressions like, "all four corners of the Hexagon" while Descartes and Fermat revolve in their graves.) I'm afraid we will not be quite in the Texas of France, as French pilots like to call the area around Bourges. It turns out that my friend did not pick the place as I would have done, with the aid of a contour map (the fewer contours the better) and a list of French gliding records, but instead with the Guides Michelin and Gault-Millau and a wine atlas.

When one member of the party is looking for triple-Diamond country and the other for triple-rosette country, compromises have got to be made. I am reconciled. Apart from occasionally fighting for control of the menu, and setting aside a few quibbles over how to pronounce basic words like corkscrew, room temperature, magnum, medium rare, cream and truffle sauce, it is about as different from mountain-flying as you can get. Thank Heaven!

recently been set by a British woman pilot. When asked by the press what she felt about this, our ex-record-holder was diplomatic and just said, "If it's all right by the FAI it's all right by me." I suggested that she should have said, "If it's all right by the British Medical Association it's all right by me" or better still, "It couldn't happen to a nicer chap" but facetiousness was not her style.

I imagine, though the rules are lamentably vague on this important issue, that the FAI would prefer it if a male pilot did not complicate things by actually changing sex during the flight, or, horrors! within 48 hours of distributing the glider over three counties. (Note to Peter Fuller. We don't need a cartoon for this bit, thanks. Ed.)

Out & return (1999)

Saturday March 27 was one of those wonderful but rare early days in the season, with unlimited visibility, well-behaved thermals and cloudbase nearly 5,000 ft. Even getting down to 900 ft – a considerable feat of ineptitude in such easy conditions in an ASH-25 – caused no worry; there were hundreds of excellent fields to choose from. The ground had barely woken up to the fact that real sunshine was tugging green shoots upwards.

On the last leg of our 312 km task, from East Swindon to Dunstable, my partner said to me, "That's Fairford, north of Swindon, where the B-52's bombing Yugoslavia are based." I didn't know this, because I have recently tried to give up newspapers and television in favour of the Times Literary Supplement, the Scientific American and books of an improving nature. A few minutes after my friend made this observation two vast black shapes appeared to the left of our track, trailing clouds of dirty smoke from eight engines apiece. Their pilots were gently letting down after unleashing cruise missiles, or whatever was their ordnance that day, with what effects I don't know. I don't suppose they know either.

Shadows falling across an otherwise flawless English spring afternoon. Some pilots fly for money, some fly for fun; but there is a third, compelling reason for taking to the air, which we don't care to think about until we absolutely have to. I wonder how often we shall see them this summer. ∎

Survival of the fittest, fastest, most cunning, devious etc

Younger readers start here: once upon a time, by which I mean about 30 years ago, pilots in a competition could take off more or less any time they liked, and depart on course whenever it suited them. The launch time was not held, nor was the start of a race. In fact the only things that were held in those days were parties.

As the number of gliders in championships got bigger, congestion at the launch point was eased by issuing each pilot with a numbered disk with a hole in it. The pilot then placed the disc on one of hundreds of nails that had been hammered into a large board, each nail representing a launch time like 1120, 1122 and so on. The order of choice was rotated every contest day, as take-off times are now. This was supposed to make the system fair, or at least not quite so grossly unfair.

Continual gamesmanship around the board took place, since a disc could be moved by the pilot at any time, any number of times. It is said that Nick Goodhart, finding the lottery had left him with no launch time near the moment he desired, gave the appearance of thinking long and hard; he then carefully placed his disk two hours away from the time that the general consensus believed to be the best. The lesser contestants began to wonder if they had not made a ghastly error, and a few of them nervously took their disks out of prime time and shifted them close to Nick's. A hole opened up and Nick pounced, taking the prime launch slot that he had coveted all along.

Playing with one's disc – touching anyone else's was taboo – could occupy the entire afternoon, especially if the weather was grey and all the cumulus tantalisingly on the horizon. The system kept pilots too busy and out of mischief: every now and again someone would launch and probably fail to soar, and whether we followed them into the air was our own decision, which we continuously pondered. We had no opportunity, as have today's competitors, to stand around in mutinous groups for hours whinging about the management until the day is scrubbed.

Once the task was set early in the morning, it could not be cancelled. This kept us on our toes. Anybody, just some guy with no talent but a deal of persistence, might rig a third time after two outlandings and two road retrieves (air retrieves were not allowed) and sneak away after a six o'clock launch and scoop 1,000 points by drifting 50kms or so downwind in the dusk when everyone else had given up. I did it myself once or twice and very satisfying it was too. The value of a day was not scaled down, as it is today, according to the number of contestants failing to exceed a substantial distance like 100kms.

In short it was a grossly arbitrary, chancy and unfair system, except that the same pilots seemed to win the whole time. Maybe fairness is crucial to the second-raters – they talk of nothing else – but is nothing special so far as the real champions are concerned. No matter how you fix the rules to eliminate luck, those same people will get lucky again and again.

The art of coarse gliding (1964)

The best way to define Coarse Gliding is by stating what it is not.

It is not as described in *On Being a Bird* or in *The Soaring Pilot* or in films that start off with seagulls and the usual pretentious voice-over droning on about, "Man's Age-long Dream of Flight."

From reading such books or seeing such films one realises that there exists a super-race of real glider pilots, known in the trade as Pundits. They own airworthy gliders, launched by serviceable tugs, retrieved by roadworthy cars containing tireless, devoted crews. They have infallible radio with a sixty-mile range which they use in brisk military style. They have new batteries; they describe thermals in knots, never in feet per second. They really use the John Williamson Calculator.

They understand the UK Contest Pilot Rating System. They are allowed to fly foreign prototypes straight out of the box. Their crashes are forgiven, however serious. Their barograph traces look like shark's teeth. They have swung their compasses. They come out of clouds pointing the right way. They write brilliant accounts of their flights.

As I was saying, the Coarse Glider Pilot is not one of these. The best-sellers of aviation literature are written for, but not by or about, Coarse Pilots. They are the submerged 99% of whom no bard sings.

Coarse Pilots are easy to identify. They can be seen feverishly doing their Certificate of Airworthiness in July. They live always for "the great day" and are never ready when it

and are never ready ...

comes. Their gliders, trailers and cars show the ravages of time, brutal handling and inspired improvisation. Coarse Pilots sneer at the pompous phrase, "sound engineering practice." If the wing fittings begin to get sloppy, bending the pins slightly will restore the feeling of a good push fit. They build trailers in mid-air, so to speak, without plans or jigs. Gap-filling glue was invented for Coarse Pilots.

Every coarse-built trailer is different and will sometimes not take a glider of identical make to the one around which it was built. Coarse trailers are often finished on the first day of a contest and may be coming apart on the last. One basically sound trailer for which I was 50% responsible had rather crude doors which, for lack of time to construct anything better, had to be nailed shut and opened with a claw hammer or jemmy. This door fell off repeatedly until one day it disappeared alto-

gether during a retrieve, which was a great relief. The trailer in question had one white-painted side, green mudguard and fourteen-inch wheel and one side painted in grey undercoat and never finished, black mudguard – scrap-heaps rarely yield neatly matching items – and thirteen-inch wheel (the spare from the A35 tow-car). If there had been any accidents (which, incredible to relate, there were not) it would have been interesting to hear the witnesses contradicting each other.

Competitions bring out the worst in the Coarse Pilot. He has no hope of winning but is content to have a vicious feud with the pilot who is a few points in front in 23rd place. Simply to see this one rival flop to earth below is pure nectar. It is one of the few occasions on which the Coarse Pilot will break into song as if intoxicated. The only other occasion is when he is intoxicated. Asked what is the greatest pleasure in gliding, he says, "Grinding the other fella's face" with disarming honesty.

Pundits go to briefings and appear to understand the weather even when the forecasters don't. The Coarse Pilot stays in bed till eleven, preferring to keep his mind clear and his body rested. He usually remembers to enquire what the task is just as the canopy closes. He'll find out about the weather when he gets up there. As one of them says, "Give him an old Esso road map and a packet of cigarettes and he's happy."

As a matter of fact, 1964 was a real Coarse Pilot's Nationals. Pundits prefer not to mention 1964 at all, and I believe steps may be taken to expunge the whole ghastly episode from the records, like Russian history. The Wrong Chap won.

The really damning case against the Coarse Pilot is that he does not cultivate public opinion either in regard to himself or the gliding movement. A recurring bad dream of a Senior Pundit must surely be this...in the lounge of a four-star hotel he is convincing a Cabinet Minister what a fine, clean-limbed body of men glider-pilots are, worthy of limitless government subsidy, when in shambles a gang of scruffy, unshaven oicks, the sort of people who steal locking-wire and never return screwdrivers. Having no sense of occasion they hail our Pundit loudly and ask him what he was doing down in that silly little field. Making ribald references to his last crash, they produce a pack of beer-stained cards and insist that Pundit and Minister join them in a game of five-card stud poker, pot limit £15. Each big winning hand buys a round of hard liquor. At every opportunity there are allusions to what the Actress said to somebody, which evoke raucous guffaws without fail. An hour later the Minister is cleaned out, cuff-links and all. He declines a generous offer of a lift home in the trailer and departs, leaving our Pundit in tears. Collapse of grandiose million-pound Government plan for gliding, ruin of gliding's image, etc., etc. . .

Bad dream? Heavens, it really will happen one day, and the rotters won't even be sorry.

After 36 years I am touched to see that the upper limit of technical sophistication was to know how to use a simple plastic circular slide-rule. Now a contest glider contains more computing power than the entire US Air Force possessed in 1964. In 2000 AD if you turn up at a competition without a full-time Information Technology Manager in your crew and your own IBM PC pre-loaded with the turnpoint data and all the relevant programs to take to briefings, you'll just flounder. I was going to say They won't speak to you, but that's not true. The scorers and competitions management will speak to you at great length, slowly and very patiently, but you won't understand a word they are saying.

How the sore people saved the world (1971)

In 1971 the Royal Air Force base at Newton, near Nottingham, was the venue for the British National Championships,. The competition director was Ian Strachan (pronounced Strawn, this being a Scots name, I explain to our readers abroad) who had in the mid-1960s strayed from the True Path and taken what was considered an eccentric interest in gliders that could launch themselves with engines. The meteorologist was Ron Cashmore. The competition was won in an Open Cirrus by Bernard Fitchett, possibly the most naturally talented and intuitive soaring pilot ever. Platypus also flew in this competition, to no special glory except that for once he did not break anything. He does remember paying handsomely for crops that he laid waste with his Dart 17. The weather was awful, but contrary to galactic leg-

end we did actually leave the ground a few times. I have the farmers' receipts to prove it.

The despot of Jupiter, known to his subjects as the Frekon, sat enthroned in his palace, plotting his impending invasion of Earth. He summoned his chief intelligence agent, Pewkon. "O Pewkon, how fare your enquiries into the mind-ways of the Earthlings, that we may know how best to subjugate these creatures?"

Pewkon delivered a snappy triple-clawed salute. "O Frekon, the boys in Socio-Psychological Intelligence (known to the monster in the street as SPI) have come up with something pretty weird just when we guessed we had the guys on Earth figured out OK."

"Pray illuminate the Frekon's mind. Our invasion cannot commence until all the Earthlings' ways are known to us."

"Well, a couple of days back we put Burpon to work on the In-depth Video-scanner but with a difference; instead of sweeping the whole Earth continuously we focused on one spot for 48 hours. And boy! I tell you what Burpon saw was real spooky!" Pewkon whistled through his mandibles.

The Frekon's claw waved impatiently, bidding Pewkon to continue.

"As I said, little old B was zeroed in on Lat 53 degrees N, Long 1 degree W; he reports he saw a hundred-and-fifty earthlings converge on a morning-prayer meeting, after which they rushed out and opened 40 boxes on wheels (about 20 cubits[5] long, give or take a claw). They began to assemble enormous white birds, about 40 cubits in spread. Some used little trolleys, trestles and very few earthlings, and were quickly assembled. Others used many earthlings and no scientific equipment and were only assembled after much blaspheming, cries for help and even the loss of blood."

"Such urgency and suffering means one thing," observed the Frekon. "The birds are machines of war and must be prevented from taking the air against us."

"Well, hold on there," squeaked Pewkon, "these guys are proud of the total uselessness of their birds from any military standpoint."

"Then surely they must be essential to the support of their homes, the nurturing of their young or the prosperity of the coming harvest?"

"Well, not even that," said Pewkon, "the boys in Economic Warfare said that the great white birds are a drain on the earthlings' pockets, they don't see their kids for most of the summer and the effect on the harvest, if they ever get airborne, will chiefly be to reap a lot of it before the farmers are ready."

Pewkon scratched his carapace thoughtfully and went on, "Psychological Warfare said the suffering and expense would only be justified if the whole exercise was essential to – er – the reproduction of the species."

The Frekon's eye lit up. (He only had one eye.) "You mean sex?"

"Well yes, kinda. That was the idea anyway. But they found that the birds hampered rather than helped the mating process and many of the great-white-bird-fanciers are quite celibate, all capacity for love, devotion and sacrifice being dedicated to 40 cubits of glass-fibre."

The Frekon interrupted the meeting briefly to instruct his Air-Marshals to hold up mobilisation for the invasion.

"To get back to Burpon's report," continued Pewkon, "the 50 birds were towed to the middle of a vast field and set out in rows pointed towards the East." He paused to let the significance of this sink in.

"Then what did the earthlings do?" demanded the Frekon.

---

[5] A cubit is about half a metre, being the length of a human forearm. Owing to the massive gravity of Jupiter, the inhabitants are only about a cubit tall, so the size of Earthmen's sailplanes, useless though they are, deeply impresses the Jovian rulers.

> ### Shocking perils of competition flying (1998)
> *I felt particularly responsible after John Glossop invented a novel form of electric chair when he hit a farmer's power line with a lot of volts – and a lot of amps, too, which I believe is what really cooks people in Sing-Sing. He was roasted by the metal in his parachute harness and seat belt and by the coins in his pockets, ending up in Stoke Mandeville hospital, where I paid a tearful visit as the brutal task-setter who had nearly sent him to a fiery end. For months after that I went around with no change in my pockets (like royalty), for fear of scorching vital parts in similar circumstances.*

"Nothing. Absolutely not a thing," wailed Pewkon. "They just sat there all day. Then at the end of the day they took the birds back, dismantled them and put them back in their boxes."

"And the next day?"

"Exactly the same. The whole rigmarole repeated from start to finish. Burpon said he'd have a nervous breakdown if we made him watch for a third day so we switched him to the World Series Baseball for a rest."

At this point Burpon entered, apparently fully recovered, waving excited tentacles. "I've just been re-running those tapes. I've got it!

"The earthlings are the unhappy slaves of two priests, Strorn and Ronmet, generally known as the Taskmasters. Those two control the weather."

"Even we on Jupiter cannot achieve that," gravely intoned the Frekon. "How can you be sure?"

"By the abuse that the earthlings (who because the word 'Sore' is one they use with most frequency and reverence, I call the Sore People) heap on the Taskmasters when the weather is bad. No intelligent life-form would blame their priests for bad weather unless the priests controlled the elements."

"Very true," murmured the Frekon, "but why do the priests tolerate such abuse from their slaves if they are omnipotent?"

"It is a harmless safety-valve for the frustrations of the Sore People. Besides, Taskmasters need not worry about popularity when they have the satisfaction of knowing that they can make the sun shine at will."

"If they can do that, why do they not make the sun shine?"

"Because they know what the Sore People do not, namely that it is impossible to fly without propulsive power. Fine weather would simply tempt the Sore People to throw their great white birds into the air and destroy them. You see, the birds are made of glass!"

Even the Frekon could barely resist a smile at the folly of the Sore People and the cunning of their Taskmasters.

"The Sore People," continued Burpon, "vainly hope that they might one day, like angels, defy gravity and fly without power. This manifest delusion is perpetuated by superstitious ceremonies designed to placate the God of Gravity, the field being named after Isaac Newton himself."

"These Taskmasters, do they share the Sore People's delusions?"

"They certainly do not! Strorn has been observed flying around in a white bird but with a little engine. Thus while the great white glass birds lie stranded on the ground, he can humble the slaves with his mastery of the heavens."

"Perhaps we should follow their example to keep our own subjects under control," said the Frekon. "Pewkon, I appoint you CFI and Arch-taskmaster. Forget about the Earth Invasion and set up a Jupiter Nationals immediately."

"Gee, boss, that's just swell!" exclaimed Pewkon.

"Oh, and one other thing. I would be grateful if you would stop watching all those old American movies on the Video-scanner. Peace be with you."

Legendary lager lout (1974)

There are two types of pilot that enter competitions regularly: those that enter despite the evident fact that contests bring out the worst in human nature, and those that enter contests precisely because they bring out the worst in human nature. There is no obvious correlation between bad behaviour and success: noble, selfless traits can be found at every level from World Champion down to the rookie. Aggressive, selfish, cowardly and downright vicious traits are likewise randomly distributed over the skill spectrum. At this point I feel the laws of libel closing in. However I am confident that the subject of this next piece will not sue for defamation. Indeed I think he is secretly rather proud of the character that this article reveals.

Whenever *S&G* prints an article by, for or about top pilots, we are always inundated with letters from peasan – sorry, from less experienced pilots who will never be champions and who want to hear about the struggles and triumphs of ordinary chaps struggling at the bottom of the pile. This month our reporter 'Q' interviews Platypus, a proudly self-confessed peasant-pilot who, practically single-handed, has made British coarse gliding what it is today – a blood sport second only to rat-catching. A refrigerator full of free Australian beer was the only inducement as our soaring skinhead bared all to the tape-recorder.

Platypus, in 1972 at Pissoire you came in 69th, but in 1974 at Bad Freidegg you came in 45th. What explains the difference?

I think I can confidently attribute that vast improvement to the fact that at Pissoire there were 69 pilots competing, whereas at Bad Freidegg there were 45.

Oh.

Pass that tube of Foster's, there's a good lad. Ta.

Do you think pilots of your calibre should be recommended to fly at demanding international contests such as Angers and Hahnweide?

Well, the people at Angers recommended me to fly at Hahnweide, and the people at Hahnweide said I should fly at Angers, and everybody in Britain says the more I fly abroad the better. So I guess you're right.

Tell me how your mind works when you're really keyed up on a competition day.

On the ground, I can say without fear of contradiction (I smash their teeth in if they do contradict) that my mind works faster than anyone else's. Especially on the old pilot-selection take-off times: when it comes to switching those discs around the board, my gamesmanship is designed to fox the competition completely – the disc is a blur in my hands as I shift it from nail to nail. You should see the others panicking to get to the board!

Is this because the other pilots want to launch the same time as you?

On the contrary, mate – pass me another lager, I hate stretching – the chaos is due to the other blokes all desperately switching times so as not to take the air within half an hour either side of me. That, and my skill in asking trick questions at briefing, has been known to cause other pilots to fly round triangles the wrong way and get disqualified.

Fantastic! But what I was really interested in was how your mind worked in the air.

I can tell you, the moment that towline goes taut an amazing transformation comes over me.

Go on.

I will if you don't keep interrupting. (Pour me a Foster's, lad. Ta.) Yes, at that electrifying moment – my adrenaline begins to flow with the speed of frozen treacle and my brain switches off totally. The old CFI noticed that very early on in my training in the T-21. Sent me solo in no time as a result. Well, he had a wife and kids, I suppose. "Better just you than us both" he used to say. What a card he was!

Longevity is the better part of valour, I dare say. But getting back to contest flying, don't you find this inability to think once airborne something of a handicap?

Not in the slightest. It accounts for my being so relaxed and without a sign of strain. The other pilots worry and make fresh decisions constantly. They get worn out, poor devils.

Quite amazing. Now, Platypus, on the finer points of closed-circuit racing: what is your inter-thermal speed-to-fly philosophy?

Very simple. I have two speeds: 50kts and 150kts. The transition between the two I make on the spur of the moment. My mind may work slowly but my arm muscles work fast.

Isn't that inefficient from the point of view of optimising cross-country performance?

In theory, yes. But it means no other pilots dare fly within a height band of 1,000ft above or below me.

Are you a loner, or do you like gaggling?

Gaggles? I don't remember seeing one ever, except occasionally at a distance. Why they all leave such lovely thermals in so much of a hurry I can't imagine, but I blame those damn silly calculators.

You mean John Willy computers. You don't use one?

Pah. If you can see it you can reach it, I always say. (Hell, who's been keeping food in the fridge? Panic over, lad – I found a six-pack of Victoria Bitter.) If you can't see it, stay good and high, then do a kamikaze on the place when it comes into view.

Isn't that, er, inefficient?

Yeah, theoretically – but I've seen other competitors pull out their brakes and land short in six-foot-high maize rather than cross the line when I'm finishing.

One up to you Platypus: Now, what are your views about water?

Never touch the stuff: you know what fish do in it, don't you? Next question.

What do you see as the major obstacle to your future as a competition pilot?

The insurance companies, definitely.

It says here that your gliding career started in earnest after you went solo at Castle Bromwich in 1949.

Yes, but my expulsion from the Air Cadets put an end to that, regrettably. Really the 1950's around the various sites were the formative years of my pubescent life in all ways except one, though I believe some clubs have remedied that deficiency recently. Hey, you know, I've heard....

Er, yes, fascinating, but what I was really interested in was whether you feel age and experience are more important than youth and vigour.

Well, that was what I was on about

In competition gliding, I mean.

Oh. Well, I am the only pilot I know who was ever grounded for senility, but I think that was just a dirty manoeuvre by the Flying Committee.

What makes you say that?

I was only 24 at the time. However, when I bought my own ship, it was as though I had suddenly taken the elixir of youth: they said I could fly as far from the site as I liked, preferably downwind in a gale. That was real vote of confidence, and I've never looked back since.

Platypus, where are you flying in 1975?

Oh, California, Uzbekistan, that sort of thing. Hey, Q, where are you off to?

New Zealand – on the next jumbo!

That splendid body of men & women (1984)

I've just been asked, by someone who should know better, to set the tasks for a little competition this season. Naturally I accepted. But how did they guess that I had sadistic tendencies? (Maybe they just read your column. Ed.)

I have always said, of course, that task-setters were a splendid body of men, sadly maligned, misunderstood and under-appreciated. (You've never said anything of the kind! Ed.) Well, if I haven't said it, I've always thought it, particularly since That Day.

It was in a National Championships in the 1970s; a triangle not much short of 300km had been set and no sooner had the task-board gone up than the blue skies turned leaden grey, with a solid base of 1,800ft, and stayed that way for several hours. In no time at all a trade union committee claiming to represent all fully-paid-up contestants was convened, and was in continuous session all morning and right through the lunch hour. Fraternal delegates drafted manifestos. Bunched fists were silhouetted against the unrelenting heavens as little knots of malcontents pledged solidarity against The Management. The chief trouble-stirrer amongst these agitators suggested – nay, demanded – that we should all sit on the ground and refuse to take off till The Management made a better offer such as 1) Smaller Task or 2) Immediate Scrub and General Retirement to the Bar – the

latter Composite Resolution carrying the union block vote by a landslide.

Management, however, was not merely stubborn, it was diabolically intransigent. Near-mutinous pilots were straitjacketed whinging into their cockpits and towed belly-aching into the grey flatness that still stretched from horizon to horizon. There seemed no option but to glide it out from release and maybe flop down in a field ten miles or so down track. Mutter, gripe, whine etc etc. At around eight miles from base, however, the universal grousing quieted down as variometers began to speak up – a much happier noise. To cut a long story short, it was a pretty good day by British standards, with half a dozen finishers.

Natural modesty prevents me from saying who got back first and took the Daily Prize. All I will say is that since then task-setters have been pretty OK by me and can do no wrong.

That was indeed the only day I have ever won in any National Championships. One brief hour of glory, which did so much for my self-esteem that I rammed the Kestrel into a hedge on the last competition day. "What do you mean, I'm going to have to land soon? Let me remind you that you're talking to the winner of Day Five!"

Mrs Plat then wrote the glider off totally on the motorway during the retrieve when the engine blew up at 70 mph. Glider pilots really should study Greek literature, especially the stuff about Hubris and his close companion, Nemesis.

Don't blame the competition reports, blame the competitions (1984)

Wandering around the 1984 BGA Conference exhibition, I bought an ancient copy of *Sailplane & Gliding*, with the results of the 1950 National Championships, flown from my favourite other site in Britain, Camphill, home of the Derby & Lancashire Gliding Club. It's a favourite site for reasons of ego: that's where I won the only competition I've ever won in my life.

Philip Wills knocked off the winner's prize as easily as he penned a page of prose, and gave me to think: why are competition reports of those days – long before even I did my Silver C – so fascinating to read years later, and competition reports today so incredibly tedious? Since I write many competition reports myself, I am as much to blame as anyone – if the wretched reporters are to blame at all. No, don't shoot the messenger. It is because competitions themselves are now becoming boring to anyone except the participants – and even to some of them, I suspect.

When Philip Wills flew in his Weihe from Camphill to Boston on the Lincolnshire coast, and nearly made it back, landing with his big wings and tiny airbrakes amongst the stone walls in the little fields at the bottom of the valley, out-and-returns were virtually unheard of. It was something new, not just in contest flying, but in British gliding altogether. When Nick Goodhart declared Portmoak from Lasham in 1959 and got there using streets, cu-nims, ridges, wave, indeed every source of lift except sea breeze, we all relived it vicariously – every club pilot learnt from it and was inspired by it.

In 1964 John Fielden showed us what distances could be flown along sea-breeze fronts on coasts east and west. He left the pundits way behind to take the winner's cup, which made them all grumble that it obviously cannot have been a proper championships. He was not invited to join the World Team. If it was a freak, it was a wonderful freak which made splendid copy in our magazine.

Competitions were where new parts of the country were traversed, new sources of lift explored and where we extended what was possible in the sport. Hence the competition reports were intrinsically interesting to all of us, regardless of whether we were competitively-minded. Now *nothing* new happens in the Championships – because the task-setters and the organisers (people like me under my other hat) work manfully to *prevent* anything interesting from happening. If I stood up in front of the Nationals pilots and said, "Today's will be a really different and unusual task..." there would be panic and rage and a lynching-bee would be rapidly organised before I'd even finished. Tow ropes would be put to novel uses, not to mention winch-axes.

Seven triangles all going through Husbands Bosworth with 80% finishing is what they want – and that is just what is served up to them, God willing, by us, the craven contest directors. But to say that a blow-by-blow account of such a week will not make the average reader's blood race is a very British understatement.

The situation has since got worse. I doubt if speed or distance records will ever again be broken in a British competition. A regulation FAI triangle, with no side bigger than 28% of the total distance,

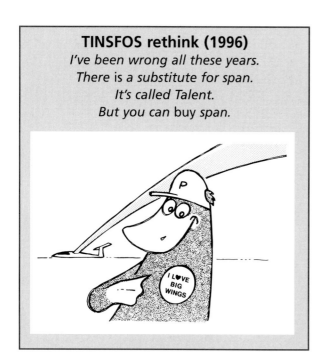

TINSFOS rethink (1996)
I've been wrong all these years.
There is a substitute for span.
It's called Talent.
But you can buy span.

is almost impossible to set as a task now. With the twin constraints of airspace and the pilots' aversion to going anywhere near the sea, a big task on a good day looks like an exercise in advanced origami. The route has so many folds in it that I should now say, "Seven polygons (not triangles) all going through Husbands Bosworth."

I might not of course be reckoning with the ingenuity of the rule-makers: someday soon they may allow a task with five or six turnpoints to count for a record or a badge, and an aspirant for a 500km diamond will be able to achieve it without getting out of sight of the club, even in British visibility.

Brain surgeon wipes out memory (1992)

In a recent competition at Issoudun in France the famous transplant surgeon, Mike Thick, and ASH-25 pilot took with him as navigator a famous brain surgeon. (No, I'm not making this up, honest.) One day the navigator managed inadvertently to delete the waypoints from the GPS, and was seen spending the afternoon – wet and windy and nothing else to do anyway – sitting in the rear cockpit of the glider in a far corner of the field, patiently re-entering all the latitudes and longitudes one at a time. There can be as many as 250 of the damn things, so the sooner the input-process can be automated the better. There will be at least one keen customer.

Of course we can do that just now in seconds. Assuming of course that you have the connectors and cables and the right software in your IBM, and the computers are on speaking terms. Otherwise you may still find yourself spending hours sitting alone in a corner of some foreign field.

Thoughts of Superchamp (1984)

Not many multi-millionaires have taken up gliding, most preferring the social cachet of ocean-racing. Having observed at close quarters a rare, flamboyant instance of such a man in our sport, Platypus wondered how he himself might have behaved if had been blessed with two gifts which he has always longed for: soaring talent and the ability to make quick and hugely lucrative deals.

Time is money. Don't know who first said that,[6] but it's my favourite cliché. The 64 million-dollar question (actually the 65.372 million dollar question, but let's not mess with small change) is, how do I sew up the Qatar oil deal, buy next year's coffee crop, lease that place in Threadneedle Street *and* win the Nationals at the same time? In spite of my business pressures, yesterday's win was pretty conclusive, though Jonesey was griping about the navigational help I had all round the course from my crew – Hands, Knees and Bumpsadaisy – who were using a computer linked to a satellite to track the transponder in my Blunderbus 4. (Damn cheek; it *was* my satellite.)

Naturally Day 6 is pretty tense, but as usual I play it, very, very cool. It really psychs me up and, better still, it psychs them down...

0925: Breakfast in bed. Croissants flown in from Le Touquet, devilled kidneys, scrambled eggs, etc. The Grauniad business section has a piece about my triumphs in the city, but full of typographical errors. Mental note: after the Nationals I'll buy that rag and get some new proof-readers. They can't even spell the names of my racehorses, let alone my name.

0932: Accept call from contest director congratulating me on five daily prizes in a row and regretting that I have not been able to show up to accept any of them. I suggest with a light laugh that he presents the daily prizes to me *in advance* before I take off. He clearly thinks this very droll; he says the pilots have banded together to buy me a clock, so if I get something ticking in the post, that's all it is.

0950: Leap out of bed. Good time for highly confidential telephone call in shower to Lee Kwan Yew (standing in another shower in Singapore) to fix supertanker deal. Exit feeling refreshed and richer.

0955: Am driven to City in the Bentley. H, K and B call on car radio-telephone (the one with the built in Met-map facsimile machine) with details of task. Glider is rigged and watered; maps fully marked up and onboard microprocessor fully programmed. Not bad. May not have to sack them after all. The servant problem is a real pain these days. I keep them waiting while on the other line I buy a football ground, a baseball team and put in a

---

[6] I've since been told that Benjamin Franklin first said it.

Platypomes (1983)

Whenever I fly on a task I find myself churning out limericks about the towns that represent the turning points. The limericks have nothing to do with gliding but help keep the mind occupied – so as not to waste time on such trivia as navigation, calculating rates of climb, average cross-country speeds, final glides etc. Since everyone will soon have computers to do all those things for us, there should be no need for the brain cells to do anything but meditate. Contest pilots could be given a theme by the task-setters immediately before take-off and the winning pilot would be the one who had written the best sonnet – or epic poem if it's a 500 km triangle – by the time he gets back. The prizes for speed and distance will of course be awarded to the manufacturers of the glider and the onboard avionics.
Thus, for a West Country turnpoint:

A daring young nun of Devizes
Has a habit the Bishop despises
It's not the cut of her cloth
That brings on his wrath
But her love life, which rather surprises.

I like the double entendre on habit, geddit? No? Oh well, please yourself.

There's also the Ghoulish young lady of Frome, who likes to make love in a tomb, and to the north the Cunning old craftsman from Goole. The list is endless.

Flying eastwards is trickier. Bury St Edmunds and Cambridge aren't very amenable and the editor won't let me do the one about the young lady from Diss. The number of times she says this is a family magazine – has she seen what they get up to in family magazines these days?

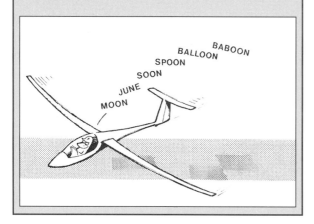

bid for a gliding club where I can build an exclusive private hangar.

1015: BBC Panorama and Money Programme teams fighting to get into my office to interview me. Double-booked. Don't know how it happened. Sack secretary.

1107: H, K and B call. First take-off due 1230. At current launch rate I'll be airborne at between 1242 and 1244. I tell them I don't care much for their lack of precision, they'd better sharpen up. Spirit of Francis Drake. "Plenty of time to make a small fortune and beat the Spaniards," he said, or words to that effect. All right for him – the Armada was hurtling up the Channel at all of three miles an hour, so of course he had bags of time. Damn good PR, all the same. Must cultivate same studied nonchalance.

1130: Address audience of young executives on the virtues of thrift, modesty, how to be a good loser, humility etc, etc. They all applaud like mad. Imbeciles. Wouldn't hire one of them

1225: Down to the helipad on the Thames. Up and away. Hackenheimer rings me from New York – from his helicopter, would you believe? These Yanks really take the biscuit when it comes to ostentation. Time for my man-of-action-but-few-words act. "Yes. No. Fine. Maybe. No. Yes. OK. Done. Goodbye." Sixty seconds later I am worth 400,000 smackers more.

1243: My pilot has some trouble getting any sense out of Dunstable Control as he seeks permission to land. It seems the airwaves are entirely gummed up with pesky Nationals pilots and the Startline yammering away. My arrival is delayed by 75 seconds. I am helped, still in natty Savile Row pinstripes, into the old bus. (I say "old" for purely sentimental reasons; it cost 50,000 green ones. In fact it's so new, when we opened the trailer door on the morning of Day One, three *gastarbeiter* from Schempp-Hirth fell out. They'd been fettling and polishing away frantically to beat the penalty clause I always insist on.) I close the canopy with a bang on H's fingers as the towrope goes taut. Do that again, young fella, and I buy a new crew and you buy new fingers. Nevertheless, precision timing, I have to admit, and you can see everyone around is pretty impressed as we stagger off towards the pig farm and the power wires.

Now for the hard bit. "Hey, Bumpsadaisy, what are all these bloody knobs for..?"

At the pharmacy (1985)

I have in the past mentioned the inadvisability of testing polarising specs at the chemist's by wagging and revolving the head while staring up at the sky, on account of the imminent arrival of the men in white coats. It occurs to me that I am extremely lucky that my behaviour at the local pharmacy has not led to the arrival of men in blue coats, or even the Plain Clothes Branch from Scotland Yard.

I stroll into the small suburban emporium, intent on the next competition and aware of nothing except my usual pathetic state of unreadiness for it.

Be careful of the men in white coats.

"Some camphor blocks, please," I say calmly, trying to keep my head absolutely level and hoping they have forgotten the Polaroid glasses episode of the week before.

"Got a bad chest, then, dearie?" she says, handing me the merchandise, shipped all the way from the People's Republic of China.

"Thank you, Madam, but my chest is in as good shape as your own." (A gross exaggeration, but never mind.) "If you are desirous of knowing my purpose, I intend to set fire to this stuff to make clouds of dense black smoke."

I notice she is edging towards the telephone, so I ask her for a notorious brand of cheapo hairspray which smells like a Bangkok bordello on a Saturday night, but fixes a trace in a trice at half the price. (I really don't know why I hire copywriters to do advertisements for me when I have all this unused talent.)

She is about to promote a brand more in keeping with my status as a mature company

director and respectably married ratepayer of this parish, but thinks better of it and just gives me an odd look. I have not got the time to convince her that the only thing about me that is bent is my metal Caproni two-seater, following a ground-loop in a meadow last month.

The methylated spirits (for cleaning maps) and clear plastic bags (for you know what) go into the shopping-basket unremarked, as do the aeromodelling requisites: old-fashioned razor blades, please, not the new-fangled sealed-in kind, and soda-siphon capsules for carbon-dioxide motors. The demand for castor oil is countered by her kind advice that more palatable laxatives are now marketed; I say that what goes for my chest also applies to my bowels. I explain that I am about to take part in a Rubber Event and that castor oil is a very good lubricant, though a mixture of soft soap and glycerine, carefully simmered for hours, is preferred by the cognoscenti. Mrs Platypus often tells me that my desire to explain things in detail is a mistake; in this instance she is spot on.

The last straw is when I ask for hypodermic needles – to make tiny droplets of glue for the construction of microfilm models to fly in Cardington airship hangar. My eyeballs are carefully scrutinised for signs of addiction and/or criminality; the proprietor is hauled out of his back room and I am interrogated at great length.

However I doubt if any of the foregoing compares with the scene that must have taken place years ago when George Burton discovered the ideally resilient material for mass-manufacturing total energy diaphragms...

Competition paranoia (1988)

There are days when for the first hour or so I can't get my act together (let's forget the years when for the first month or so I can't get it together) and it seems the glider won't climb, while every supposedly inferior ship whiffles up past me, and in the glide I get lower and further behind. There is no point whinging about it on the radio; you just hear Ralph Jones jeering, "Get a Nimbus!"

Unwilling to admit that my flying could be at fault, I glare out along the wings and wonder whether I have bolted them on upside down or left the dive-brakes out. I know what it is, the flaps aren't connected. Wish I could see the damn flaps from here; my neck is hurting trying to crane round and under. "Look out you idiot!" Oops, sorry. Another 15m Class goes past. What is wrong?

You know what it's like when you have a tiny sore inside your mouth and it feels like a golf ball? Well, one midge squashed on the wing looks the size of an elephant when you're in this self-pitying frame of mind. Wait, this is galloping paranoia – haven't all the other gliders got monster bugs, too? Yes, but they've got smaller wings so they catch fewer bugs. It's not fair.

Then I think I have left the wheel down, and it has taken on the dimensions of the wheel in the little diagram down by the undercarriage lever, which makes the wheel look the size of the front roller on a traction engine. How can a fellow soar with a steam-roller wheel dangling out in the breeze? No, the wheel is up. It must be something else.

Can't get my act together.

Yes, the instruments; they can always be blamed, why didn't I think of it before? The pipes are full of weevil's eggs; and they've been hooked up wrongly by some fool, probably me; the terminals have been reversed by a saboteur (probably me again); the batteries are defunct and should have been scrapped months ago; the solder joints must have crumbled after yesterday's landing, I know it. The more good reasons I find for not being able to soar, the worse my flying gets.

Then WHAM! Quite by chance I hit a corker; all the little gliders dwindle below and behind, and I even begin to get some of the big ones in my gun-sights. The steamroller and the elephants vanish, the wings, flaps, brakes, pipes and wires have suddenly been reconnected the right way, the weevils hatch out and fly off, the gelcoat sparkles and yesterday's landing was a baby's kiss after all.

What *was* all the fuss about...?

What a waste! (1989)

Time was, if you said to your CFI "Chiefy – " (I'm assuming he was not the sort that would an ground you instantly for calling him Chiefy, though personally I would never have dared to, not even when I was young and bold) " – on my next gliding holiday I want to put as many hours in my logbook as possible. I want to fly as many miles as possible and to see the widest variety of countryside and generally get the most out my glider, my talents and the British weather, all of which are pretty limited. I'd also like to get a Gold badge or even a Diamond. What do you advise?" then the instant answer would have come winging back, "Enter a competition, of course! Best of

Galloping paranoia.

all, see if you can get into a National Championships."

And of course a contest was indeed the ideal way to achieve all those noble aims. With expert weather briefings and aerotows laid on; with a crew madly eager to drive thousands of miles from dawn to dusk, and from dusk to dawn again; and finally with distance tasks that started in the very first thermal of the morning and ended in a long, floating descent from the last thermal of the evening. Many pilots, in gliders of lower performance than those in which people now go solo, averaged seven hours a flight, seeing not just the countryside but the coastline, often from many miles out to sea, from Cornwall to Scotland in the same week. From dawn to dusk no thermal went unscathed. It wasn't just worth 50 hours in the logbook, it was beautiful and hard to forget.

Dreadful tales are told of the extermination of the American bison in the 19th century; people would shoot the poor beasts just to cut out the tongue as a delicacy and leave the carcass to rot. That's what the unholy alliance of competition pilots and organisers increasingly do to magnificent, broad-shouldered soaring days that could effortlessly carry hundreds of gliders round this land for seven, eight hours or more. They carve out a two or three hours in the middle of the afternoon and discard the really interesting bits at either end. Like a dead buffalo, a great soaring day never, ever comes back. It is lost for all eternity.

Rib-tickling fun (1984)

I have broken or cracked a rib three times in three years and hope my little run of misfortune has now stopped. The first was while walking down some ice-covered steps carry-

ing skis (No, I emphatically was not drunk. I wish everyone wouldn't automatically assume that.) The second was at an Enstone competition in 1982; I was bicycling energetically up a hill coming back from the phone in the nearby village – the sole phone at the club being commandeered for Control – having just reassured my wife, ironically as it turned out, that I was in alive and well.[7]

The folding bicycle, borrowed from a revered ex-chairman of the BGA, collapsed without warning just behind the hinge-point (a dodgy weld proved unequal to my Reg Harris musculature) and precipitated me brutally onto the road in front of a car. The driver, who proved to be the local churchwarden, kindly gave me and the wreckage a lift to the club while lecturing me on the topic of the foul noise made by the Enstone microlights. "Sorry, nowt to do with me," I groaned as I counted my remaining sound bones. From previous experience I knew that the rib would be at its worst on the third day, by which time I was being lifted into and out of the Nimbus cockpit like a sack of potatoes. I flew it in much the same way too. Outlandings were more than the usual Hell, of course.

The revered ex-chairman of the BGA agreed not to sue me for wrecking his bike if I agreed not to sue him for lending me a bike without a C of A, or at least at C of R. We both tried to sue the bike company and got nowhere, as you might expect.

The third time I broke a rib was on a retrieve from a field which I had picked during a cloudburst during an Open Nationals. I used to think cloudbursts were peasant inventions like air pockets, but I now hear that under some circumstances it's not a bad

---

[7] The sad reason for my having dashed to the village public telephone on two wheels, which I did not mention in S&G at the time, was that two young pilots in K-8s had collided at a services contest not many miles away. Both had been killed. I heard the whole dreadful thing over the radio while I was airborne in the Enstone competition, and by the time I landed I expected the media to be full of it, as they usually are. I wanted to get the message to my wife Veronica before the news hit the television screens. We all must have been in a similar state of concern at one time or another, especially when the news given out is unspecific as to names, and places and aircraft, or worse still, when it is plain wrong.

description of what clouds actually do. And anyone who goes around sneering at air pockets is likely to find themselves in one, and serve them right. The older I get the more I believe in old wives' tales. Anyway, the steep, narrow, soggy track offered no purchase to the tyres of my swish new saloon car. Wait till I win a million on Premium Bonds and can afford a Range Rover. So the ASW-20 (change of glider) wings had to be carried by me and one female crew member (Marjorie Hobby) in the gathering dark and stowed in the trailer while it was pointing up a 20-degree slope and leaning over perilously. Pausing for breath was fatal; the wing was determined to push me back down the rain-soaked hill.

A last desperate heave while standing on the angled, mud-covered ramp threw the sweating, cursing pilot violently against the trailer entrance and crunched his rib a third time. Our notorious hostility to field landings in competitions reached a new peak.

I can only say when it comes to rigging and derigging with a cracked rib on the third day, the ASW-20 demonstrated vast superiority over the Nimbus. I'm quite reconciled to the little ship now.

Which kind are you? (1988)
Ask your partners – if you dare

When it comes to getting everything right, from practice to pitots to paperwork, there are four classes of competition pilot:

Superstars are totally organised at least a week before the contest begins.

Pundits get their act together by the end of the first day of the Competition.

Coarse pilots are sorted out by the end of the last day of the Competition.

Peasants are totally disorganised before, during and after the Competition, and usually manage to roll the trailer over on the way home, just to round things off.

The superstar partially achieves this pre-champs perfection by hiding the glider where nobody else can find it, especially the peasants. No syndicate should have more than one superstar in it, nor should it have more than one peasant: the strain on the others is too great.

And another lesson is that borrowing an un-roadworthy bicycle to go and tell someone you are in good physical condition is about as good a definition of Tempting Providence as you can get.

Enterprising competitors (1992)

Some years ago during one of those rainy afternoons in the middle of a Nationals the pilots were given their customary opportunity for a whinge-in as a substitute for flying. Wearing my tasksetter's hat (What, you've never seen a task-setter's hat? Well, it comes only in Extra Large size, it's complete with ear protectors to prevent pilots from trying to bend your mind, built-in orange shades that make the sky look a lot better than it really is, and most importantly it's really thick to protect against very hard, or very wet, objects accidentally dropped from a great height) I asked them how they would like tasks that enabled them to get the best out of the day, but with a possibility that luck or unfairness might creep in. To a man they declared passionately that if there was the slightest risk of unfairness they would rather not fly at all, thank you very much. I found that rather depressing at the time, but it still took years for me to see the light and send in my entry for a contest in which there is no nonsense about fairness, in which held start-lines don't exist and in which protests are outlawed.

A task-setter's hat.

What a splendid event Competition Enterprise is, what a splendid site Sutton Bank is, and what a splendid combination the two make! But you have to get used to the fact that Enterprise is like no other Competition. My first day in an Enterprise was a disaster owing to a failure to engage the brain. I landed back at 5.30, having fumbled the wave after a derisory little out and return, muttered, "Oh well, that's that," put the glider to bed and headed for the bar. It simply hadn't occurred to me that I could immediately re-launch into the east wind wave, which was visibly full of gliders up to 10,000ft. These were to roam around for another three or four hours, covering as much as 400km before darkness herded them home. By the time I realised my mistake I'd grounded myself with a pint of Yorkshire's best bitter beer. Blast. Conventional competition tasks aren't like that. They're usually over by bar-opening time. Better still, you don't have to think about where to go, when to go, what to do or anything. That's why they are so popular.

— ∞ —

The commonest illusion about Enterprise is that it is anti-competitive in spirit, and that contestants are too gentlemanly to trample their opponents into the dirt if the chance presents itself. *Au contraire*. The variations awarded for kilometres flown in different directions are so arbitrary and so large (a few degrees more to the west and your bonus can be 100%) as to encourage devilish ingenuity in designing your itinerary. It is only when the less cunning pilots struggle back at dusk, quietly pleased with their efforts, that they discover they have been stitched up by some chap who spent an extra 15 minutes devising his point-maximisation strategy. This sort of scheming appeals to me enormously, and next year I will go into Richard-the-Third mode from sun up on day one.

— ∞ —

At Enterprise the possibility of soaring the Channel is always in one's mind, John Fielden having prepared the way with the airspace bureaucrats. Many Enterprisers have in readiness passports, foreign currency and maps of France and even the Low Countries and Germany – so there is much earnest discussion and head-scratching in anticipation of The Great Day. The whole business is meteorologically trickier than I thought, leaving aside airspace problems. If you want to cover any distance on the other side you have to get to Kent

by one o'clock, and then you might find that sea air compels you to start the crossing not at the coast but several miles inland. There will be sea breeze effects for even further on the other side, so you need enough altitude to cover twice the 20 miles of the Channel itself in order to arrive at the first usable thermals sufficiently high to work them.

Well, with a 20kt tailwind and a modern glider, no problem, you say? Not exactly. In the 1985 Enterprise John Bally, starting from Sutton Bank, just scraped in with 700ft clearance over Cap Gris Nez, having discovered that if the wind is more northerly than 300 degrees when you depart from the White Cliffs it can change to a north-easterly half way across. Something to do with the wind being deflected by the landmass of the Kent peninsula. That margin works out at less than one per cent of the width of *La Manche* measured at its narrowest point. To any one who has watched a J. Bally final glide, it was nothing special.

The more we discussed the problems of the crossing, the more astonishing seemed Geoffrey Stephenson's 1939 cross-Channel flight in the Gull from Dunstable to le Wast, with a glide angle of about 20 at a best speed of 30kt.

What's the flap all about? (1986)

I wonder if anyone will offer the latest Standard machines with optional tips to produce the unflapped 17 metre of the 1980s, as the Dart and SHK were to the 1960s? Without the extravagance of flappery it could be the best performance-for-money package in town. Come on, you guys!
Well, 12 years later the LS8 came out with tips that stretch to 18 metres, and a great success it is, too. I do occasionally get it right.

Bloody competitions (1993)
(Originally written for the World Championships Newsletter, Sweden 1993.)

Competition flying does not bother me, but competitions do bother me. What I mean is, the flying from A to B and back again is the easiest part. The most stressful part of the contest is coping with the mountain of detail under which the sadistic organisers and other bureaucrats bury you:

Panic two days before the Championships in Patagonia when you find that your insurance cover specifically excludes Patagonia, and the insurance agent has gone on holiday and is unreachable.

Excludes Patagonia.

Hysteria when you notice that your ground radio licence has been mislaid, so you can talk to your crew but they can't reply.

Apoplexy when the Transylvanian border guards tell you that you are very naughty trying to import a glider into Transylvania illegally and they are going to impound it for two weeks. (The fact that it was made in Transylvania and you have a written personal invitation from the Transylvanian president to take part in their Nationals makes no impression.)

Then the contest proper starts – if you ever get there and if your documentation is accepted. However, your misery is only just beginning. Indeed the chief reason for the vast popularity of two-seaters is the need for a private secretary/lawyer to carry – and ideally to memorise – all the rule-books. The list is endless.

Photographs must be the biggest cause of grief in competition flying, in the same way that rum used to be the biggest source of trouble in the British Navy. All of the following have been done by the very best pilots:
1. Taking photos of the right TP from the wrong angle. I have donated far more points to my fellow-contestants by out-of-sector pictures than by my flying errors.
2. Being in the right sector but somehow failing to get the TP itself onto that little 36mm by 24mm rectangle.

3. Failing to photograph the clock after you have landed. After a hard day's work a pilot should be allowed to roll out of his cockpit and stagger off to the bar without having to remember such nonsense.
4. Forgetting to put any film in either camera.
5. Finding out after processing that although the time appears correctly on the camera back, the processed film is not registering the time.
6. Having a camera that switches from hours/minutes to date without your noticing it.
7. Mounting the cameras on the wrong side.
8. Having your cameras stolen after a field landing.
9. Taking the film out of the camera before an official has witnessed this solemn event.
10. Forgetting which start sector to photograph.
11. Running out of film, especially on a post task.

(Forgetting which way to circle before the start is not much of a problem, since the other competitors will gently remind you with the politeness for which contest pilots are famed, even in moments of imminent danger.)

— ∞ —

Barographs are another source of pain:
1. You find that a barograph acceptable for contests in one country is not accepted in another country.
2. If it is clockwork, you have the opportunity variously to forget to ink it, smoke it, wind it, seal it or get it witnessed.
3. You can put a clockwork barograph in the wrong way up, so that the stylus is hanging under the foil and not touching it.
4. If it is electronic, its battery dies or its memory gets indigestion, so it stops recording half an hour after it has been switched on.
5. In either case, you can forget to switch the barograph on, or can do all the above things correctly but for one small error – you simply forget to put the barograph in the glider before take off.

— ∞ —

You are going to say the GPS will put an end to all that stress, worry and opportunity for mistakes that cameras and barographs have caused up till now.

Good heavens, when were you born?

— ꝏ —

Having an aversion to water, possibly after being bitten by a rabid dog, I personally have never got into trouble for having too much of the horrible stuff sloshing about in my glider, but some people do. (When I use ballast I have trouble with the electrics or the pipes and most of it ends up in the cockpit, so I do not usually bother with it in temperate latitudes. In hot countries it is different: a soaking wet cockpit is rather pleasant.) But the fuss everyone makes about it! The time wasted at the 1991 World Championships in committees arguing about small quantities of this supposedly magic fluid amazed me. We all know that it takes 100 litres to make any measurable difference to sailplane performance, but the amounts that are the subject of heated debate by distinguished panels of arbitrators could be drunk by a baby camel in ten seconds.

Thank God it's over; we've only lost 500 penalty points, a personal best, and our plastic bomber is still in one piece. Now we can drive home without a care in the world. Goodbye, dreary BGA Rulebook! Adieu, nitpicking officials and pedantic scorers!

Hold on, what's that car with the flashing blue light on top, and can that siren possibly be wailing for us?

"Good evening, sir. Yes, it is a beautiful evening for the time of year, really lovely. Did you know – just a second while I get my big notebook out, this is going to be a rather lengthy chat – that your trailer (a) has a malfunctioning brake-light? (b) has a number plate

Finishes are the end (1993)

Finish lines give me a lot of trouble, especially if I arrive before everyone else, or, more likely, after everyone else. What I like about a sailplane with nearly 60:1 glide ratio is that it gives me plenty of options when I fail to cross the correct finish line at the correct height from the correct direction. If I do not hear those sweet words, "Platyplaneur, good finish!" I can do a dozen leisurely figure-eights around different parts of the field in the hope that one of them intersects the finish line before the ground comes up and hits me. On the other hand this does not go down well with the business jets, helicopters and parachutists that are trying to use the same aerodrome. In ordinary day-to-day gliding, if the manner of your flying indicates evident mental confusion, the people in charge on the ground are only too eager to tell you where to go and what to do with your big toy in the interests of safety. In contests, however, the officials are sworn to silence, apart from telling you tersely that you have not done a proper finish. My crew are now briefed to station themselves next to the finish line observers with a transmitter (the licence having been found in the cat basket at the last moment) ready to prevent me doing something truly stupid.

Of course, all the necessary information is usually printed out and given to the pilots, so you can end up with a sheaf of paper – make sure you have shredded yesterday's sheaf of paper – which I now bind together in a folder. Then after launching I find that the folder has slid irretrievably down behind the seat. Hence the popularity of doppel-sitzers with secretaries, as I said.

Cartoon by Enzo Centofante

different from the one on the car? (c) was being towed at 30% over the speed limit for trailers? (d) appears to be overweight for the size of car? (e) is being driven by someone who appears to have been celebrating recently...?"

The sky's the limit, if we stop being stupid (1996)

A classic is a work that does not age. George Moffat's "Winning on the Wind" is 22 years old, but most of it – leave aside the reviews of sailplanes now applying for membership of the Vintage Glider Club, such as the Capstan – is fresh, relevant and required reading still. A true classic. One of the most memorable chapters is Low-Loss Flying, better remembered for its subtitle "Winning By Not Losing."

This deals with the little cumulative gains that you make when you pay attention to details like efficient starts and finishes, entering thermals cleanly, then leaving them before the lift falls off and so on. Having flown in innumerable contests and having helped to manage quite a few, I have concluded that if George brings out a new edition of the book to take young glider pilots into the 21st century, then "Winning By Not Losing" requires an extension, which he might call "Winning by Not Screwing Up." The greatest and the humblest of competition pilots alike would benefit.

The points gains George offers in "Winning by not Losing" are small but important. However "Winning By Not Screwing Up" (WBNSU, pronounced Woobensoo) offers absolutely gigantic increases in points, as I shall demonstrate with a number of some real-life examples. The names are concealed to protect the guilty.

In the era before GPS one of our finest international pilots, on a day in the World Champs, increased his score by 900pts over the previous day. "Unbelievable!" you will say. Not really. He did indeed fly well on the second day, but his real WBNSU triumph was to remember to put film in his cameras for a change.

In the Dunstable Regionals in 1992, the club chairman similarly made a vast improvement in score from one day to the next. He managed to go round all the correct turnpoints as specified by the contest director, and

not round a task of his own devising. The winner of the previous day (modesty forbids me to say who that was) suggested in his witty speech that the chairman's lovely wife should buy her man a GPS for Christmas. I think she did, if only to help moderate the language around the house.

I could cite several cases from my own career in olden days before GPS, where I have earned substantial points gains as a contest wore on, so that by the very last day I was remembering to switch the barograph on before take-off (then, even better, remembering to put it in the glider), to go round the task the right way, to take my pictures in the right sector, to photograph the start-board before, and the fin and the clock after, the flight, and generally avoiding a host of little irritations and punishments. What a rare joy it is to the coarse contest pilot to see his name on a score sheet quite unsoiled by Administration Penalties. *Admin Penalty* on the score sheet means, "You've done nothing really wicked but you have been a pain in the bum to the organisation, and we are going to make you suffer for it."

"Ah, but now we are in the era after GPS, and free from the problems that turnpoint photography brought," you interject sagely. "Nowadays such spectacular opportunities for Winning by not Screwing Up surely do not arise?"

If you believe that you'll believe anything. One of my friends, in a goal race to another club (on a day when the weather man thought that getting back to our own site was impossible) did a fizzing final glide to a field so empty of gliders that he congratulated himself on leaving his fellow competitors well behind. It was only on the approach that the truth dawned on him: he'd entered the GPS co-ordinates wrongly with his banana-like fingers.

Pilots in England (not to mention France Spain, Algeria, Mali, Upper Volta and Ghana) can earn excellent WBNSU points by correctly distinguishing between east and west co-ordinates. Let your competitors forget to tell their GPS which side of the Greenwich meridian the turnpoints are, but you will remember, won't you?

At least 50pts can be gained by remembering to re-program the GPS logger from 30sec to 10sec intervals, because a fast, tight turn on the slow 30sec setting will often fail to show your presence in the sector.

Using fresh batteries in the logger, remembering to clear its memory before take-off, studying the map for prohibited airspace, knowing where the Finish line is, reading the Rule Book – oh, there's a host of ways in which you can quietly accumulate points that your rivals are spilling all over the place, like a drunk with a tray of beer.

I think we should encourage pilots to Win By Not Screwing Up by giving an award to the Administratively Most Improved Contestant (AMIC) during the competition. This would be the competitor who, regardless of soaring performance, shows the biggest reduction in penalty points between the first and last contest days. But exactly what should this much prized, avidly contested WBNSU trophy – which I could have won myself countless times – consist of?

Do write in and make suggestions. But for the moment I suggest a wooden spoon.

Since I wrote this I learn that a French former World Champion lost 1,000 points in a GPS-regulated World Championships by missing a start-line entirely. In the 1999 World Championships

Platypus takes on an even bigger list (1983)

While we are making lists (I love making lists, particularly those intended to remind me to do useful things. However, I usually lose or forget the list, unless I put on a second list a reminder not to lose the first list, and so on ad infinitum...), here is my little list of loves and hates:

LOVE

The sight of my nearest rival struggling at 500ft while I'm at cloudbase.

Emerging from the top of a cloud the right way up, pointing in the right direction.

Swooping in on finals to see that none of the other contestants has arrived.

A thermal smack over the turnpoint .

The first thermal of the season.

The first cross-country of the season.

The yawstring on my canopy.

Gin-clear visibility.

Gin-clear gin.

Task setting.

Tasks.

Final glides.

HATE

The sight of my nearest rival at cloudbase while I'm struggling at 500ft.

Emerging from the bottom of a cloud the wrong way up and pointing in all directions in quick succession.

Finding one has swooped in on the wrong airfield.

!@? Where is the *!?@ turn point?*

The first landing of the season.

The first field landing of the season.

All other instruments.

Standard British murk.

Water, except as ballast.

Meteorologists.

Task setters.

Final glides.

an American Open Class champion entered a slightly wrong name from the turnpoint database into his computer and lost most of his points for the day. The very best pilots foul up as easily as raw beginners, and GPS, as I predicted, has not repealed Murphy's Law.

Big wings, small whinge (1996)

More about span. And more about contests. Last week I finished a Regionals with a position smack in the middle ranks, right on the median. Boring, boring. On the previous five occasions that I had flown big gliders in British handicapped competitions I got a 4th place, a 3rd and three 2nds.

Why not first, you ask? Indeed, why not? I must lack the killer instinct. It was the same when I played table tennis in my youth: I would get to 19 pts to the other guy's 12, then I would lose concentration and start thinking about something else like girls, or when the bar was going to open, or maybe it was just nerves at the relentless pressure of being in front. Anyway the ball would start flying erratically all over the room and the other player invariably stormed past me. I didn't mind them winning as long as they didn't gloat too much.

If you want to win you really have to hate losing. My friends should have done me a favour by gloating more so as to make losing less palatable. They failed me, they really let me down. If this was the USA I should sue somebody.

The reason for my distinctly lacklustre performance in 1996 was chiefly the unusually good weather and short tasks on most of the days. Pilots do like getting back, so I don't blame the organisers at all for the small tasks. I do blame the weather, though. The weather let me down badly. (Difficult to sue the weather. So far, that is. I bet the lawyers are working on it. When government or business start tinkering with the weather, it will be a feast for litigators.)

In the five previous competitions there was so much rain, wind and overdeveloped cloud that the airwaves were constantly rent by plaintive cries from little gliders plummeting into pastures. As I sat drinking ice-cold lager after yet another finish, the loudspeakers would regularly boom out the delicious message, "Crew of number XYZ to control!"

Halleluya, I'm a glider-pilot! (1981)

You have surely all read the priceless anecdote from the 1960 World Championships about the American pilot who had the standard pre-printed sign written in German saying, "I am a glider pilot, please help me," which he showed to a passing Frau after an outlanding. That good citizen rummaged in her handbag, produced a Deutschmark, gave it to him and went on her way.

Whether the dear woman knew he wanted a retrieve is neither here nor there. What the story proves is that the German public, who are vastly better informed about gliding than our own (hardly difficult, I admit, since the British public's knowledge of gliding is a minus quantity – that is, most of what they know ain't so) immediately bracket the words "Glider pilot" with pauper, vagrant or itinerant bum. In short, a beggar, liable to rattle a tin cup at any passing bourgeois with a whinging, "Give a poor fellow the price of an aerotow, guv!" Try that on a British passer-by and you'd get nowhere unless you'd persuaded her that a glider was a nearly extinct specimen of bird, the prevention of cruelty to which was your sole vocation in life.

Who's a pretty boy then?

LESSER SPOTTED KESTREL
Please give generously

soon followed by another sweet sound, the hollow rumble of somebody else's trailer heading for the open road.

However, global warming is wrecking all this happiness. There is too much sunshine and the little blighters are getting back too often. I don't ask for continuous foul weather, just a band of stratus about 20 miles across, preferably in the last stages of the task so that everyone passes Y to make it a 1,000 point day.

Here comes an undisguised, self-interested plea for a change in the handicapping system to restore things to their proper order.

The handicapping system was initially based on the glider's polar curve (hah!) applied to the British Standard Thermal (hah! again). When I was first introduced to him – or her – The British Standard Thermal delivered a climb of 2.4kts to a Skylark 3 (ask Granddad what that is) climbing at 35 degrees of bank.

Years of recording all-day climb rates from the Peschges for our syndicate ASH-25 shows an average of 2.0kts[8], though that includes hundreds of hours flying around when nothing else is staying up at all, not even Skylark 3s. So the British Standard Thermal has probably been a reasonable estimate of the lift you get typically between noon and the Happy Hour.

The trouble is, averages are clumsy tools, which frequently fail to describe the real world. For instance, my favourite statistic is the fact that the average Englishman spends 14 days of his life in jail.

So it is with average thermals on which handicapping is based. Very simply, if the rates of climb average 3.0kts or better, the big gliders have to achieve record-breaking speeds to overcome their handicaps, which are in the region of 125-130. If the lift is only half as strong, big wings triumph. So if you mix 15 metre and 25 metre gliders, the contest result is almost entirely decided by the weather and we are reduced to vapid untruths like, "Well, we are only flying for fun here, anyway." The needle, the urge to match yourself against rivals, disappears.

It is perfectly feasible to compensate for strong days and weak days by taking the speeds of the fastest pilots and comparing those with the speeds they should have achieved in standard British thermal. Where the speeds are lower than theory predicts, the handicaps should be spread further apart, penalising the big wings. Where the speeds are higher than theory predicts, the handicaps should come closer together, reducing the penalty on big wings. I know how I would do the mathematics, but the BGA might think I had a vested interest.

Scales of justice (1997)

One terror that faces all pilots in international competitions, and in national championships in which I have flown in America and Australia, is having your glider randomly weighed before launch on any day to make sure it doesn't exceed the all up weight limit for the contest. This weight limit may well be less than the safe limit stipulated by the manufacturer or the airworthiness authorities, so the rule is a matter of fairness as much as safety.

However there's one country where I have never seen that solemn ritual – the finger pointing at the chosen glider, somewhat like the National Lottery; the tedious measuring process under a relentless noonday sun; the red-faced shame when a few kilos of excess weight are discovered by the high priest; the pilot's face turning pale and stricken as points are deducted far beyond any advantage gained – and that country is Britain.

Massive amounts of waterballast.

---

[8] In Australia over the season 1990-1991 it averaged exactly 4.0kts, precisely twice as strong as Britain.

So we find that, in the home of the one knot thermal, contest ships stagger around the course weighing 200lbs more than would be allowed in Texas, home of the 10kt thermal.

When I pointed this paradox out to a fellow contestant, while waiting on the grid at nearly 4pm for the third re-brief of the day (you can tell it was England) a few weeks ago, he said, "So what? It can't do them any good!" Possibly not, but clearly many pilots believe it can do them good. And maybe it does, especially if the task is short and the final glide is a large proportion of the total distance.

One day I started a final glide 500ft higher than one of these airborne reservoirs, thinking, "I've got you cold, mate!" only to see it streak away from me at a good 10kt faster than my MacCready speed, despite my height advantage. When I was calling, "Finish line, one minute!" I could see the four great plumes of water streaming from its tanks as it pulled up to win the day

Food – or drink, anyway – for thought. With global warming we might soon see an alien ritual become as British as, say, Burger King and Foster's.   ∎

Those magnificent flying machines

There are other sports that use machines to exploit human muscle or nature's forces: rowing, sailing and cycling come to mind. But in none of these activities has the technology, or the resultant performance, changed so much as it has in gliding. Rowing boats, yachts & racing bicycles are not much different in design or speeds achieved from 40 years ago when I first entered a gliding competition in 1960. That was in the London Gliding Club Regionals: I landed the club Olympia in some pasture or crop every day, sometimes twice in an afternoon after a retrieve that was even more perilous than the flying itself.

The impetus to greater performance comes from a simple fact. A boat that goes slower than another boat does not sink to the bottom of the ocean; it just crosses the finish line somewhat later. A bicycle that is a bit sluggish does not roll into a ditch, unable to move again, requiring a friend to come with a car to get you home. Gliders are quite different. A glider that cannot reach the next thermal, or that cannot climb in a thermal, actually does sink to the bottom of its ocean, namely the ocean of air in which we strive to stay afloat. On most days of the year in northern Europe it is still difficult for average pilots in average gliders to stay airborne for long enough to do a cross-country and get back safely to the site. People who work Monday to Friday and who share a glider with friends can go for months without a decent flight.

The frustration of being unable to soar, or having to be retrieved from a ploughed field and taken in haste to the nearest repair shop, is a great spur to the designers and builders of sailplanes. Thank heaven most of these wonderful engineers live, work, and attempt to soar in northern Europe, and not in Spain or Texas!

A material difference (1989)

Long before designer stubble had been invented, there was a potterer-to-end-all-potterers to be seen around Dunstable every weekend with what looked like a perpetual two-day-old beard, his moustache and fingers stained, not yellow but dark brown, from the chain-smoking which eventually killed him. Ron Watson was untiringly helpful with any job you wanted done, from a variometer calibration to a Cornish retrieve. He was also untiringly dogmatic, as when during one of the great downwind-dash Nationals (1961) he refused to stop his vintage Bentley to let his fellow crew members telephone Control to see if their man had landed. "Look at those cloudstreets, nobody could get sunk in those conditions" he snorted, and swept past the hapless pilot and onwards, another hundred miles down the peninsular, before the blunder (the pilot's blunder, not Ron's, of course) was discovered.

To look at him in his dirty beret, messing around with bits of wire in the Ottley Building, you would hardly have guessed that he was a distinguished scientific civil servant in one of the aviation ministries. When I asked him why government-financed aircraft always cost about ten times what they were originally budgeted to cost, he said cheerfully, "Well, if we went and told Members of Parliament what we thought the wretched things would really cost, none of the projects would ever get off the ground, would they?" He would have been a marvellous character in *Yes, Prime Minister* foxing both the bureaucrats and the politicians with his technical knowledge, his pawky wit and his total lack of respect for rank.

I asked him (this was more than 25 years ago) whether tailless gliders had a future, and he said, "There is nothing wrong with a tailless glider that can't be put right by adding a tail." Which firmly ended that topic of debate.

Swept past.

Then I asked what he thought the biggest strides forward in glider design would come from, and out of the portion of his mouth that was not engaged in gripping a cigarette he said simply, "Materials" and went on bashing out the most recent ding in the 1930s four-wheeled ashtray that served as his car.

He was right. Exotic designs like the Horten flying wings have got nowhere. Neither did the metal variable geometry Sigma – too complicated by far. And though a plastic variable-geometry SB-1 won the 1978 15 Metre World Championship in the hands of Helmut Reichmann, that monstrously expensive prototype never entered series production. But materials – glass, then carbon, then Kevlar – have successfully made possible higher aspect ratios, stiffer and more perfect wingsections, more effective controls, wider ranges of wing loadings from dry to fully ballasted – all of which have helped, along with better aerofoils, to double performances of the wooden gliders of which we were so proud a generation ago.

Perhaps it should have been a matter for lamentation rather than celebration when a British Skylark 3 won the World Championships in 1960, since it helped to reinforce our insular attitude to new materials. One of the gliders on display on that occasion was the still very new glass reinforced plastic Phoenix, which was described by a distinguished British aerodynamicist in his famous drawl (not Ron but another scientist, still very much with us) as, "A schoolboy's idea of what a glider should look like," which was true but perhaps missing the point. The Phoenix was the direct forerunner of the Phoebus and the inspiration to all modern GRP gliders. Apparently all of the eight 1950s Phoenixes were still flying well into the 1980s and for all I know are still flying today; I only hope the latest plastics last as long.

When Slingsby's finally decided that wooden gliders had hit the buffers, they plunged in 1968 for an American design in metal that had not been meant for series production. No American glider of World Championship calibre has ever been mass-produced, the main reason being the horrendous US government bureaucracy which put certification of commercially produced gliders on a par with that of Boeing 747s. Their best gliders were always brilliant one-offs with EXPERIMENTAL sten-

cilled on the side. So the British HP-14c flopped. It seemed that Slingsby's wanted to do anything rather than touch the dreaded glass-fibre technology. Eventually the first British GRP glider, the Kestrel 19, based on the Glasflugel Kestrel 17, flew in the UK Nationals in 1971 and became generally available in the 1972 season. (I loved the Kestrel, and had three of them between 1973 and 1979; don't let's go into why I had so many...) But Britain had lost its lead in designing gliders and, after the Vega, dropped out of the world market altogether.

This whole story of decline and fall was a microcosm of British industry in general over the same years.

I often wonder what dry comment Ron, had some miracle of medical science saved him, would have uttered about this sad tale. It could have been one of his hour long dissertations, brooking no interruption or disagreement; on the other hand it might have been extremely short and pithy.

Apropos the above, gliders have changed incredibly little in planform since the late 1920s. What kind of performance, I wonder, could you get from a modern carbon-fibre replica of the 1930 Fafnir, if you cheated with a 1980s aerofoil, flaps, brakes etc? Now there really was a schoolboy's idea of what a glider should look like. Mike Russell would doubtless throttle me for the blasphemous suggestion that we should build fake plastic replicas of old gliders with modern wing sections. But my point is simply that the best designers had basically got it right 60 years ago, and if there has not been any fundamental change in glider shapes over the past 60 years, there is unlikely to be much in the next 20. But I would love to be wrong.

The judgment of Solomon (1984)

At the World Championships in South Cerney in 1965 the prime, and very simply applied, qualification for a Standard Class glider was for it to be wheeled between two poles (no, not two Poles; they were another story altogether) stuck in the ground 15 metres apart.

Well, this spanking new ship arrives, straight off the drawing board, and promptly gets wedged between the two, er, posts. It is manifestly too big. A brilliant legal defence of this oversized prototype ensues. "M'lud," intones the designer/builder/pilot, "this glider is indeed exactly 15 metres in span in its natural state, ie, viz, namely, to wit; when it is aviating. Which it isn't right now, being quite evidently in an unnatural state of earthboundness." All the jurors weep at the plight of this grounded little bird just longing to get into its proper element and assume its rightful wingspan. "Thusly, its poor wings droop, denied of their inherent dihedral, which was built into the design and which it possesses in full flight. Ergo..." but he had no need to perorate and throw himself on the mercy of the court since this forensic display had already prompted a standing ovation amongst the spectators. Come to think of it, they are already standing, so it was just an ovation, I suppose.

The judge is unmoved. Nay, I tell a lie; he is deeply moved, but being British he concealed this with iron self-control. For a while he balances in his mind the eloquence of the little pleader standing before him with the obvious chaos that would follow if the argument i allowed to stand (Hell, what is a natural airspeed – 140kt?) then delivers the judgment that is an example of true wisdom and an object lesson to law-givers. "OK, you win" he says, "on one condition. I'll let you in the Standard Class when I see you fly that thing between those two posts."

Collapse of articulate pleader. Case dismissed.

The only thing wrong with that true story (apart from the fact that I made most of it up) is that the judge may have been not a he but a she. I actually believe that this rule has indeed been changed since 1965 and bendiness of wings is taken into account.

In a sailplane made for two (1981)

How nice to have a new share in a really fizzy high performance two-seater, a side-by-side Caproni Calif! A terrific fun-machine.

The received wisdom is that top pilots don't like flying two up because they require single-minded concentration to give of their best. Speaking for myself, I need all the intellcctual, moral and physical help I can get; two brains, twenty fingers and four eyes is the minimum I require to get any aircraft safely from A to B.

On one occasion, flying solo on a free-distance day, I unexpectedly found myself flying off the map and had to find and refold a North of England map. I spent an alarming twenty minutes wrapped in intractable fablon-covered paper which seriously impaired vision, control and language. Eventually the map was not refolded but had been pummelled into the approximate shape of a football, across which crumpled globe I managed to navigate up to Ilkley Moor, (which does actually exist, worms, ducks and all, in Yorkshire). A full-time co-pilot would have dealt smoothly with that problem and conserved the mental and physical energies of the pilot-in-command.

In the first two-seater I had, a Schleicher K-7, the best navigator was a young chap with a Clark Gable moustache who eventually became Chairman of the BGA and navigated that very well too. It was in the days before audio variometers and he used to sing, the pitch going up and down as the vario rose and fell, so that the P1 could keep a good look-out. One moment it was Caruso, the next it was Chaliapin. His voice has never been the same since – nor after a couple of heavy landings *(ie* crashes) has his coccyx (for the ignoramuses amongst you, that means the lower vertebrae). The trouble with navigators is they can get ideas above their station. During one epic struggle in the 1961 Nationals, this dialogue took place:

Future Chairman, BGA: You're not making much progress.

Platypus (snootily): Will the co-pilot kindly confine his observations to those of a purely navigational nature?

Long Pause.

Future Chairman, BGA: Navigator's Report coming up. The little Cotswold village we are

A great number of functions.

over now is the same little Cotswold village we were over half an hour ago.

Shortly after, we ran into a solid wall of sea breeze mist drifting inland from the Bristol Channel and, though thermals continued miraculously to bloom in this dense miasma, nearly every solo pilot got lost. In the K-7, however, our division of labour into thermalling and navigating brought us to an almost deserted Nympsfield – the first contest race that I (sorry, *we*) had ever completed. Happy days!

Of mice and Platypi (1982)

Last Saturday, during the haphazard poking about that I call doing a C of A, I found a mouse in the all-metal Caproni. *(Waiter, there's a mouse in my Caproni, call the manager!)* That's nonsense for starters, of course. First, I saw no mouse, just a wee nest made from chewed-up quarter-mill maps and Opal Fruit wrappers. Second, it's well known that there's no such thing as *a* mouse in the house – if there's one there are at least a dozen. A whole tribe, scampering from tip to root, from rudder-post to rudder-pedals. Breeding all over the place. Not only parturating, but masticating. Not to mention micturating and all the rest. It's the masticating that really bothers me at present. (Though I'm not too keen on the thought that a small amount of zero g while I am dolphining might be all that is required to suspend a troupe of furry creatures weightless and slowly revolving in front of my unbelieving eyes, not to mention the effects on any female passengers.)

No, as I say, it's the masticating. Having succeeded in getting the radio to receive for the first time in years, by a process of trial and error using an electrician's multimeter (he's just not a pretty face, you know) I could not get the thing to transmit. Then I noticed that a great bite – or hundreds of little bites, I prefer

to think – had been taken out of the spiral plastic microphone cord, right through the covering, wires and all. It was practically severed. Why Jaws, or whatever his name is, gave up at this point I don't know. I'm only glad that it isn't a wooden glider ...

Furry creatures in front of my eyes.

Talking about radios, you all know of course that Platypus's first law of radio warfare states: *The length of a radio message is inversely proportionate to its importance.* Thus a revered late chairman of the BGA (I'm using *late* in the British sense to mean *ex-*, not in the American sense which is rather more final) wished to convey this message last year while soaring – or in the case in question failing to soar – in the Alps. 'I am in a spin or spiral dive from which I cannot recover, I have lost 4,000ft, the aircraft appears to be breaking up, I cannot bale out because of the *g* forces and I am in rather pressing need of some practical advice on what to do next.' All he said, with commendable economy, was, "HELP!!" which brought advisers sprinting to the groundset, especially his partners – or as the French call them, *co-proprietaires,* which rather better expresses their material interest.

By extreme contrast, this is the sort of thing you hear, usually in the middle of a very busy competition:

Cabbage White Base from Cabbage White, do you receive?

Silence. Well not *silence*, there's a competition on. But silence from Cabbage White Base.

Cabbage White Base from Cabbage White etc, etc, repeatedly. The fool goes on like this for ages, without thinking of transmitting his vital message – if he has one – blind. It hasn't occurred to him that either (a) CWB isn't listening or can't receive (in which case why say anything at all?) or (b) CWB is receiving OK but has poor transmission on his groundset so the pilot can't hear the reply. But the silly berk still goes on trying to get a response from CWB *before* sending his message.

Ah, at last – CWB has come back from the bar. Now civilised conversation, intellectual intercourse and wit, badinage and repartee can coruscate across the ether to the edification of all the rest of us – whether we want it or not.

That you, Ron?

Where've you been?

I've been fixing the trailer (liar). It's got a duff bearing, I think.

(Long description of this real or imagined crisis.)

Well, I'm over a little village with a church with a spire, can you find it on the map? It's got a pond to the south-east, no sorry, the south-west, etc, etc.

This description of precisely where Cabbage White is goes on for ages, and since his finger hardly ever comes off the button he can't hear people bellowing: "Shaddup! Can it! Pipe Down! Belt up! Can't you hear there's a competition on? etc, etc." (CW isn't in the contest, of course. Competition pilots aren't gods, but they do deserve a small share of the radio action. The better they are the smaller the share they want.) Even if he heard them he'd only think what a selfish, uncouth and callous crowd, with him lost and no one to assist him with the navigation. The punchline is when you hear, willy-nilly, as the cut and thrust of CW and CWB's dialogue crackles merrily along, that CW is at 4,000ft and is only local soaring anyway. Our collective fury knows no bounds.

When I was flying at Hahnweide in 1975 someone made a joke on the radio (at least I think it was a joke, my German not being up to much, but there was a lot of Hoch-Hoching and general bierkeller bonhomie) and instantly there boomed out from the contest direktor, "*Achtung! Funkdisciplin!*" which nipped all that Bavarian jollity right in the bud. Quite correct too. What we need is some *FUNKDISCIPLIN* in this crowded little Isle.

— ooo —

To those who heed not, I pronounce with bell, book and candle: May a pox, a murrain and a hundred assorted other plagues smite your rotten radio. May mice devour your microphone and rats your co-ax. May the Lord flatten your battery. May foul growths form on your terminals. May you always receive "Rigoletto" on Radio 3 when you want your crew in an emergency. May you get laryngitis, streptococcal throat and inflamed tonsils. May you be compelled to write out a thousand times – nay, a million times – SILENCE IS GOLDEN.

TINSFOS again or History as it should have been writ (1993)

In ancient times, a great warrior was the scourge of the Hebrews. He was a Philistine, which I think means that when he was bored with breaking heads he liked nothing better than to watch Match of the Day with a six-pack at his elbow. One day a brave young fellow came forth, took up his sling and hurled a pebble at Goliath, for that was the big fellow's name. The pebble whistled past G's ear. G stepped forward with a snort of contempt, and "Whap!" the poor boy was laid stone dead. This carnage went on for months. Finally, whether by dint of assiduous practice or sheer luck, a youth named David confronted Goliath, and "Ziiing-Whap!" – the giant fell on his face. At this, all the scribes and chroniclers leapt to their feet, seized their clay tablets and papyri and crowed with one voice, "Now at last we have something worth putting in that great book we are writing!"

Thus it comes about, children, that people the world over believe that the little guy will always beat the big guy, just as from reading another ancient book they discover that a tortoise will beat a hare any time. So people who

> **My favourite (& cheapest) instrument (1984)**
>
> *Oh for a return to the open cockpit and the fresh breeze on one's brow! Or on one's ear, if you flew like me. The instrument I'm still addicted to is the yawstring which is the next best thing to a faceful, or earful of wind. However, my partner hates yawstrings; they don't have them on 737s for some reason, so he rips it off every time he flies and I stick it back on again every time I fly. You can easily tell who flew the glider last – as if you couldn't already guess from the leaves, rooftiles etc wedged in the undercarriage doors ...*

Better to be a Philistine.

read too much are deluded into thinking that little gliders are better than big gliders, and are indeed prepared to spend more on a new glider of 30 cubits than a slightly worn glider of 50 cubits, though the latter will slay the little glider stone dead today, tomorrow and unto the end of the millennium after next.

Maybe there are times when it's better to be a Philistine, what don't read much, y'know, like, than someone who reads too much and draws all the wrong conclusions .

A mere coincidence (1993)

There is a bizarre group of people who find mystic significance in numbers, and twist and manipulate them to prove anything they like. I'm not thinking of politicians, nor of mathematicians or scientists (though Isaac Newton was obsessed with weird necromantic ideas that seem to us a million miles away from the age of enlightenment that he ushered in) but of pure cranks, who will add the Queen's birthday to the square root of the height of St Paul's Cathedral and derive the date of the end of the World.

I am not one of those kinds of crank, though I may well be any other kind. But I am intrigued by something that dawned on me only last night, after finishing a six-pack. When I was 15 I got my A badge in a Cadet, glide angle 15:1. When age 25 was reached I was allowed to fly the club Olympia, with an L/D of 25. Then at 27, the K-7 with an L/D of 27. At 31 the Skylark 3 at around 31:1.[9] When I was 36 I was flying Dart 17 at 36:1. At 44 I was flying the Kestrel 19 at – you guessed it. At 47 the Nimbus 2. At 57 the ASH-25 – and just before the day I turn 59 next spring, a lovely pair of winglets promises to add anoth-

er couple of points to the 57, threatening to send the whole thing gently into earth-orbit.

All sorts of strange ideas might now seize the numerologists (I looked the word up in the Shorter Oxford Dictionary, and it doesn't exist, so I had better copyright it) who will see a clear case of cause and effect: "Think of the amazing performances we could get in the 21st century if Plat goes on till he's 100!" I can see myself being kidnapped from my rocking-chair by a gang of aged alumni of the akafliegs, bearing duelling scars, cropped hair and heavy accents, "Put der olt geezer on der life-support machine, Gerhard. Maybe ve can sqveeze anuzzer five points out of him!"

Rational-minded people will rebut the theory with an elegant *reductio ad absurdum*. When Platypus was born in 1934, gliders should have plummeted straight into the ground the moment they were launched. Well, lots of them did. But one would have to admit that a few of them were covering the countryside pretty effectively. So much for the pseudo-science of numerology. All the same, if I celebrate my 80th birthday with a new glider capable of, yes, 80 to 1, I shall start looking over my shoulder...

I have been invited to fly in eta, the 31-metre glider mentioned elsewhere in this chapter, in yar 2000, sometime between my 66th and my 67th birthday. Perhaps the older I get the more such invitations I shall receive from the akafliegs.

Don't look down (1992)

I was enormously impressed by Keith Nurcombe's recent cross-countries in the Tutor in, a 1930's machine of hideous handling and pathetic penetration inflicted on us beginners in the 1950's. How we hated it! How

---

[9] The 36:1 claimed at one time for the 18m Skylark 3 was an optimistic revision, quite unjustified, of the original much lower manufacturer's estimate. The same goes for the 30:1 claimed for the 15m Skylark 2 at the same time. When the Skylark 2 was rigorously tested at Dunstable in the late 1950s the figure was nearer 25 than the 30 claimed for it. The news was never disseminated, in the best British tradition of least said, soonest mended. The Skylark 2's big sister was probably over-hyped to the same extent.

we yearned for real performance – unaware that at our fingertips we had a ship that could leap effortlessly cross hill and vale.

Hell, I shall always yearn for performance. The moment a brochure arrives guaranteeing that an extra 2.5ft of carbon-fibre on each tip – every foot costing more than I earned in the year that I joined the club, 50 weeks of miserable pen-pushing toil that I shudder to recall – will reduce my minimum sink by 9/16ths of an inch per second, which in turn will improve my glide angle by 3.3%, I'm pleading for them to dispatch the merchandise by Federal Express, adding 75p for nails and glue and string to fix them on, and a pathetic PS: please fax and say, "When you are going to stick vertical winglets on to the horizontal tiplets to shave another 3/16ths off the sink? Here's my signed blank cheque ready for you to fill in the first number that enters your head." I must be daft. I need counselling by an aged, wise aviator, begoggled and with long streaming hair, on the benefits of wood, canvas and open cockpits to the health and pocketbook, not to mention the National Ladder.

Anyway, back in 1958 one of our group, an attractive female Tutor pilot (who went off and married a chap with more experience than me, by which I mean he had 50hrs in his logbook against my five) used to end all debate about better glide angles by flatly stating, "Performance is irrelevant: you either get the next thermal or you don't." Despite having wrestled with formal logic at our most ancient university, I could not figure out why that was supposed to be such a knock-down argument. I think it was just the confident way it was stated; it would have floored Wittgenstein.

Now, 34 years later, I see that she was right; if you have the right mental approach, you

Yearn for performance.

can ignore performance. It is rather like those cartoon films where Tom and Jerry race out over a cliff and don't drop until they look down. Top Tutor Pilots Don't Look Down, that's all.

There's no Segelflugzeugbau like home (1993)

Home-building is like motherhood: no gentleman knocks it or mocks it. Not being a gentleman, however, I shall take a dig or two at this sacred institution, though with caution. In the USA home-building is a religion: in that expansive land a man feels a pang of shame if he cannot boast of having been born in a log cabin that he constructed with his own hands. (When I next go to the USA I shall wear heavy disguise and deny I have even a nodding acquaintance with such a cur as Platypus.)

Home-builders are more rare in this country than in the USA, so I am a bit safer. Most of us in this island have taken to heart Belloc's sad tale of Lord Finchley, who tried to mend the electric light

"It struck him dead, and serve him right.
It is the duty of the wealthy man
to give employment to the artisan"

We British are clearly much more sensitive to the need of the artisan to be kept in work. "If a job's worth doing, someone else had better do it," is my father's guiding principle, and I have followed it. If I am elevated to the peerage – and I know some very idle people who have achieved that eminence – I shall have that motto inscribed on the family shield in Latin, surmounted by heraldic Platypuses (Platypi? Platypodes? Platypussies?) some rampant, but most of them recumbent, or even dormant.

I only know of about three people in Britain who have made a modern glider with their own hands. However there are quite a few more, masochists one and all, who have put thousands of hours of painstaking, immaculate workmanship into building exact copies of gliders that were terrible fliers even when they were first designed 60, 80 and even 100 years ago. Such is their fidelity to the original, they still fly abominably, to the absolute delight of their creators.

The most bone-headed argument given in favour of amateurs building their own gliders is that it offers the economic path to happy soaring. Baldercock and poppydash. As one greyheaded American said to me, in a low whisper for fear of being overheard by a lynch mob of crazed do-it-yourselfers, "It's cheaper to get a job in a gas station at a dollar an hour and buy your glider with your earnings than to build your own, but they don't want to know that." Only if you value your time below that of convict labour can it be more profitable for the amateur to build a sailplane rather than scrape an honest living and buy a good second-hand one with the proceeds.

— ooo —

The problem about building one's own glider is that the job always takes far longer than anticipated, so the constructors never get into the air. While the cumulus blossom overhead against cerulean skies, these toilers shut themselves away in a shed, sawing and banging, drilling and polishing. Years go by, and finally they emerge, pale and blinking, into the unaccustomed sunlight. The splendid – or is it hideous? – moment of truth has arrived. Their first flight in the new toy is a traumatic initiation not merely for the glider but for the pilot, since the truth is that by now he has practically forgotten how to aviate. It is said that some home-builders fly their creation just once, and if they survive they put the machine in its box, where it stays unflown forever. That story is manifestly a gross libel on a fine body of men. All the same, a comparison of the utilisation of those gliders specially designed for home construction with the utilisation of Schleicher or Schempp gliders would make an interesting statistical study. Especially after 15 years or so have elapsed since the date of construction.

— ooo —

Did I not praise such devoted, hardworking people in an earlier Tail Feathers? Yes! Am I a turncoat, therefore? No! To build gliders for love makes all the sense in the world, as it does to do anything for love. But to pretend it is economic is silly. That's all I'm trying to say.

> ## More TINSFOS[10] (1983)
> *A little while ago I kissed a tearful goodbye to my lovely 21 metres Nimbus 2 and acquired a share in a dinky little glider, an ASW-20. After landing short at Totternoe a few times, I have two thoughts on this change:*
>
> *Little gliders are ideal for doing the short safe outlandings that you don't have to do if you have a big glider.*
>
> *Little gliders are ideal for doing the de-rigging and re-rigging that you don't have to do if you have a big glider.*
>
> ---
>
> [10] *There is no substitute for span.*

Instruments of torture, or, Assault and battery (1994)

I am invariably sunny and benign with people (Say again? Ed) but inanimate objects get the full force of my irritability, especially if, like cars, computers, radios and other gadgets, they are supposed to be animate on demand but instead just lie insolently doggo, feigning death. My particular hate these days is nickel-cadmium batteries, or Ni-Cads as they are called by people who feel on speaking terms with them. I am certainly not on speaking terms with the blasted things, and am not going to call them by pet names.

I have scores of these wretched nickel-cadmium batteries littering the house and car and glider, and none of them works with any reliability. After hours of charging, the hand-held 720 channel radio gives a brief hiss and all 720 channels expire after a minute or so. And the same goes for the two expensive batteries I bought as backups for the same radio.

Then there's my computer which dares to call itself portable and independent (Hah!) but, after the lapse of a tenth of its advertised duration away from the comfort of mains electricity, what happens but its batteries threaten to destroy my work and send it to the great data-bank in the sky unless I plug it in again NOW? "Be reasonable," I plead. "This is the Gobi Desert, and mains sockets are not in evidence." I get a total ignoral. Burp. Clunk. Whirr. It blinks twice and goes belly up.

"Ah well," murmur the technically wise, or those who know it is perfectly safe to pretend to be technically wise in my presence, since they will never be rumbled, meanwhile giving the 720 a technically sophisticated wallop with the side of a fist, "What you've done is run the little thing down and charged it up again the wrong way. As a result of your ill-treatment the poor Ni-Cad has developed a memory, and so is continually imprinting itself, so to speak, with a pathetic level of charge."

"A blinking memory?!?" At this point I am running up the clubhouse wall and across the ceiling in a frothing paroxysm of indignation. "What the heck right has a miserable lump of nickel and cadmium to go round giving itself airs and having a memory? I suppose the nasty little creep is writing its ruddy memoirs?"

Dear Diary, I gave my master the most splendid seizure this afternoon when I arranged for his GPS to die just as he was attempting to locate one of the BGA's best loved turnpoints, the road-bridge over the river Kennet at Marlborough, – the road, the bridge and the river all being quite unfindable when the trees are in full leaf. A fine January turnpoint, they all aver, but May to August, forget it. Ah, where was I? Oh, yes, hopping mad he would have been, except you can't hop much when you're lying on your back at 600ft. Serves him right, he didn't exercise me properly. I like to be taken for walkies. After all, I'm only human.

It's high time these expensive little monsters and their arrogant reminiscences were put firmly in their place. Why isn't there a device that, especially throughout the winter months, shows the precise state of all my batteries on some display that even I can understand, or better still arranges for them to be automatically discharged or recharged from the mains and, while we're about it, lobotomises their naughty little memories whenever they show signs of behaving like Samuel Pepys?

They can do it. I know and love these designers of gadgets for glider pilots; they are crazed rocket scientists and loopy nuclear physicists, every one. One of them 17 years ago built a trailer with the clear intention of getting himself and Platypus into the Guinness Book of Records for shoe-horning the World's Biggest Glider into the World's Smallest Trailer. These boffins will invent a brilliant battery-monitoring device which does everything I ask. BUT they will have made the nursing of all 30 of my nickel-cadmiums depend – you've guessed it! – on one nickel-cadmium battery, which I will find next March to have given up on its guardianship duties shortly after Christmas and since then to have been writing its autobiography...

If it looks right it'll fly right, or will it? (1994)

For 21 years, from my third-storey eyrie – and it's an airy, eerie eyrie – overlooking the Thames, I have been able to watch the Oxford and Cambridge boats flash by in their historic annual bout. Well, I do so if the weather does not suit gliding, and very frequently in March it does not suit anything better than sitting in comfort with a hot whisky while two brave crews catch pneumonia. But what's this I see? Following countless computer simulations and tests in water tanks, both eights have now put the most hideous modern oblong or trapezoidal paddles on the ends of their oars, so much at variance with the elegance of the traditional oars and of the boats themselves.

I was just about to write to the Times – I am always on the point of posting furious or witty letters to the Times but never get around to it – when I thought, "Hang on, what about those lumps that you have just stuck on the wingtips of your ship? Not only are the sticking-up bits not very pretty, but the leading edge of the new flat bit on to which the new sticking-up bits are stuck comes back at an angle instead of a curve as before. Can you convince yourself that the whole ensemble is pretty? Come on, be honest!" Then the letter to the Times about the ugly oars on the Thames goes in the bin.

So whatever happened to the old aviation proverb, "If it looks right it'll fly right"? Was it

ever true? Well, the Spitfire looked right, and so did the Sabre jet fighter, and so does Concorde.

Obviously technology changes and tastes change with it; there is no resemblance between those three famous aircraft, but they were all three right for their time. The Kite 1 and the Weihe and the ASW-12 looked right too, and for the same reason. But in each case that was before the computer took over our lives and our toys. By helping designers to discover minute little tricks of hydrodynamics or aerodynamics, the computer has brought into being hideous new keels for yachts, and added all sorts of baffles and other unsightly junk to racing cars. Can any sane person possibly say that a new Formula One car is as good looking as an old Mercedes racer?

The answer is No. I'm afraid that creeping uglification is here to stay, and we shall have to live with it.

But there are two consoling thoughts. First a tour round any art gallery will demonstrate that over the centuries fashion fools us into believing that the most extraordinary costume is in immaculate good taste, once people get used to it. Thus in a while gliders without winglets will begin to look somehow incomplete. Even now I feel cheated if I get aboard a Boeing 747 that hasn't got winglets. Why are we being fobbed off with second best? "We want our winglets!" we yell as we bang our spoon on our dinner tray, and are only mollified by a trip to the flight deck and a second round of free drinks served by the captain.

The other is that for any proverb, however profoundly true it may be, there is an equal and opposite proverb that is just as true. Bear in mind that an ugly glider soaring is always a more beautiful sight than the prettiest glider sitting in a ploughed field. So in place of the now unfashionable, "If it looks right it'll fly right," we new realists say,"Handsome is as handsome does." ■

A more beautiful sight...

People, partnerships and passions

Syndicates, like marriages, are made in Heaven (1988)

I have had shares in 14 gliders since 1958, and on average have had 2.9 partners per glider. The two could just about stand me, but the point-nine was driven wild. No, I get my sums wrong; the continual swapping of shares means that the total number of people I've been partners with must be over 60, and, amazingly, many of them shared a glider with me for a second or third time as we struggled up from Kite 1 and Cadet (singular) through Skylarks and Kestrels (plural). I shall always feel grateful for their long-suffering tolerance and good nature. Or maybe they were just desperate for someone to share the financial burden, and at least my vices are a known quantity. There *are* worse partners than me, *incredible dictu*. Better the devil you know... Someday, somewhere, someone will write a sociological treatise for his PhD at a modern, concrete university on the nature of glider syndicates and how, like marriages, they come together – and how they come apart.

Take syndicate wives – by which I do not mean a form of polyandry or polygamy but simply the respective wives or spouses (spice?) of the partners. One famous syndicate wife, who deserved a gold medal for devotion above and beyond the call of duty, would run her finger under the leading edge and lower her lovely eyebrows fiercely not at the chap who was about to fly but at his *wife*, for neglecting her duties. (What women's libbers still don't realise is that it's not the men who create the shackles of slavery but those women who don't believe in women's lib, having found other, time-honoured, means of getting their own way.) There are a number of techniques whereby the less dedicated wives (*ie* all other wives in the whole world) can avoid a clash in this situation, which we donate free in case it arises again. One is to stay at home. Another is to come equipped with a typewriter and reams of paper and hammer away at the keys while smoking furiously. (No one interrupts a woman author at her work, for fear of being put in her next novel. You'll be in it anyway, but with luck and good behaviour you won't be too recognisable.) Another ploy is to turn up wearing stiletto heels and fingernails two inches long, obviously on the point of going to a cocktail party or a Buckingham Palace reception. Fake plaster casts, bandages, wheelchairs and white sticks are another method, though smacking of cowardice and hardly a technique that can be kept up for years at a time.

Some syndicates have contracts drawn up by lawyers, and rotas of whose-day-to-fly drawn up by drill sergeants. Some have none of these. The first is like being back in the Army. The second like a (doomed) hippy commune. If you have to choose, Army is better.

A real stinker – Can you beat it? (1984)

A friend of mine was in the bar of a golf club in Rye some weeks ago, when he overheard an old chap exclaim, "Fellow's an absolute boundah – shot a swan during the Two-Minute Silence!" Apart from one's delight at hearing the antique expression bounder being dusted off and given an airing, there is the true astonishment – one nearly said admiration – at a rotter who could do two socially and morally unacceptable things at one and the same time: a double-barrelled cad, so to speak.

Mrs Platypus thinks the only comparable action in gliding would be, "a partner who ran off with a pilot's wife while he was away on a cross-country – "

" – and forgets to leave the trailer keys behind!" adds Platypus.

I would welcome any (printable) suggestions from readers as to what other villainy would qualify a glider pilot to be called a bounder – I mean, a boundah – in the same league as the Armistice-Day swan-killer.

Forgets the trailer keys.

A Tribute to Veronica (1986)

Being married to Veronica was the greatest blessing of my life. She was kind, warm, intelligent, humorous, hospitable and lovely in every possible way. Scores of friends and colleagues have written to me to underline those marvellous traits in her character.

She knew for 40 days that she had inoperable cancer. She died as she lived, bravely, lucidly, without a trace of sentimentality or self-pity, seeking only to comfort those who loved her. Believe it or not we had quite a few laughs in those final weeks: that was her special gift.

Her rare excursions into writing for S&G were so good that I would occasionally forget their true authorship and take credit for them myself. Only then might she look just a little stern.

Mrs Platypus's advice to those about to marry gliding enthusiasts – DON'T! (1976)

When Platypus proposed, he made his priorities perfectly plain.

"We could get married at the end of May," he suggested at breakfast one morning (all the best proposals take place at breakfast), "because that's when the Nationals are on. One of my syndicate partners will be flying the Kestrel so I shouldn't be able to glide for a week anyway and could take you on honeymoon."

Arrived at the Registrar, Platypus patted his pockets, found the 2p he keeps for retrieve phone calls, and not much else. Like Royalty, Platypus rarely carries cash, and while I don't usually mind too much being his purse-bearer, I felt it unseemly for a bride to ferret in her handbag. So I waited demurely while Platypus asked the Registrar (a Mr Peacock) if he would accept Barclaycard or a cheque. Mr Peacock, with a guffaw, declined; and Platypus was just contemplating a whip-round among the witnesses when he came upon the fivers he keeps for retrieve dinners and the situation was saved.

Our honeymoon, on which Platypus pointed out several gliding sites into which I declined to be inveigled, ended up at the Nationals, which by an amazing coincidence lay directly on our homeward path.

I knew that the first flush of romance had really worn off by an incident some six weeks later. I accompanied my new husband to a competition in France – the first gliding competition with which I had ever been involved.

On the first day, on the launch point, French tug pilots were whipping the gliders into the air with ferocious speed and efficiency. I was standing dreamily by the trailing edge of the wing, watching the glider piloted by Platypus being attached to the tow rope, when I noticed all about me had scattered and were bellowing urgently. I drifted off and it was explained to me severely that I could have been decapitated by the tailplane.

Recounting the incident to my bridegroom in bed that night I was touched when he sat up in alarm.

"You must *never ever* do that again," he said. "You could have *severely* damaged the tailplane."

All this was some years in the past. Now as a gliding wife of some years' experience, who has been blooded by a retrieve which earned Platypus a trophy for the worst retrieve of the year (why did Platypus collect the trophy, I ask myself, and not the crew?) I feel qualified to pass on some words of advice to those about to marry gliding enthusiasts.

First, unless you have to, don't.

(I didn't have to. I just loved Platypus.)

If you do, you will have to accept that gliding is going to come first with your husband. For instance, your sex life will to some extent depend on the weather.

"Your sex life will depend on the weather."

"You wouldn't *DARE* write that!", said Platypus in bed this morning.

I would and I will.

— ∞ —

On weekend mornings, Platypus springs from bed and tweaks open the curtains. If the sun is shining, I know I've got to get my clothes on fast if I want to accompany him to the club. If on the other hand he returns to bed, I know it's a poor gliding day....

"I think gliding is a substitute for sex," I once remarked, when considering the Freudian aspects of the sport – the phallic symbolism of high-performance gliders thrusting into thermals and waggling their wings in uncoupling rituals with tow planes.

"Nonsense, sex is a substitute for gliding," said Platypus briskly, and there are times when I think he wasn't joking.

The second thing you have to decide is whether you intend to be a gliding widow or a gliding wife. You can either opt for widowhood, waving him off to the club each weekend and taking up golf – or a lover; or you can accompany him to the club and take the consequences.

If you opt for the second alternative, and you don't terribly care for hard work and being shouted at, the line to take is that one simply could never aspire to be a second Kitty Wills or Beryl Stephenson, and it would be sheer presumption to try. Regrettably, one simply isn't of the calibre required to drive a trailer 400 miles through the night, nor has one the physique to throw together a Kestrel 19 with effortless ease and good grace. I do occasionally hold Platypus's wing tip (though dropping it from time to time ensures that it is only occasionally) and last season I did retrieve him from the field next to the club. Of course, you will have to cultivate some alternative skills instead – provide syndicate noshes willingly, feed crews, map-read intelligently, listen wholeheartedly and generally offer moral if not physical support.

The most endearing thing about Platypus is his absentmindedness. At a very early stage, his friends warned me that I should have to watch him like a hawk to make sure that he didn't get airborne while still in possession of the car keys. I also try to prevent him from taking-off while he is sitting on his maps, and try to find the things he loses – keys, maps, sunglasses, tools, shoes – last week it was the inspection panel.

By a man's friends you shall know him, they say, and Platypus's friends are a particularly Stout Bunch (speaking purely metaphorically). Not many people would endure conditions rather worse than trenches in World War One to retrieve him in a snow storm, nor

"200 miles in the wrong direction."

de-rig in pitch dark in a field knee deep in cow pats, nor drive 200 miles in the wrong direction and 200 miles back again (French villages have similar-sounding names) and still remain on speaking terms with the instigator of all this suffering. Platypus's friends, however, do all this and more. For my part, I have learned to understand their jokes. At the beginning, when they reported picking up Platypus on the radio at 500ft over Evesham (when in fact they had not heard from him at all) they were puzzled by my phlegmatic calm. It was however ignorance rather than a humourless *sangfroid;* I just didn't know how low 500ft was. Now I giggle politely and hope it is a joke again.

I have learned a lot of things since taking up with Platypus. I have learned, for instance, never to go on a retrieve in a mini skirt – apart from the difficulty of climbing barbed wire fences, the horse flies near some Continental gliding sites are vicious and ungentlemanly. So I always arm myself, when going anywhere near a gliding site, with trousers, Wellies, sunglasses, fur coat, sun hat, food, knitting, reading matter, money, a corkscrew and a complete change of clothes (see note on cow dung retrieve). Thus prepared for any weather and all eventualities, I can await Platypus's return in as much comfort as possible.

I have learned that Platypus is generally sweet-tempered and tolerant. Two things, however, drive him into a frenzy. One is when I do something wrong when towing the glider to the launch point, and the rope snaps.

The other thing which can prove greatly disturbing to the serenity of my home life is a letter from Kirbymoorside bringing tidings of another mandatory modification. Four-letter words echo around the house and we have a bad half hour before Platypus regains an even keel.

Putting into effect the mandatory mod, of course, takes its toll of Platypus's time and temper as well. As does trailer painting/maintaining. Fortunately the weather is nearly always too wet or too dry. If it's pouring clearly he can't be fettling, and if it's fine he's flying.

— ∞ —

One thing *you don't* have to worry about if you marry a gliding enthusiast (well, not much, anyway) is the Other Woman. His glider is his mistress, and takes up so much of his time, energy – and money – that he hasn't really any to spare for anyone else. You have the advantage of knowing the enemy intimately and being able literally to take her apart any time you choose. The ultimate sanction, of course, is that you can leave her stranded if he takes off with her and doesn't return to you – you can refuse to retrieve him if he's paying her too much attention – but he'll never abandon her for you, so if you want to see your husband regularly you'd better just accept her. You don't have to overdo it, of course; Platypus often invites me to join him in rubbing her

"We can't go on meeting like this."

down or touching her up, but I don't consider this to be my scene at all. I do have to lend my hairdryer to dry out the water in her wings and my hairspray for her barograph (not to mention bits of my carpet to pad her trailer more comfortably) but that's as far as it goes.

I've just had a thought. How about an *"AUNTIE"* Platypus column in *S&G*, with advice to worried gliding brides, etc?

"My husband is spending longer and longer at the club, and keeps mentioning Libelle in his sleep. Should I worry?" Only if he lands out in her.

"My boyfriend spends hours in his trailer with a girl he says is a member of his syndicate. He says they're weatherproofing it. Could this be true?" Probably.

How about it, Editor? (We've got enough problems without inviting any from readers. Ed.)

Anyway with all said and done, life with Platypus is never dull, and I wouldn't have it any different for the world.

He has viewed the prospect of this article with some trepidation, and at one time I offered to suppress it.

"Not at all," he said generously. "As a matter of fact, I think I'm quite flattered at the thought of you being a kind of Boswell to me. I'll give you a Johnsonian quote if you like," he offered.

So as I pinched the title from Dr Johnson, I'll pinch the last line, too.

"When a man is tired of gliding," says Platypus, "he is tired of life."

Postscript from Plat: It was in fact not Dr Johnson but Punch about 150 years ago that gave the negative advice to people on the brink of matrimony. But I was never in the habit of correcting Mrs P's copy.

Mrs Platypus's Bedtime Reading (1978)

Platypus was reading *S&G* in bed. Ever thoughtful of my comfort and well-being, he handed me something with which to occupy myself until he had digested *S&G* down to the last small ad. In this case, what he handed me was the Index to Volume XXVIII 1977, compiled by our old friend Rika Harwood. The Index had fallen out of *S&G* when Platypus picked it up.

Now you might not think that the Index to Volume XXVIII is the most riveting bedtime reading around. However, as clearly nothing more interesting was going to present itself before Platypus had read every last syllable of *S&G*, I decided to fritter away an idle hour with it. And I have to report that the Index to Volume XXVIII is a quite amazing document.

For instance, did you notice a letter in *S&G* in 1977 entitled "The Aim is for Maximum Enjoyment"? Or a feature by A D Purnell entitled "Try the Tiny Triangle"? (As the actress said to the bishop, presumably.) Mr A Wills apparently asked "How Could You Fail?" whereas Mike Beach confidently maintained "We Can Do It" and Gren Seibels noticed a "Disconcerting Phenomenon."

Was it just, I wondered, my overheated imagination? Or were all the Indexes (Indices?) as full of delightful double entendres as dear XXVIII? I rustlcd up XXVII, Index to Volume, 1976, to check. I was not disappointed.

There was J. Wills, declaring "Behold the Dreamer Cometh." Ann Welch wrote about "Too Much or Too Little" and Ruth Tait complained "Only 270 Minutes More." Under "Record Breakers" we were advised "See Also Bigger and Better."

Among the more bizarre entries was "Rodwell, R R, Amid the Vultures and the Kites, 164; The Press can be Very Helpful (letter)."

The entry "A Task Week for the Over 65s" reminded me of a story about the Family Planning Journal, which announced in 1969 that in a forthcoming issue they would be publishing an article on "Sex and Contraception in the Seventies." They were besieged by anxious correspondents who wanted to know, was contraception really necessary at that age?

Back to XXVIII, however, I felt that "Angela's Antics" might not be out of place in Penthouse, while bondage fetishists were catered for with "And a Lot of Rope." A Mr Harris gave it as his opinion that there is "No Substitute for Experience."

"What are you doing?" Platypus demanded, as I giggled to myself over some of the choicer items.

"Reading about A Plea for Regional Activity," I quoted to him. "I know all about the Avoidance of Arrival Accidents."

But Platypus was fast asleep.

Mrs Platypus: Platypus and the little people (1981)

Mrs Platypus reveals that the male of the species doesn't hibernate during the winter but takes up a scaled-down flying interest

Platypus has recently revived a dormant interest in aeromodelling and I have wholeheartedly encouraged him in this. As my friend Gwen Bellew says (her husband Jim is an aeromodeller too) the retrieves are so much easier.

I have to confess that I haven't excelled myself as aeromodelling crew any more than I have at crewing for the full scale versions of Platypus's models. In both cases, I'm afraid, I have managed more or less to write off something dear to Platypus's heart. A psychologist might assert that there is no such thing as a true accident and that the incidents are evidence of a subconscious desire to eliminate my rivals for Platypus's affections. I do freely admit that I do regard almost anything with wings as a rival.

However in the case of the Kestrel trailer which I overturned on the M1, I was exonerated by the insurers who said that the accident was caused by a fault in the car engine, though I have never felt able wholly to exonerate myself. In the case of the little rubber model to which I set fire in Richmond Park, it is even more difficult to free myself from guilt.

Platypus was holding the aircraft, lovingly constructed over a period of months from balsa specially imported from America, and being test flown prior to an important competition. I was lighting the de-thermaliser fuse. Suddenly – whoosh! the whole thing was in flames and Platypus was jumping up and down stamping vigorously on his model, looking rather like Rumpelstiltskin. I was helpless with hysterical laughter – largely nerves, as apart from anything else it was one of the few dry spells we had that summer, Richmond Park was like a tinderbrush and I thought that I had probably started a forest fire.

Within seconds all that was left was a charred patch of turf, a propeller, and a disconsolate Platypus who maintains to this day that it was the best model he had ever built.

We repaired for consolation to the house of a fellow aeromodeller who poured whisky into Platypus and, looking on the bright side,

Prop salvaged.

said how splendid it was that the prop had been salvaged in such excellent condition. Aeromodellers are very supportive of each other, I've noticed. At a recent competition for microfilm models (I wasn't invited to crew, Platypus evidently feeling that his chances were better without me) he reported afterwards that his model hadn't flown very well, and one of his fellow competitors had breathed on it. Things got rather confused because I misunderstood and became very indignant at this unsportsmanlike behaviour and suggested that the perpetrator should be reported to the FAI, until it was explained to me that breathing on the model had enhanced its performance and had been an act of unselfishness enabling Platypus to come sixth.

Anyway I did feel truly sorry about my first and last act of arson, and as a penance I betook myself to Henry's Models and bought Platypus hundreds of pieces of balsa. The advantage of accidents to Little Gliders is that there are no hassles with The Insurers, of course. I also bought PIatypus his very own stripper, which cheered him up no end.

The disadvantage of being involved with Little Gliders and Little People is the Little Shavings – all over the house. However I know that in big gliding, wives are not immune to this kind of problem. A friend of mine had to leave her car out in the cold all one winter because a full scale trailer was being constructed in her garage. She rang me,

Platypus's little trailer.

complaining about the bits that were trodden into her hall carpet as the men came in and out for cups of tea not to mention, she said, having to vacuum the carpet in the garage all the time: her garage is carpeted. I won't say that her standards of housekeeping are higher than mine, though they undoubtedly are, but they are certainly different.

At least her trailer couldn't get lost which is what happened to Platypus's Little Trailer a couple of weeks back. It's a large cardboard box, like the one I bring groceries in each week, but special, and it simply vanished. I was suspected of having thrown it away and the children were interrogated in case they had converted it to a puppet theatre or something. Finally it came to light in the loft, a bit squashed but still competition-worthy.

The bonus of being married to an aeromodeller is the fascinating literature which comes into the house. Platypus subscribes to magazines from all over the world. I was leafing through some French ones in bed the other weekend, waiting for Platypus to decide whether it was gliding weather or aeromodelling weather or neither, when I came upon this amazing guide to aviation vocabulary in French, German and English.

"*Angle = winkel = angle*" it began. Having thereby captured the reader's interest in the first few words, as all good journalists are trained to do, it continued:

"*Epais = dick = thickness.*" No, I am not making it up. It is absolutely true.

It was, of course, a very selective vocabulary. It was preoccupied with thrust. There was *traction = thrust, cabreur = upthrust, vireur = side thrust, piquer en plane = downthrust* and *butel a billes = thrust ball bearing*. After all that I wasn't at all surprised to come upon *helice = airscrew*. I loved *bracelet caoutchouc*, and in case you can't guess what it is, it's *gummiband* in German and rubber band in English. *Balsa tendre* sounds like a French endearment. It's soft balsa. *Enduit de tension* is dope. *Chrono* is a timekeeper. *GC* (whatever that is) is CG, but *PLM* is mysteriously H LG.[11] A *tube* is a tube, it said, and a *canard* is a canard.

"What are you laughing at?" Platypus asked me. In the ten years that I have lived with him, I told him, I have laughed more than in all the preceding years of my life. Ah, he said suspiciously, but was it because he was being intentionally or unintentionally funny?

---

[11] CG, of course, is Centre of Gravity. HLG, less obviously, is Hand Launched Glider, and its French equivalent is PLM, or Planeur Lancé à Main. (Plat)

"Does it matter?" I asked. "Probably not," he said graciously.

It was two nineteenth-century philosophers, Julius Charles Hare and Augustus William Hare who said, "Few men are much worth loving in whom there is not something well worth laughing at."

Or perhaps, to end on a slightly less lofty note, it's just that little things please little minds.

It is not strictly true to say that retrieves are easier with model aircraft. On one occasion in Richmond Park Jim Bellew (The Lord Bellew to give him his proper moniker) insisted on climbing a big tree to get my glider down. As he teetered way out on a high branch I had awful visions of the Fleet Street press, being obsessed with titled people, having a great time with headlines like, "Peer Tries to Grab Model in Tree, Breaks Neck." I myself would have been publicly excoriated for my cowardice in letting a nobleman 16 years older than me risk his life for my bit of balsa.

On another occasion I was apprehended by the police in the same park, because a woman had reported me for "being in possession of an offensive weapon." I had been trying to get my model down with the aid of a fishing-line attached to lead weights thrown up by a catapult, which I'd made on the spot from twigs and a length of Pirelli rubber-motor cannibalised from another model. The poor woman had thought I was trying to slaughter squirrels or birds, I suppose. By the time I had pacified the police and got back to the tree to retrieve the model, I found that a young chap had climbed up and stolen it. The guardians of the Law had gone by then. And they say full-sized gliding is frustrating.

Soaring voices: Platypus writes an opera (1995)

Gliding people have a pretty relaxed attitude towards culture. They don't go quite so far as Göring, who said that when he heard anyone mention culture he took the safety catch off his revolver, but most of my mates can take it or leave it alone, shall we say.

(What you mean is they're a right bunch of Philistines? Ed. You said it, not me. Plat.)

Nevertheless, art in nearly all its forms has put itself at the service of our great sport.

Poetry, songs, novels, oil paintings, sculpture, etchings and graffiti have celebrated the whole gamut of gliding experiences: competitions, cloud flying, crashes and the deflowering of farmers' daughters. I have (he coughs modestly) even written a trilogy of short plays, humorous in style, but deadly serious in their moral message. But there is one supreme art which has failed, so far as I know, to take gliding as its theme. Yes, I mean opera. Grand opera. What an ambition it would be, to celebrate the start of the new millennium, to hear Pavarotti sing, "Your tiny pitot is frozen" before a royal audience (assuming we have any royals left by the start of the new millennium, January first 2001) enthralled by a simple, but magical and moving, tale of noble gliding folk and their ungovernable passions.

"What's he talking about, Fred?"

"The ungovernable passions of us noble glider pilots, Bert."

"You could've fooled me. Another pint of Theakstons, Mabel. As I was saying, Fred, the trouble with grommet-knurdling rings is..."

Well, you can't please them all. This project will go ahead.

First, I want to make it clear that I shall not sneakily borrow tunes from famous and popular operas: I shall steal them wholesale. Composing is not my forte, but any idiot can write a *libretto* (that's Italian for a little book). All you need for a plot is an assortment of Babylonian kings, inquisitors, sorcerers, assassins, bands of brigands, gods, ghosts, torturers, gypsy temptresses, dungeons, secret trapdoors, magic bullets, love potions and fire-breathing serpents – the sort of thing you can easily find around any gliding site on a damp Sunday afternoon. You stir up this brew, mixed together with the six deadly sins, some incredible coincidences and some utterly self-defeating behaviour, and there you have your little book. I shall become a *librettist* (that's Italian for a little bookie).

The more alert among you, or at least those who know a thing or two about sin, will have observed that I seem to be one deadly sin short. Well, I have never considered sloth a sin, especially not a deadly one. If it had been a deadly sin, somebody would certainly have attempted an opera about sloth. If somebody did, then he was too idle to get around to finishing it. It's Lust, Gluttony (which includes excessive drinking), Pride, Avarice, Envy and Rage that I shall depict.

What a gliding opera needs is some good choruses. Well, let's not be too fussy. I mean large choruses, masses of bodies all bellowing forth on the stage. I'm talking quantity, not quality. Why? Because for every person appearing on the stage half a dozen friends and relations will buy tickets. Choruses mean solvency, so long as the stage doesn't give way in the over-zealous pursuit of profit.

In act one the Anvil chorus from Il Trovatore, for example, will be belted out by Ralph Jones's team performing a delicate fuselage repair with seven pound sledgehammers. Pilots below World team standard will be rounded up as an amorphous mob for mystical, religious get-togethers such as briefings and prizegivings. Crews get specially brutal treatment, but also the best choruses.

I only have space here to describe the last three scenes in rough outline.

Lucy (I suggest Suzy Edyvean) is a strapping, ambitious, newly-joined member of the Lammermoor gliding club. She has today been given a wizard forecast by the High Priest Zarastro (played by Tom Bradbury). Zarastro, being a top Freemason, has had a hot tip from God (played by Barry Rolfe, if we can get him to stop dyeing his whiskers black and let them revert to their natural, distinguished, snowy white) that the morrow will be her 1,000km day. Lucy only has to get airborne before 10 o'clock and the diploma is guaranteed by sorcery – but *for that one day only*. Let slip that chance and she will never get another. This opportunity, says Zarastro, is her divine reward for guarding her virtue for 15 years and still being *intacta*, though none of the two dozen gliders she has flown is *intacta*.

(There's not a huge amount of room for humour in opera, but knowledgeable members of the audience will get a chuckle out of the subtle way in which I hint at the name of the club in the south of England where she spent the previous 15 years. The *cognocscenti* will know that she was in no danger whatever on that site, and that Zarastro, for all he is a fount of spiritual wisdom, is, on the worldly plane, a pretty naïve guy.)

The dawn breaks. A sweating, toiling mob of Soaring Crew Union Members (SCUM) sing the Chorus of Hebrew Slaves from Nabucco while rigging their masters' and mistresses' sailplanes, as the ferociously mustachioed slave driver (British team manager Bob Bickers) lashes their naked backs to encourage them.

At Zarastro's briefing the other pilots are amazed at Lucy's calm, Mona-Lisa-like half smile, as if she knows something the others do not. She seems positively nonchalant, while they are possessed and made frantic by all the five deadly sins. (Just five? When it's a possible 1,000km day, they have no time for lust, so the remaining five passions boil over in a tremendous scene in which most pilots call upon God, but another, played by Brian Spreckley – in a Faustian subplot which I have no time to describe here – privately sells his soul to the Devil, played by Derek Piggott.)

At only half past nine Lucy strolls across to her trailer. Nothing like this has been seen since Sir Francis Drake played bowls as the Spanish Armada swept up the English Channel at all of two knots. But a restless, shimmering undercurrent of violins in a minor key suggests trouble. The stuff is about to hit the fan.

Suddenly, Lucy spots a note nailed to the trailer door. The reading out of a letter is a great dramatic device in grand opera. Everything else is sung: even such banalities as "Be so good as to pass the peebags" and "Where the hell are my quarter-mill maps?" will have to be sung *recitativo*, but letters are read out straight, which makes a gripping contrast. She goes ghastly pale as she declaims the hideous contents: "Darling Lucy, You will be so pleased to know that I have decided to fix that little chip in the gel coat on the starboard wing. I have taken the outer panel back to my castle and it will be back in 24 hours. Your adoring partner, Edgar." The ensuing shriek cuts through the Hebrew Slaves' Chorus with stunning effect.

Lucy departs precipitately, or at least as quickly as convention allows. This being opera, she is compelled to reiterate the line, "I must haste away, for my thousand-K" about 20 times, while the mixed emotions of a whole quintet interweave other lines such as, "Edgar is a nice chap, his heart's in the right place" (sings Justin Wills) and "it won't be when she gets to him" (replies Martyn Wells) and more of a similar kind appertaining to the folly of being a member of a syndicate of more than one.

Finally, at the climax of the quintet, Lucy gallops off to the castle. (She hasn't got a horse, she just moves like that naturally.) Andy Davis sings "That woman sure does move" (*La Donna e mobile*) as a furious cloud of dust heads towards the battlements which dominate the horizon.

More dramatic and tragic irony will be wrung out of the mistaken belief on the part of Edgar (Jed Edyvean) that Lucy has rushed to his workroom high in the castle solely in order to reciprocate his passionate love for her. All she wants is the starboard outer panel, and he teasingly keeps getting between her and it in the hope of catching a kiss, or maybe a bit more. And so he does. Donizetti does not show this particular scene at all, only its terrible aftermath, and maybe Donizetti was right. He knew about women, though not a lot about gliding syndicates.

What follows, of course, is the inevitable Mad Scene. Lucy slowly descends the wide, curving staircase before a horrified crowd. Under her left arm a white wing panel spattered with blood, in the other hand a Schempp-Hirth main wingpin. (With respect to Suzy, I believe that only someone with the power of Joan Sutherland could carry off this part. I don't mean the role of Lucy, I mean the 100lb wing panel.) From a gothic window a shaft of sunlight fails on her face. In that very instant she calculates, without benefit of any clock, from the azimuth of the staircase and right declension of the window and the latitude and longitude of the castle (I hadn't mentioned she was a mathematical genius, had I? Just another little surprise in the plot) that it is 10 o'clock. She has blown it. The pianissimo way that she launches into her simple, almost childlike, aria (Due Cappucini Per Favore) indicates that she has totally flipped. A chorus of men in white coats move forward and gently lead Lucy off to the funny farm (Booker GC).

The drama has yet another climax, however. The last act is a trial, presided over by the imposing figure of the Grand Inquisitor (played by Bill Scull). He asks Lucy if she has anyone to defend her on a charge of premeditated murder: her aria an route to the castle, "I'll do him in, I'll do him in" (Offenbach's "We'll run them in, we'll run them in" will do nicely here) had been cited convincingly as evidence of premeditation.

A mystery figure swathed in black – it's like Verdi's Masked Ball, except that every part of him is masked – steps forward as the lawyer for the defence. After a moving address in which he extols Lucy's virtue and beauty to a packed jury (I don't mean rigged or corrupt, I just mean the jury box is crammed with pilots and peasants and glider repairers to help the opera break even) he is at the climax revealed to be none other than Edgar himself! His head wound had indeed bled profusely from a glancing blow with the wing pin, but he had only been momentarily concussed.

The GI (Grand Inquisitor) forgives Lucy, on condition that she marries Edgar that afternoon and promises to retrieve for him uncomplainingly for 100 successive soaring days. She begins wistfully to eye the wing pin again, but it is removed from her reach, and with a sigh she eventually submits.

The jurors all dance with the slaves and the men in white coats, and the final drinking song by members of the RAFGSA led by Mick Boyden, energetically swinging great foaming tankards of ale, serves to remind the audience that there is something more to life than gliding and sex.

The seven deadly sins: lust (1990)

For male pilots it is well established that sex is a substitute for gliding, not the other way round as supposed by Freudian psychologists. The reason is fairly straightforward. Male pilots assume that their womenfolk (I'm talking about those men that have womenfolk; large numbers of gliding men don't want anything to do with women) are available for their pleasurable company at any time, whereas the combination of an available glider and good soaring conditions is so rare a moment that it must be seized – *Carpe Diem* – and everything else can wait. But I wonder if the men don't assume too much.

There must be huge opportunities for a ruthless seducer at gliding clubs. Think of all those bored, neglected women, their men miles away, in mind if not in body. Now I myself have never stooped to take advantage. I have to say it is mainly cowardice rather than conscience. Think, for a moment, of the consequences if you actually stirred a fellow member to a fit of jealous passion. (Hard to imagine at my club; about the only thing that would stir a fellow member to any kind of jealous passion would be if you sneaked your glider into his place on the aerotow queue.) Then, imagine, halfway through the take-off run you discover you have 200 lbs of water-ballast in one wing and none in the other; or the elevator is disconnected; or you go into cloud and the terminals on the turn & slip have mysteriously been reversed. You are playing with fire. That is why at gliding sites, in comparison with what I'm told goes on at golf clubs or fox-hunting circles, I hear so little scandal. Or maybe I've just got cloth ears.

There is one small exception. Well, it is a pretty big exception really, and it's called *****. I am told it is rampant at ******. Rife. Long before those terrible gales it was a rule at ***** that the caravans had to be tethered firmly at both ends with steel hawsers – they didn't worry about the gliders or trailers, so they blew all over the place in the last hurricane, but the caravans have to be secure. I think the committee were more concerned about noise pollution rather than about the caravans getting loose and bouncing their way down the perimeter track in broad daylight. Besides secure tying-down, a well-greased suspension reduces unwanted squeaks, if you are concerned about attracting undue attention. At least, so I'm told. I wouldn't know myself.

I've often thought, since for the reasons I have mentioned it's not a good idea to do it on one's own doorstep, that it might be fun, on a day when my partner has the glider, to nip down to ******* and make a few low passes, so to speak. But I know that with my luck and my character, at the end of the day it would be an emotional disaster of guilt, remorse and self-recrimination. Because, when the tom-cat crawls home at the end of that day of debauchery he will switch on the answering machine and hear his partner's voice: "Hello Plat, this is Fred at 9.00am. I have been re-rostered and have to fly a 737 to Frankfurt this afternoon, so the glider's all yours, rigged and ready to go. Looks like a 600km record day. Happy soaring!"

Aaaaarrrgghhh! What have I done? What a stupid, mindless waste! (Bangs head against door.) Miserable, lascivious wretch! This is your punishment; the Day of Days, thrown away in a caravan with the blinds drawn! Where's the gin bottle? etc, etc.

The moral is: men who are tempted to infidelity, stay faithful to your loved one, do not stray, for that can only lead to woe. That's right, stick with your glider. Take a cold shower every morning and go up to the club without fail. You never know, the Lord may smile on you and drop the wingroot on your partner's foot or ground his airliner in Dubai. Your reward shall be in Heaven – ie anywhere over 5,000ft clear of restricted airspace. Here endeth the lesson.

PS. My apologies to women glider pilots for leaving them out of this farrago. Researches into this small but increasingly important group are only just beginning. Offers of information and assistance gratefully accepted. First-hand accounts preferred.

It's a snip! (1984)

I've seen some intriguing advertisements in *S&G* in my time but the recent one offering sterilisation operations is the most enterprising for some while. The aversion of male glider pilots to the responsibilities of parenthood is legendary, so the clinic in question could be on to a good thing. On the other hand, the mainstay of most clubs are those monastic fettlers who year in, year out make the workshop their cell and the trailer park their cloister: I don't see them succumbing to an uncontrollable tidal wave of desire – not unless they spot an original Minimoa rudder lying intacta in the hangar roof.

In the 1930s they had other, less subtle ways of reducing the propensity to breed, viz the heavy landing in an unsprung primary; the very thought of which brings tears to the eyes. A London Club member was deprived of one of the essential parts in just such a prang (the word *prang* is pure onomatopoeia – the sound of flying wires and landing wires parting company under protest) but a year later fathered a child and went around boasting that he could still fire on one cylinder. I bet he didn't fly primaries again, though.   ∎

> *Charlie Spratt says that a simple way to assess whether a youth is progressing from boyhood to manhood is to ask, "Which would you rather do: see a woman naked or set off a bomb?" However one teenager stumped Charlie when he replied, "How big's the bomb?"*

Heck, it's Supposed to be Dangerous, isn't it?

I am an expert on safety the way burglars are experts in the law. That is to say I have not had a systematic education in the subject, but I do have a hazy awareness that safety and I are somewhat at odds. Like the recidivist burglar I can speak from experience of having done unsafe things, but am insufficiently deterred from repeating the offence, despite the frequent punishments that are exacted.

Such a confession, I realise, shows low intelligence on my part. That makes sense: the experts say criminals are indeed people of low intelligence. What they mean is the criminals who are in jail are of low intelligence. I am convinced there are master-crooks of genius who live amongst us as respected citizens. Likewise there are pilots of the first rank who are deadly, but who so far have never had to fill in an accident report or make an insurance claim – yet. They have caused others to make out accident reports and claim on their insurance, but their own record is spotless. The two reasons I do not name such pilots are that 1) I have to share thermals with them in the coming season and 2) with their low insurance premiums they are among the minority who can afford to buy my book.

Washout (1971)

It was really a form of frustration that was to blame. Here it was, the last weekend of June, and I hadn't had a decent cross-country at a time when I'd usually done hundreds of miles. That was simply because I'd opted for a latish contest and my partners enjoyed the brilliant conditions of the early part of the season. Luck of the draw. But all the same, that did not prevent my pencils being chewed to matchwood as cumulus burbled past the office window, framed against a dazzling blue background.

At last the glider, the pilot and the weather were to meet. It was like one of Nelson's tars finding his first woman after umpteen weeks at sea. Caution was thrown to the winds. The winds threw it back again, gusting to 40 knots and howling round the windsock to the accompaniment of millions of marble-sized hailstones that pummelled and rocked those gliders that some fools had been rash enough to rig. To hell with that. I was going to aviate. The gods of thunder and lightning could go hang.

The moment we saw a patch of blue sky large enough to make the aforementioned sailor's pants, we launched. First tentative, then successively brisker, updraughts bore us heavenwards as the wind at the same time obligingly whisked us out of controlled airspace into the flatlands of East Anglia. I had no plan but to get to, say, Cambridge, attain a vast height and, with luck, hack my way back home against the wind.

In fact, I had devised a simplified way of navigating in cloud by dead-reckoning[12] that turned out to be the only success of the day. I was delighted, after an hour-and-a-half out of sight of earth, to pinpoint an unmistakable landmark though a small hole in the cloud at 8,500ft. Having satisfied scientific curiosity and personal pride, I headed for home, which was now about 50 miles away. I had also satisfied myself, unjustifiably as it turned out, that the wind speed and direction were as forecast at all times, all places and at all heights. On average, this was generally true, but at particular places it turned out to be a fallacy.

The return home was not so easy. I had bargained for the headwind, but the vast clogging-together of black cu-nims was demoralising. It was increasingly difficult to identify the up-and-coming cauliflower, head for it, locate its core and wring height out of it before hail and ice had taken their toll.

Eventually, after pursuing a ripe-looking cloud and being driven off by a totally silent but very purposeful bolt of lightning, I decided to glide it out.

---

[12] Again, the use of such an arcane expression will help historians date this piece. For younger readers, "dead-reckoning" is a corruption of the term "ded(uced) reckoning", which entails drawing vectors (lines) on paper and assuming constant wind-velocity at all heights, and steady speed and heading of the aircraft in level flight with an accurate compass and air speed indicator, and meticulous time-keeping. In short my navigational triumph was a pure fluke.

There was the question of finding a decent place to land. On the edge of the Fens, the low-lying fields were like row upon row of mirrors reflecting the broken sky. I rejected landing in any of these paddy-fields. It wasn't just the prospective nightmare of organising a retrieve. There was a real danger that on touchdown the wheel would sink in, possibly flipping the Dart over on its back. Even if that didn't happen, how would I be able to turn the wingtip single-handed into wind every time the squalls hit, let alone to tether it down? No, I had to land on a large, well-drained surface near to people/ telephone/ road – and facing into wind, of course.

Through the patches of broken cloud at 1,500ft. I saw a village and felt confident that a usable field would be found near it. Then village, fields and sky were blotted out by a blanket of low cloud that doubtless represented the last belch of a departed thunderstorm. Despairingly I watched the altimeter unwind until it fell to 400ft; only then did I break cloud.

There were no indications of wind at all – no washing, no fires. What do you expect with all that rain? The few trees in that area gave no sign, their leaves heavy with water. Raindrops on the canopy compelled me to peer irritably through the clear-vision panels. A bare minute remained for the search. I was only grateful that it had momentarily stopped raining, though the sink seemed as bad as ever.

Then I saw it: The ideal field. A sports-ground, all of 250 yards long, running up and down wind, give or take 30 degrees. Trees on the approach but less than 20 feet high.

Leafy landing-places (1995)

My first reaction as we climbed out on tow on the practice day of the April 1995 competition at Chester, South Carolina, was "Help! Where does anyone land?" Trees stretched to the horizon on all sides, and navigational landmarks were scarce. I asked a local, what happened with older gliders in the days of 28:1 and no GPS? "Oh, they piled into the woods all the time." There are a lot of people in Britain and the USA with a nostalgia for 28:1, and even more yearn for 15:1. The first principle of nostalgia is that anything that works well cannot be lovable. Love therefore is expended in inverse proportion to efficiency.

The field was so big that the boundaries of the cricket field only occupied about a third of its area. White-flannelled figures were stealing some play between showers. I decided that if they did not see me and make obvious movements away from the centre of the field I would prolong my crosswind leg and drop into the adjoining field, which looked rougher but was without obstructions. (I only wish now that they had ignored me altogether!) As the bowler ran up I was sure that the batsman would swing, heads would turn my way and I would be seen. Sure enough, the ball pitched, the batsman struck out and heads turned. Figures stood transfixed for two seconds then made an orderly sprint to the edge as I pointed the nose at them with a dramatic waggling of wings. I felt positively smug at this coup; the ideal field and 22 brawny pairs of arms to manhandle and de-rig in any conditions. A nice long bomber-type approach at 65-70 knots, skimming over the little trees, touching down a third of the way up the field. Too easy.

It was only after covering a hundred yards on the ground (about four seconds) that I noticed that my wheel-brake was having no effect and that my groundspeed was still immense. A healthy loathing of groundloops made me pause a further second or two, then with a mere fifty yards left and a collision inevitable I forced the wing on the ground and kicked on full left rudder. The sports ground, however, was finely mown and very wet, like a greased billiard-table, so the wing-tip discovered what the wheel had already found out – there was hardly an ounce of friction in it. The rudder discovered (earlier than I had) that our airspeed was not as high as our groundspeed and that it could make little impression on our path over the grass. The astonished cricketers saw their uninvited guest whistle past them, turn through barely 20 degrees and without a pause pile noisily into their ten-foot high fence.

Two massive concrete posts reinforced with multiple steel bars were severed by the cockpit and starboard wing. Flannels rushed up with anxious queries of, "Is he alive?" and were reassured by the pilot sitting up in the debris and swearing, "I am a..!"

After the early moments of shock I was able to stride about on sorely bruised but intact limbs (thank you, Fred Slingsby and the invention of glass-fibre) to measure the 175 yards from touch-down to the fence (176 yards if you allow for the vital amount of "give" in those newly-appointed arrester-wires). The caretaker was very kind. "We were going to move that fence anyway." What you call making a virtue of a necessity.

Then, wetted finger up, I tested the wretched wind. No doubt about it. It had swung through 120 degrees. A *downwind* component of nearly ten knots, coupled with a buxom 70 knots over the boundary to cope with a non-existent wind gradient, amounted to a pile of kinetic energy which that beautifully-kept surface could never dissipate.

There is only one moral to this tale: there are days when you shouldn't leave the ground.

The seventh sin (1980)

Of the deadly sins. O Brethren. the deadliest is Pride. It takes many forms, and one shape in which it manifests itself amongst glider pilots is, for example, to refer to those ordinary members of the general public who have the sense not to spend their time messing about in gliders as "peasants." Another form, particularly virulent before the war but still endemic, is to regard power pilots with disdain, as yachtsmen do motorboat-owners. This error was briskly sorted out, so far as I was concerned, more than twenty years ago by an ancient aviator who had soared and motored through the air for countless hours over untold years, man and boy, peace and war. Cornering us brats in the bar where he had overheard some cocky remarks like the above, he demanded to know (rhetorically, being quite uninterested in any answers) whether we had ever flown at night, or across oceans, or in fog, or monsoon, or bliz-

zard? Had we? Of course we hadn't. We were a bunch of fair-weather fliers who only knew a fraction of what aviating was about. That shut us up.

Of course since then I have flown gliders in torrential rain, hail, snow, ice, fog (or at least very, very low cloud) and have groped my way onto the ground in near-dark. (Your insurance brokers are on the phone: shall I tell them you're out? Ed.)

But in all those cases I had started out flying in sunshine with no intention of grappling with the murky elements. Fair weather fliers in such situations begin to feel very humble and sit there promising fervently that if they get back on the ground in one piece they'll never do it again, honest, cross their hearts.

Powered aircraft are able to get into situations that gliders cannot get into, That's why a power pilot needs to be better than a glider pilot in dealing with bad weather. The times, however, that a glider pilot can get into an unaccustomed bad-weather plight are when he is on tow, usually when retrieving or ferrying a glider from A to B.

My worst fright ever (and that is saying quite a bit) is something I intend to bore you with right now.

There can be some very good soaring weather at Easter, especially if the wind has a bit of north in it. But that can mean snow, too. One Easter Weekend day many years ago I enjoyed myself soaring back and forth along the front edge of a massive and impenetrable snowstorm, which gradually pushed me south-westwards until I decided to land at a friendly site 20 miles downwind before I ended up in Cornwall. I rang my home club and told the member who answered where I was, and that I would call again later when and if I wanted an aerotow retrieve.

Upright fellow (1999)

For some reason that I forget, George Moffat and I found ourselves talking about wheels-up landings on hard runways. He capped anything I could boast of by stating that he once landed a Nimbus 3 wheels-up on the asphalt – with full water, which is a heck of a lot of extra weight. It ground such a pronounced flat on the bottom of the Nimbus that the glider remained perfectly upright after it stopped.

I was quite specific because in the few minutes between landing and making the call, an inch of snow had already fallen and in half an hour the place looked like the North Pole. To my surprise, in the first clearance a tug landed with two of my clubmates aboard. They had been told, incorrectly, that I wanted an aerotow retrieve. It was sunny and soarable back at base – so they couldn't hang about, since the tug was urgently needed by my fellow members. I muttered about the threatening low clouds, was assured that there were some gaps we could get through and was rather unhappily towed off.

What followed was the most hair-raising hour of my entire gliding career. Within minutes the promised gap had closed and the tug vanished ahead of me in a billion snowflakes. The turbulence was equivalent to the average cu-nim or wave rotor cloud, with the added discomfort that the ground was steadily rising as we crawled into the buffeting headwind across the range of hills that separated the two sites. There was no question of my pulling off and landing since we were all of 300ft above the high ground which was only occasionally visible in the blinding whiteness of the storm. A score of times the tow line snaked back in loops that swayed far under the glider or way out to one side, then without warning it would go violently taut as the tug reappeared amid the whiteness, often 40 degrees above or below or to one side. On some occasions we found ourselves flying in formation – trailing the line between us in a wide "U." A collision, a line snarled around the wing or a linebreak were each time on the cards. Why the line didn't break. I can't imagine. It must have been the toughest towline since D-Day.

In desperation I tried to keep the line straight by using airbrake – though fearing that excessive use of brake would lose us our precious 300ft (there was no question of flying higher, since the occasional glimpse of the rugged winter landscape was navigationally essential to our tug driver). As I moved the brake lever, the undercarriage warning horn sounded loudly – so I remembered to create some drag by lowering the wheel. Then I learned how to skid with crossed controls in anticipation of the line slackening and things gradually began to come back under control. I was learning fast. Eventually we broke out into brilliant blue skies quite near home after a massive, meandering tour of the countryside. It had taken an hour to cover 20 miles.

It took me another hour of gentle local soaring under the post-frontal cumulus to recover my nerve sufficiently to land.

I do not think lessons on how to be aerotowed in blizzards are relevant here – other than don't. The only proper lesson – apart from making sure that whoever takes your retrieve message writes it down and repeats it to you verbatim – is, if you don't want to go, *don't* go. The lethal sin of pride embraces the desire not to lose face, not to thought a coward, not to risk being a nuisance and therefore unpopular. Don't give in to it.

Postscript: This ordeal took place at Easter 1975, and the friendly gliding site was Booker. It occurs to me 25 years later that I was saved by the nose-hook in the Kestrel, which of course could not back-release. Long-distance aerotows with a belly-hook in rough weather carry a big risk of shedding the glider through back-releasing when there is slack in the line.

The tug pilot was Terry McMullin (subsequently killed in a road collision in his sports car). The passenger was Murray Hayes, who with nothing to do except pray for this hour, had the worst time of all. The Supercub which was left in Terry's will to the Club, bearing the name "Terry Mac," is still there, still towing. It is now painted vivid yellow, so if it ever tows a glider into a blizzard again it will at least be easier to see.

No old, bold pilots? (1981)

A letter in a recent *S&G* that caught my notice fired a charge of buckshot at Mike Fairman's suggestion that, in contests, field landings away from approved sites should be discouraged by deducting penalty points. The writer pours scorn on what he sees as a pathetic failure of nerve that accompanies creeping old age, and sarcastically suggests people who feel like that should take up knitting instead. Who, I ask as I read, is this virile young daredevil challenging us to get out there and risk all? Not merely the boldest pilot of our time, member of the Caterpillar Club (or its equivalent depending on the brand of parachute) and Open Class National Champion many times, but the uncrowned King of the glider-repairers.

The last time I saw Ralph Jones (if one excludes the dreary meetings with the insurance assessors and wailing next-of-kin, ie partners) was at a party during an especially destructive contest. He arrived tanned, flashing gold accessories, in an immaculate cream-coloured suit, looking for all the world like a character out of "Dallas" whose oil-well had just come on line. He was entitled to, since in that little local competition the weather and visibility had been terrible: there had been a mid-air collision, widespread field landing crashes and six or seven canopies written off. I wouldn't for a minute suggest that his profession colours his views, since he has always flown the way he works – hard. All the same I can imagine JR doffing his Stetson to RJ and drawling "Smart fella!"

Home sweat home (1983)

It was terrifying. They came out of the sun, they zoomed up from under my tail, or tried to jam a wingtip in my eye. They drove in on collision courses from all angles. Whenever I left to find a new thermal they followed and resolutely circled in the opposite direction. If they thought I was not centred they immediately circled half a diameter away and challenged me to hold my ground (or my air, rather). They flew right under me so that I was petrified of stalling – the ASW-20 will drop like a stone for a hundred feet or so if you overcook it – or they ran their wheels gently over my canopy and blotted out the sun.

Where was this? The *Huit Jours d'Angers* (or the Eight Days of Danger, as it is called)? Or Hahnweide, up against the ex-Luftwaffe's finest? Texas? The UK Nationals? No. It was an ordinary non-competitive afternoon at a club whose name is concealed so as to protect the guilty. Indeed had it been the Nationals I would not have minded. You have a pretty good idea how many hours (and how many crashes) each pilot has. You know whom to get close to, and whom to avoid. By their contest numbers ye shall know them. But at an ordinary club all you know is that these maniacs are not experienced at mixing it, so what they are doing is presumably done out of sheer

Landing "Aux vaches" or How to make a cow really mad (1969)

The Annual Accident Reports make dismal reading again, and I only hope that our reaction is to say, "There but for the grace of God..." and, "What can be learnt from those poor fellows' experience?" rather than showing smugness or patronising pity for the unlucky pilots.

All the same, I am intrigued by the pilot's statement which contained the self-exculpating explanation, "collided with running cow." What was wrong with just saying, "Hit cow"?

Well, for a start, it would look un-British. Leaving aside the odd bounder in our midst whom we can not longer dispatch to the Colonies to spare his family from embarrassment, we are not the types to shoot at sitting pheasants out of season, or ram browsing cattle with sailplanes, right in mid-cud, as it were. The other implication is that it was really all the cow's fault for running into the glider's path; had the ruminant's nerve not cracked, the whole fracas would have been avoided.

Fair enough. However, I suspect that she was one of the last of the anti-invasion breed of 1941, trained to charge enemy gliders. These are recognisable by a strange lack of milking-gear, a ring through the nose, and answering (if you have time to ask) to the name "Bruce."

ignorance. Having mentioned this to a number of contest pilots at the Nationals, I learned that the club in question is not unique; it is pretty perilous in most places. Either I am getting more cowardly as time wears on, or it is that

25 years ago really inept pilots couldn't soar at all, especially when only winch launches and strutted trainers were available.

Nowadays, the sky is full of expensive glass-fibre, superb variometers and dunderheads with suicidal tendencies.

French gliding clubs have marvellously witty cartoons as wall posters stressing different aspects of safety. We over here generally manage to make safety seem boring. Perhaps my colleague, Peter Fuller, could be persuaded to put some life-saving humour into a series of Do and Don't posters.

Here are Reichmann's Do's and Dont's for circling in thermals:

1. First sailplane into the thermal sets the circling direction for all later entrants.
2. Newcomer must fly such that already circling sailplanes are not inconvenienced: that is, work your way into the circle spirally from the outside.
3. Anyone displacing his circle must not hinder other sailplanes in the old circle.
4. If outclimbing another sailplane, the worse climber must not be hindered.
5. As a general rule, never fly closely right below another ship; the other plane has almost no escape route, particularly at low speeds.
6. Always observe your airspace and know who is where, when.
7. Attempt to fly such that the other pilots can always see you.

The only alternative is that other, not quite obsolete, French device for dealing with anti-social nuisances...

The art of coarse ground-handling: or do cars and gliders mix? (1984)

I'm afraid that my insurers have suffered more from my misfortunes on the ground than from any flying mishaps, though the latter have, er, happened from time to time. One expensive prang took place at two miles an hour when a tiny pin fell out of the tow bracket as I was towing a Kestrel down a steep gully at Dunstable.

When I heard the clunk as the bracket came undone, like an utter moron I applied

the brake instead of motoring gently on down the slope. Result: the trailing edge of the rudder slowly crumples against the rear bumper. A repair bill of over £1,000.

Another slow-motion catastrophe, while on a towline behind a car, occurred during a competition in which two gliders had just collided in mid-air (without injury, amazingly) and everyone on the ground was clearing the runways in a panic. My driver started forward just at the moment I was putting my arm through the clear vision panel to pull the release knob. The canopy of the Nimbus 2 disintegrated slowly but inexorably around my arm, which remained relatively intact, though my voice cracked somewhat.

I draw useful lessons from all such incidents, though it doesn't help much. I am reminded of the Colonel who wrote of a subaltern, "One thing I can say for this officer is that he never makes the same mistake twice. He always comes up with a brand new mistake every time."

If I can buy it, I can fly it, or, Physician, cure thyself (1980)

In America, I was told, there is a "Doctor's Syndrome" that causes many accidents. A doctor or other successful professional or businessman, who after early years of hard work and poor pay, when he had no time or money to learn to fly, becomes successful in middle age. He now takes flying lessons and buys himself an aeroplane. (Or worse still, the other way round.) He then, with very few hours in his logbook, takes up his friends or family to show off his new toy and kills off the whole lot in very short order. That is what you can really call a tragedy. Newspaper journalists use the word tragedy to describe any sad event,

Caterpillar corner (1984)

Having recently had the experience of watching from cloudbase as two gliders plummeted towards the woods below, then seeing parachutes opening, I am resolved to treat parachutes with even more tender, loving care than before. By the way, I always make a point of getting out of a cockpit with the parachute on, however uncomfortable that may be. The reflex action of undoing cockpit straps and parachute before clambering out is, to my mind, lazy and potentially dangerous.

Quote from an American publication, The Warrenton Democrat: *"If you are one of the hundreds of parachuting enthusiasts who bought our Easy Sky Diving booklet, please make the following correction: on p8, line 7, the words 'State Zip Code' should have read 'Pull Rip Cord'."*

I wonder if that tiny misprint was drawn to their attention by their Complaints Department.

from a mother of five being struck by lightning to Spurs losing at home to AC Milan, but I am using it in the proper Greek sense to mean the destruction of a good man by *hubris*, best translated into aviationese as over-confidence.

Successful middle-aged professionals have got where they are in the world not by humility but by giving orders. They are used to telling others what to do; they expect to be deferred to. They don't take kindly to being lectured or grounded by instructor-chappies half their age and earning a tenth of their pay. Nobody can tell them anything. In England I can think of at least two or three fatal cases of this happening to well-to-do men (not doctors: they don't get so rich over here) buying high performance gliders immediately after solo and then getting far out of their depth. Their still surviving confrères might read this or better still, read John Williamson and Bill Scull.

Attachez vos ceintures! A true story (1988)

Not long ago a British syndicate chose to take delivery of a new glider from a central France by flying it to England on aerotow. So much

speedier than trailing by road, the theory says. However long-distance aerotowing is not much fun, even in poor weather. In perfect soaring weather it can be Hell. On this day the lift was rampant.

Shortly after setting off from the factory towards the Channel, as they bumped their way through the thermals, the tug pilot was surprised to look over his shoulder and see the glider spiralling down out of control to crash in a field.

Panic ensued when they landed and dashed over to the wreckage, to find no pilot. He, however, presently arrived, clutching armfuls of parachute, in the company of the local fire brigade.

He had been catapulted through the canopy by one specially powerful bump, and promptly hit the silk. They went straight back to the manufacturers and told the astonished management that the new ship had lasted less than one hour, and could they please have another one immediately.

The prize for chutzpah goes to the glider pilot for asking the manufacturers for a volume discount on the grounds that they had bought two sailplanes in one day. I don't know what their answer was but one can guess.

Postscript from Bob Bickers
I found that my former ASH-25 partner Bob Bickers was the tug-pilot and without wanting to duplicate the pretty full account in Wally Kahn's book, here is his story from the moment the tug landed:

"I jumped out of the machine and set off at a run down the lane to the hamlet on the way to the crash site. In my best French I was shouting, "Au Secours, Sapeurs, Pompiers" at the top of my voice. I received one or two quizzical looks but nothing else, not even a following out of curiosity. After about a kilometre I arrived at the field and finally, having crawled through a gorse hedge, at the glider. There was no-one in it and no sign of any one in the field. Immediately behind the glider was a large, high, gorse thicket. I wondered if he might be in it somewhere and started searching, getting torn to bits. Still no sign of any one. As I emerged from the gorse I was in time to see a Fire engine pass down the lane at the end of the field and, Lo and behold! a somewhat bedraggled Pegase pilot standing on the back. He appeared to be shoeless but other-wise unharmed.

I returned to my aeroplane, to find the farmer shaking his head whilst surveying the field. To my surprise he was an Englishman, which made life a lot simpler for the moment. He advised me that I was not permitted to take off from the field without the permission of the Gendarmes, who were sending an officer forthwith. In the meantime I asked the farmer to part the line of hay piles which bisected the field, sufficient for me to pass through whilst, I paced out the field, and then to use his trac-tor to tow the aircraft back right to the edge of the field. On landing, the Rallye had sunk through the dry crust of the field into the mud underneath. Hardly surprising given the trout farm lakes surrounding the field I was in.

After an age convincing the Gendarme that I should be allowed to return to Le Blanc I was permitted to take off. The field was 240 paces long with a further 200 paces of trout lake and then 50ft trees. I was not sure I really wanted to do this. Eventually I set full power and wait-ed. It seemed like half an hour before the Rallye started moving, as we approached the lake I dropped full flap and just before the trees pulled back on the yoke as hard as I could. I was very aware that I had probably just grazed the top of the trees but immediately pushed the nose down and eventually climbed away. By the way my co-pilot had been left behind with the Gendarme as a sort of hostage to ensure that I would return to Le Blanc.

On arrival I was whisked away to the town hospital to the bedside of the erstwhile Pegase pilot where an official of the French Department of Civil Aviation was carrying out an accident investigation. Here I learned that

when we had hit the first thermal on climb out the Pegase pilot had been treated to the sight of his aircraft straps floating up into the air. He had then put the stick between his knees whilst attempting to do up his straps. Just then he hit the 10-knotter. The stick was taken out of his knees and he grabbed at it – having let go of the straps. He said that the glider seemed to stop dead in the air and he was ejected through the canopy, his shoes and socks being pulled off in the process. He pulled his rip-cord and floated down to a safe landing.

Now the pressures of being a serviceman and on a specialist unit began to take over. I was due to fly a Very, Very Important Person the following morning early, and there were no deputies available to fill in for me. It took a lot of persuading but I eventually convinced the Gendarmes and more importantly the Official from the Department of Civil Aviation that I should be allowed to convey the two bereft ex-owners of a Pegase back to our base.

Around 4.00pm we got airborne. The plan was to go direct to Le Touquet where we had asked them to stay open for fuel and customs outbound and then on to Lydd who we had also telephonically persuaded to remain open until we arrived. My two young would-be Pegase owners were prepared to pay any nec-essary overtime bills.

Half way up the coastline on a beautiful balmy summer's evening my two passengers were fast asleep and I was getting too warm for comfort. The Rallye has a delightful facili-ty which enables you to open the canopy in flight, and leave it open if you wish. Without thinking I reached up and pulled the canopy open. Simultaneously there was a rush of cooling air a shout of "Oh No!" from the rear seat where our inadvertent parachutist had been sleeping. He was apparently convinced he was leaving the aircraft all over again!"

R A Bickers

Plat adds: when I asked Bob the obvious ques-tion, "Why were the Pegase seat belts not fas-tened?" he said the new owner "was probably overawed by the occasion." Yes, I can see that for an inexperienced pilot, the prospect of being towed a very long way in a brand new glider, with the English Channel looming in the middle of the journey, would be quite daunting. Nerves could easily override basic procedures like a cock-

pit check. I don't normally feel sorry for insurance companies, but they deserve our deep sympathy in this instance.

The other thought I have is that it may be just as well that the Gendarmes kept Bob's passenger hostage, since it sounds as if he might not otherwise have cleared those trees...

Not another routine crash!? (1990)

One extrovert reader of *S&G* told me that he (no, I remember for various reasons that it was she) only found two things worth a good belly laugh in this magazine – the Platypus column and the BGA official accident reports. I think it is a backhanded compliment to be regarded as about as funny as a compund fracture, but never mind, any kind of praise from the punters, even the sadists, is better than none. "In that case," I said, "the best piece of reading would be an accident report involving Platypus – one, he selfishly hopes, that leaves him sufficiently whole to write it up afterwards?" "Oh yes," she chortled, "that would be spiffing! Please oblige." She slapped me heartily on the back, dislocating my shoulder, and roared back to the bar. Well, I do get pretty desperate for ideas, but having a prang in order to generate copy is going too far.

To give you a notion of how desperate I get with the old writer's block, which is not confined to paid-up union members but can happen to rank amateurs, this particular piece resulted from my using a random-number generator on my Mac II computer to decide which page of *S&G* I should open, the rigid rule of the game being immediately to write something prompted by the very first item on the ran-domly chosen page, regardless. Page 205 *S&G* August issue 1990, Accident Reports, came out of the electronic hat. So now you know just how dried-up the well of literary inspiration has become. I can only thank heaven or the microchip that page 205 wasn't an advertisement glorifying some gliding site or electronic device: advertisers can be very touchy people. You can see their point of view: they don't pay good money in a recession just to be mocked.

I did once write up a prang that I had in 1970 I turned it into a major piece in *S&G* with illustrations by Peter Fuller, on whom I so often depend to save the day. He's the one who can make a leg in traction seem funny. I had another crash in 1977 but I didn't write that one up. One reason for my reticence the second time around was that after the 1970 confession the editor was deluged under a shoal of letters, both of which deplored the poor taste of my washing my dirty underwear in public. It wasn't dirty, just a bit damp, as you might expect under the circumstances. The correspondents said that decent chaps hid themselves after such disgraceful episodes, and didn't boast about their lack of airmanship. And there I was imagining I was doing a public service.

A much better reason for not writing up the second crash was that it was exactly the same as the first one. Which indicates that if anyone had learnt anything from my public breast-beating over the first accident, it certainly wasn't me. There is a dreary, repetitive sameness about most crashery which must make people like Bill Scull despair. Truly original ways of wrecking gliders are so special, there ought to be some kind of medal: a Prang of the Year award limited, for reasons of good taste, to those that can get to the podium under their own power. ∎

Soaring costs

Men's jokes seems always to be about the things which they don't understand and are in fearful awe of: for example, death, money, women, stall-and-spin accidents and so on. Women's main source of jokes is men, except that they do understand men and are not in awe of them one bit. You ought to sneak up on a rowdy hen-party and eavesdrop if you don't believe me. Though do remember your Euripides and the ghastly fate of the guy who did just that and got caught.

The particular source of anxiety I deal with here is economics, rightly termed the Dismal Science, since it appears that whatever you do to improve things just makes things worse.

However, as in so many walks of life, you don't have to be super clever to get by in finance: you just have to avoid doing blindingly stupid stuff. (Like owning shares in four gliders at once? Ed.) Unfortunately, not doing stupid things is beyond some of us. Like moths to flames, or spacemen nibbling at a Black Hole, we can't help being drawn closer and closer....

Wintry thoughts about policies, premiums and six point print (1997)

It's perishing cold as I write this at the beginning of December 1996. A gloomy seasonal item to contemplate is insurance. The Africans have a useful saying, "Never throw stones at the crocodiles while fording a river," and since insurers are the biggest crocodiles in my particular creek, I am not going to bait them. Indeed, I think insurers of light aircraft and gliders are absolute saints. When I am inclined to grumble about underwriters I remind myself that I would not insure glider pilots or their equipment at any price. So the three following items are just observations rather than whinges.

First I was impressed during my 1995 tour of the USA by how much cheaper glider insurance is in America than in Britain. To insure an ASH-25 to the same value cost £1,000 less in the USA. That saving paid a large portion of the cost of ferrying the beast over the Atlantic to Florida. It could just be that American pilots are safer than ours – a hypothesis for which I saw not a trace of evidence. Or their outlanding places are safer. Sorry, but that's unbelievable. Or that they enjoy economies of scale in that vast country. Maybe, but would that account for our insurance costing 50% more?

Then, after 11 years without incident, I had not one but two belly landings in 1996. The second of these disfigured a handsome asphalt runway with a long and very expensive white streak. And disfigured a handsome ASH-25 with a short and very expensive black streak. As Lady Bracknell would have said, "To have one belly landing in a fortnight is a misfortune, but to have two seems very much like carelessness." Leave aside the fact that Lady B would hardly have said *belly*. Soon I was being politely but very insistently asked by the loss adjuster to furnish my pilot's logbooks for the last 39 seasons, otherwise I was not complying with the fine print in the contract, and would not get paid until I did. Of course I had not read the fine print, chiefly out of my customary terminal laziness but also because if I did read it I wouldn't understand it. So with a very ill grace I spent ages searching for old logbooks in my loft, copying competition results from ancient editions of *S&G* and cal-

Don't throw stones at the crocodiles.

culating the flight times from the speeds, and badgering my parthers to lend me the computer discs on which we have put nine years of Peschges data but with several individuals' figures all mixed up.

Finally, exhausted, I called three of Britain's most famous glider pilots to get their opinion about how to escape this quandary. The two famousest both said, "We've never kept regular logbooks since we got our Silver badge. Wish we had. Don't worry, the BGA doesn't require it after your Silver." I was quite flabbergasted as well as relieved. I thought that I was always supposed to keep a proper logbook, and that by not keeping one and staying quiet about it I was not just being an idle slob but a sneaky and dishonest one, too. The third famous pilot let me down disgracefully as a witness for the defence: unlike the more famous two, he had recorded every minute of 22 years' gliding in a series of logbooks as immaculate as his moustache, but he was an RAF type, so what can you expect?

So I sent off my 39 seasons' rough calculations to the adjuster and said wearily that that was all I could manage, expecting the roof to fall in at any moment through the combined wrath of God and Lloyds. Nothing untoward happened in fact, and the repairers did get paid. But, and this brings me to our third item, I got a courteous but firm warning, not about logbooks, but about the need to hold back the start of any repair work till a detailed inspection had been done by the underwriters' appointed agents. I think they are absolutely entitled to make that point. (Ain't that big of him? Ed.) But strict adherence to such requirements will put an end to one of the most hallowed traditions of competition flying, namely the frantic all-night repair job which is quoted for even while the dust and debris are settling, and commenced before the sounds of the crash have ceased echoing around the hills. Have we not all witnessed, or participated in, that dramatic scene, like a Victorian narrative painting? Dawn glimmers faintly on the horizon, promising, or rather threatening, an early start to a perfect soaring day. In the workshop, silhouetted against harsh lights, Ralph Jones and his sons sweat over glass-cloth and resin. Huddled under the limp windsock the ashen-faced pilot and tearful crew are praying for rain, or at least a delayed start, so as to keep the once stricken but now convalescent craft in the contest with a sporting chance.

But that will become just a distant, treasured memory, along with other romantic legends. If Lloyds have their way, never again will we see the repairers, in the absence of proper drawings and jigs, simply pull the severed tail back until the rudder cables go taut and then fill in the gap with plywood. Nor shall we hear again the advice delivered by the craftsman to the pilot, as he waited for a bungy launch in his heavily-bandaged Olympia in a Regionals on a blustery northern crag some forty years ago. "She'll fly all right, lad. But mind you don't land in the next three hours; the glue's still wet."

The dismal science (1999)

At a recent mass meeting of our club Steve Lynn, a brilliant accountant-pilot (I leave you to work out whether he is brilliant as an accountant, or as a pilot, or both, or merely that he is brilliant at the financial analysis of gliding, which is a different kettle of fish entirely) delivered the opinion that it cost so much to keep track of the launches and flying hours of club gliders that we might consider not bothering to keep the figures at all. In fact some clubs on the Continent do not charge for club aircraft by the hour but ask members to pay an all-in fee at the start of each season, so it is not a totally barmy idea, provided you have a fair system for allocating gliders in fine weather. However we still do need to know how many hours each machine has flown for airworthiness and maintenance purposes, and in our chats with government about airspace

– and even Lottery money – we need some solid statistics about what proportion of general aviation activity is carried out by gliding clubs. In short, the radical notion of not keeping the figures at all is unacceptable.

But Steve's question remains: how to we make it easy to collect and analyse the flight times? Especially as it is a rotten chore out on the field and often not done well.

Answer: technology! (Peal of trumpets, stage left. Da-Daaaaa!)

Soon, I suggested, GPS loggers will be so cheap that all club gliders and tug aircraft can have them, permanently running, to be downloaded in the office once a week. Even winches could log launches automatically. A side-benefit is that with the loggers you will, when the sad occasion arises, have an exact time and place of impact for insurance purposes. Club gliders collect an awful lot of impacts, often when they are still on the ground just fresh out of the Workshop after an earlier impact.

However that might require all club tractors and golf-carts to carry loggers too, so you can reconcile the data in the computer and discover which tractor dinged which two-seater. People love driving these vehicles full-tilt into club gliders. They are more cautious about driving into privately-owned gliders since someone actually cares about them, unlike club gliders, to the point of physical ferocity. (Now I think about it, some members should be required to carry loggers, but that is a dangerous line of enquiry.)

However the brilliantest idea came from some young wag. Well, it was Bob King, the Club Chairman, but he was retiring after a long and heroic stint at a thankless task, and must have been feeling demob-happy. (I wonder, does that term mean anything to those who were never in Her Majesty's uniform?) Why not, he said, paint supermarket bar-codes on the sides of the club gliders and make them fly past a bar-code-laser-scanner on take-off and landing?

This stunned everyone so much that the topic was dropped entirely. However I think it deserves thought. There might be a small problem about the lasers blinding the pilots in the early stages of development, though the Workshop's welding goggles, such as we used during the famous eclipse, should obviate that

danger. Pilots might not be able to see the ground or each other, but you can't have everything. Good book-keeping is worth considerable sacrifices.

Another threat may be what lasers may do to the gonads and other intimate parts. No problem. Most gliders have to carry lead ballast, and if hammered into the shape of lederhosen this protection would not be too uncomfortable to wear, once you got used to it.

I shall need technological advice, so I'll give Bill Gates and Wal-Mart a yodel.

PS By the way, if you do meet someone who truly is brilliant at the financial analysis of gliding, do NOT ask them what it really costs. It will ruin your life.

A prayer for a wing (1993)

A small ad, psychiatrists would doubtless assert, is a cry for help. "Bunny. Come back to the syndicate. All is forgiven. Cuddles. PS. Please bring wing pins with you." Some advertisements are fascinating since we must wonder how the situation came about that provokes a particular cry for help. Thus I always seem to be come across ads in *S&G* or on club-house notice-boards that say something like, "Urgently wanted: starboard wing of Dart 17." Did the owners of an otherwise intact Dart 17 leave a wing behind while on holiday in the south of France? Probably not. Or did someone run over it with a pickup truck, not just nibbling at the tip, which is a quite common and recoverable blunder, but smack across the middle, reducing the spar and brake-box to matchwood? I jest, of course, knowing the true answer. In the particular case of the Slingsby Dart, one of which I managed to spin at about 400ft above the bar of the Dunstable Golf Club within minutes of being winched off on my very first flight in the new ship in 1966, there is little doubt that the call for help in the advertisement arises from an asymmetrical impact with the ground following a spiral descent in a stalled condition. Thus one wing escapes, and a tearful call goes out for a mate.

A reader of *S&G*, smugly cosy with pipe and slippers, reads the tragic small ad to his wife, who is knitting a pitot-warmer, and not unnaturally jeers: "Look sweetie, some poor clown hopes someone else has got a spare Dart 17 starboard wing just lying around! People really are weird!"

"Well, darling, what's that thing cluttering up the loft that I'm always asking you to tidy away and you always say you'll throw it in a skip next time builders are in the neighbourhood, which they never are?"

Pipe hangs sort of suspended in mid-air...

"Great Scott! It's a – "

"It can't be – "

In unison: "It's a Dart 17 starboard wing! It's a Dart 17 starboard wing!"

At least this little scenario is what the owner of an intact port wing is imagining as he hopefully pens his ad. After all, gliders are not like power planes, with their marked preference for spins in one direction, depending which way the prop is turning. So the law of averages should send the answer to his prayer.

Pete Wells says don't joke, there is indeed a serious trade in odd wings. He was called by a chap who wanted a replacement wing for a Polish glider. Pete happened to have just such a wing, which was duly collected. However the person who called – obviously not the pilot at the time of impact, since he or she would be unlikely to forget – had not examined the surviving wing much closer than, say, a hundred yards distance. That's right, you guessed it. They were now the owners of two port wings and still no starboard wing. This was eventually bought from the manufacturers. Oddly enough, nobody tried to return the surplus wing to Pete and ask for

their money back. Shame and embarrassment make people act in ways that are not wholly rational.

Wells père (Martyn) relates a still sadder story. Encumbered with two outer sections of a three-piece Skylark 4 wing, he said one day, "This junk has to go. Where's my chainsaw?" and in a few minutes reduced the 45ft of timber to chunks of firewood, all a nice size for popping into an Aga stove.

No, I don't have to tell you what someone rang and asked for the very next day...

Blackmail (1992)

During the nineteenth century some fellow in London made a respectable income – well, a sleazy income – by writing to dozens of women, their names picked at random, saying, "Dear Madam, Your secret is known to me. Unless etc etc." Eventually some lady of impeccable reputation and a totally clear conscience (a rarity, it seems, in view the amount of money he collected) put the police on to him, and his squalid little game of extortion was up. This gave me to ponder on the various ways we try to get people to do what we want them to do.

The management of this organ have in their desperation used all sorts of moral pressure to get me to produce my copy on time – everything except bribery, that is, there being no allocation for bribes in the BGA's budget. They would, if they could, threaten me with the exposure of some guilty secret of which I am ashamed – very difficult to use on someone who has no shame. (Or is it that I have an impeccable reputation and a totally clear conscience? Take your choice.) Other more physical means of suasion are foiled by savage dogs guarding my house and especially my trailer. So the editor's most frequent appeal is to vanity. "Everything you say is read by everybody in gliding, and your advice is Holy Writ. People hang on your lips!" That doubtless explains why I mumble so much. Anyway, vain though I am, this piece of blatant flattery is transparently pathetic nonsense. If people do read, or more likely skim, what I write, they say, "He's only the resident buffoon. This is the never-to-be-taken-seriously column, as a relief from the Bill Sculls and

Leave a wing behind.

Barry Rolfes. There is not one word of hard advice or penetrating wisdom in it."

Solid proof of this dismissive attitude to my outpourings was when I saw some pictures of a comprehensively broken glider a couple of years ago, and read the account of how it had happened. What I read made my teeth grind. Much more of this stupidity on the part of my fellow pilots and I shall have worn my teeth down altogether and be gnashing my gums noiselessly. Only a few months before that sad event I had sounded off in this journal about the folly of would-be glider-owners (WBGOs) who insist on flying a machine before they buy it, and the even greater folly of would-be ex-owners (WBE0s) in agreeing to allow some stranger to stagger around an unfamiliar circuit with the WBEO's life savings, usually after a quite inadequate briefing as to what lever does what. If D Piggott (or someone like D Piggott, except that there is nobody like D Piggott) says in one of his indispensable surveys of second-hand sailplanes that the Schnurlpfii 4B is a safe and sensible glider, then I'll take his word for it and learn to like it once I've bought it. If he says it has the handling characteristics of a Starfighter crossed with a supermarket trolley, then I won't touch it, whatever the glide-angle per Pound Sterling. By the way, Derek's code for these evil traits is, "Big Glider Handling." Be warned. I'm not normally deferential to superior authority, but I make an exception for Derek.

In the particular sad case in question a WBGO was allowed by a WBEO to try out some perfectly straightforward glider, and the WBGO managed to run out of height, speed and ideas in a patch of scrub about a half mile from the site. One could say that the WBGO and the WBEO deserved each other.

However, for those people who, despite not being professional glider-fliers, believe that they will gain deep insights about a machine's performance, handling, freedom from vices etc in the course of a ten-minute flip, I offer this form which I have just devised:

"I, Fred Nurk (WBGO) hereby hand to Alf Baskett (WBEO) a banker's draft representing the full purchase price of the Rhonflieger 3, BGA number xxxx, prior to aviating in same. If following the approval flight, I decide not to keep the aforesaid aircraft, the WBEO is obliged to repurchase the machine, if undamaged, at the identical price. Arrangements have been made with Lloyds underwriters Messrs Rytoff & Rytoff that, inasmuch as the aircraft is my exclusive property for the duration of the flight, any insurance claim arising is my responsibility, including the deductible excess, loss of no claims bonus etc, etc."

You could get a sharp lawyer to knock that little notion into proper legal shape, no problem. It would doubtless reduce the demands for flights by WBGOs, but that is the whole idea.

But wait! It has suddenly dawned on me that perhaps the WBEO whose glider was destroyed was not so dumb as I thought. He collected the insurance and is now the happy owner of a spanking new ship – without getting so much as a scratch on him. So it is possible that he had read my homily and laid his plans accordingly. Good Grief! Why don't I get out the black ink and mail him a friendly note?

"Dear Sir, Your secret is known to me. Unless etc etc."

Sell, sell, sell! (1981)

In *S&G* the small advertisements always command our attention, even if we are not thinking of buying or selling. Like an investor poring over the Stock Market reports, we watch the value of our glider move up and down. Writing small ads to sell big gliders is a skill which some people have and some have not. John Delafield is almost professional in this regard and should be hired to write other people's glider ads for two per cent of the gross. What? Oh all right, John, five per cent. It

Chance of a lifetime.

would still be worth it. People like John D make the glider seem like something from outer space, an opportunity that you can't afford to pass up, the chance of a lifetime. His work on the gliders is very good, but the copy is even better.

Some sellers fear that the mere fact that one is trying to sell a glider means there must be something wrong with it. They strive to reassure the potential buyer by citing some *force majeure* as an excuse for disposing of it. Marriage is frequently pleaded; alternatively we learn that the seller is emigrating to Australia (maybe to avoid getting married) and cannot take the glider along as excess baggage. However the best excuse – or worst depending on your point of view – that I have seen for some time appeared in an ad in a recent *S&G*, which offered to undercut any Nimbus on the market. "This glider must go. A broken leg has put paid to next season's flying."

There, I am afraid, you see the hand, or at least the heavily bandaged foot, of the amateur copywriter, who has obviously done no time with J Walter Thompson. What he leaves horribly uncertain is how he broke his leg (about which of course everyone here at *S&G* feels genuinely sorry). For Heaven's sake, where was the glider at the time, and what is its state now? If he broke his leg skiing then for a few pennies more he could have made that clear. It might seem irrelevant and extravagant to go on about what happened at Kitzbühl, but it might have reassured many people who would otherwise hang on to their chequebooks.

We also wonder about that rather vindictive note, "This glider must go." He might just as well have added, "and never darken my doorstep again!" Does he blame the glider for his broken leg? Perhaps the fuselage or wing-root fell on him while rigging, thinks the potential buyer. If he was underneath at the time, the glider is probably undamaged, and the potential buyer cheers up perceptibly at the thought. Perhaps, though, the vendor kicked the Nimbus in a rage after stopping five feet short of the finishing line. I've known Spanish airline pilots do that to their planes when they refuse to do what they were asked. The mind runs riot. Hypotheses burgeon. Oh dear, oh dear.

The first golden rule of hardsell copywriting is, don't mention broken legs and gliders in the same paragraph. The second rule is, don't be afraid of long and fulsome praise for the product. The third is, eliminate the negative and accentuate the positive: don't say why you must sell, tell them why they've just got to buy.

As Dr Johnson said, "Promise, large promise is the soul of an advertisement."

Broken leg, my foot.

If you want to know the price, you'd better be sitting down first (1996)

When in the last century a millionaire acquaintance of Commodore Vanderbilt, amateur sailor and professional robber baron, inquired what it cost to run a yacht, he got the characteristically arrogant reply, "If you have to ask, you can't afford it." A similar-sounding but more endearing response was made by Fats Waller to a woman who asked him what he meant by rhythm. "Lady, if you gotta ask, you ain't got it!" When I decide that I can't afford the effort and expense of gliding I might well take up jazz piano instead. (Alistair Cooke still plays jazz at 88 years, so it is obviously good for the constitution. The BGA and Lloyds will be glad to know that by that age I shall have hung up my John Willy and will be emulating Fats, except for the bottle of gin on top of the Joanna; that stuff is death to French polish.) One advantage a piano has over a glider is that you don't have to rig the damned instrument every time you want to sit down at the keyboard, and with what it costs to fly big wings I could buy a new Yamaha or an old Bechstein every year.

Let's face it, there is more drivel spoken, and believed, about the costs of gliding than about any other aspect of the sport. Someone who talks great sense about thermal-centring, or is an acknowledged authority on glider maintenance, or is always heeded respectfully on the topic of contest-winning will, the moment the price of gliding is raised, start uttering the most mind-numbingly cretinous fantasies. For instance, Fred will say cheerfully that he has "made a profit" on his Discus because he hears that a second-hand specimen has just changed hands for more than he originally paid for his in 1984. It may be so: certainly the Discus has been the best buy of the 1980s and the 1990s, having defied every effort by other designers to render it obsolete.

But the boastful owner will ignore the fact that the pound sterling has halved in purchasing power in the past 12 years, or be unaware that the chap who got such a good price spent £10,000 not long ago on refinishing the gelcoat and rebuilding the trailer. What our smug friend does not do is ask what it will cost to replace his old ship and all the accompanying equipment with a brand new outfit.

Either he is lying to us (which is perfectly OK) or he is lying to himself (which is unforgivable) but most likely he is too economically immature to be allowed out of the house with any sum of money greater than the bus fare.

Haemorrhaging money

The fact is gliding is a ruinously expensive pastime. (For Pete's sake, I've got advertisers to keep happy! Ed.) Well, let the chips fall where they may, *ruat caelum,* is what I always say.

I have tried calculating the costs of owning a glider, and have even bounced these sums off professional accountants. Since these accountants are also keen glider pilots, you would think they would be able to analyse what I propound and quickly confirm my thesis or put me straight if I am in error. However that is not what happens. My sums come winging back to me with muttered remarks like, "Well, you could look at it that way" making me aware yet again that accounting is an art rather than a science. Obviously I have just ruined their whole weekend by compelling them to apply their professional skills to matters which they did not want to think about. It's like doctors not wishing to confront the possibility of having themselves contracted a socially disastrous disease.

The other thing that terrifies the male, seriously-married, accountant-glider-pilots is that my sums might by chance fall into the hands of their wives, whereupon the roof will rise as if in the grip of a Kansas tornado. "You said it was equivalent to a cheap holiday in Spain once a year – it's more like a moon landing every month, according to this friend of yours!"

"That'll teach you to open my mail: you were perfectly happy until breakfast time. Anyway he's no friend of mine. And his sums are rubbish."

"Are they now? Explain precisely in what way they are rubbish."

"It's too technical and complicated to explain" (desperately).

"Come on, humour me, you forget I read maths at Cambridge."

In the worst case, accountants (gliding) who have married accountants (earthbound) have no escape at all, except an elaborate web of forgery, which could prove costly if used as grounds for divorce in front of an unsympathetic judge.

"I grant Mrs Pinchpenny a *decree nisi* on grounds of severe mental cruelty and gross deception. Instead of carrying on discreet affairs with other women like any normal man, her husband flaunted extravagant new sailplanes in public while she languished at home, humiliated by his inept falsehoods relating to their true costs, which he strove to minimise with a tissue of fabricated syndicate expenses. In addition to stiff alimony, I award her, to dispose of as she wishes, Mr Pinchpenny's new motorised ASH-25E. I see he has written down this rather neat piece of kit in the books at only £8,000, so he should not feel the loss too severely, heh heh." (Judge, lawyers and public gallery collapse in merriment, not shared by Mr P.)

Raising the wind (1990)

Naturally, my sole interest in money is so I can afford to glide, and anything that threat-

Used in an invoice.

Raise the cash.

ens to stem the flow of launches or trips to Australia must be taken seriously. A few weeks ago my boss called me in and began talking to me about the amazing opportunities there were to be found in the world of consultancy. He's very subtle fellow, for I was out in the corridor before I realised I'd been fired. Nevertheless he was right about the consultancy racket. With this change of life I had to pay for a financial consultant and a legal consultant (that's the same as an accountant and a lawyer, only costing twice as much).

The first one had a plush office in St James's St, right near the Palace, and he oozed charm and reassurance. He said, "Now, Mr P, tell me all about it in your own time," and on his desk is this damn great clock, with the big hand marking the hundreds and the little hand quietly sweeping up the £5 notes. The lawyer was even smarter – she operated from a little Victorian house in Fulham, no overheads – and charged £120 an hour. Two pounds a minute! We dealt entirely by phone or post. I don't know whether she fancied me but she kept inviting me round for tea, and I thought, "Even Lyons Quickbrew takes four minutes, that's an aerotow – and this could be an oriental tea ceremony – plus VAT – and I'd have to sell the glider!" I felt that anything I said or did in her drawing room might be taken down and used in an invoice. All the same I suppose I could have done worse than have a lady friend who could earn two pounds a minute without getting up off her sofa.

So I have become a consultant myself – and there are two simple mottoes which are "the higher the fewer," and "less is more." That means 1) have nothing to do with anyone

below the rank of chairman or managing director; and 2) let them do all the talking, and send them a massive bill so they know they have been well advised. I'm hoping to get to the position where I sit cross-legged on a cushion for one hour at breakfast-time, seeing a stream of tycoons for ten minutes each, then my chauffeur can get me up to the club before the thermals start.

The men with the white coats are coming for us (1991)

No lady of fashion looks so anxiously each morning for lines, cracks, wrinkles, blotches and other signs of ageing skin as does a modern glider. The same mixture of ignorance and dread, pseudo-science, myth and old wive's tales, circulates amongst the victims:

"All you need is to get your man to rub in royal jelly and beeswax last thing at night, darling .. You must stay out of the light ... Good Lord, you don't mess around with silicones?...Sunblock 25-plus, and don't lie around uncovered, with everyone staring at you and comparing notes."

"I hate it when the young men peer at you from three inches away and say, "She's really let herself go, looks like crazy paving...""

"Don't go up too high and don't get all hot and cold, that's ruin."

"Soap? You must be mad, you might as well use Brillo pads; water only – distilled water of course, none of that London muck ... Oh my God, there's another line, I swear that wasn't there yesterday."

"Do you know Alphonse of Enstone can do you a whole new skin from face to fanny[13]? for just £10,000 plus tax?"

"It's all right for you, ducky, you've got three rich lovers."

"You absolute bitch, come outside and say that!"

"Don't be silly, I never go outside, as you know perfectly well!"

---

[13] This glider went on a trip to America and uses odd expressions like this to remind the others that she is a World Traveler

Even more galling, the 1983 glider watches the obsolete 1973 Kestrels and Libelles swanning around still crackless and lineless; it's so unfair. At least not many women have the humiliation of seeing other women two or three times their age flaunting far better skins. The dreariest thing is having to listen to the excuses manufactured by the makers – sorry, I meant the excuses made by the manufacturers. "Well, in the old days of schwabbelac (a lovely sound that, you can roll it around the tongue – the word, I mean, not the actual stuff) it was made of a mixture of arsenic and radio-active waste, and the government won't let us use it any more; it's verboten."

They never say, "Look, silly, the new method is quicker and easier and therefore cheaper, and produces a marvellous result for the first few years; then you get rid of your glider at a thumping great loss to someone who is prepared to do a lot of work on it, and we sell you a brand new one. Now put down a deposit and stop whingeing!"

Such frankness would come as a welcome breath of foul air, even if it wouldn't solve the chief problem of Britain's bankers, which is whether to re-open our 18th century debtors' prisons specifically for glider pilots.

Seriously, though (What do you mean seriously? We've got three writs already. Ed.) any well-organised syndicate should set aside about £1,000 a year solely to cover the eventuality – no, the near certainty – of either re-coating their glider or selling it at a loss in the not too distant future. A special bank account, inflation-proofed if possible. A Sinking Fund, an accountant would call it. No, I don't like the sound of that: call it a Soaring

There's another line.

Fund, sounds more positive. The Soaring Fund, remember, is in addition to the cost of depreciation, obsolescence, routine wear and tear and maintenance, annual Certificate of Airworthiness, insurance etc etc.

For most syndicates that is an extra five to ten pounds an hour just for the pleasure of watching the ultra-violet eat your wings.

By the way, I hope we are not going to have people writing in with a lot of drivel about gliders maintaining their value over long periods; 99% of the time it's an illusion caused by inflation. Of course if money is failing in purchasing power at ten per cent a year a glider will appear to maintain its value; but just try selling it and using the money to buy anything else – in particular an identical replacement glider – then see whether value has been maintained. Occasionally the price stability is a short-term phenomenon caused by waiting lists for new gliders – but then by definition an identical replacement glider is not readily available, and when it does become available it will always cost significantly more than your old machine will fetch second-hand. Let's face it, modern gliders haemorrhage money, and it's folly to pretend otherwise. Why deceive yourself?

Re-gelcoating by a competent workshop has historically produced gliders that performed superbly and lasted for years: it used to be said in the 1970s that the very best Nimbus 2s were those that were just a few years old and had been comprehensively pranged – written off, ideally – and then had the wings rebuilt and reprofiled by one of the masters of the art, like Ralph Jones. By that time the shrinkage and waviness, which is nothing to do with gelcoat deterioration but with the "curing" of the underlying structure, had stabilised and could be filled in to give a perfect airfoil that would stay put. Why did the machine have to be pranged in order to produce this happy result? Because only an insurance company could afford to pay for such a luxury as re-gelling a complete pair of wings.

It's Lloyds on the phone. They're extremely worried that people will get ideas...Ed. ■

Travel broadens the behind: gliding in Europe, Australia & New Zealand

To leave Britain's shores and mingle with foreigners was once the sole preserve of the rich and multilingual. It used to be painfully expensive to travel any distance from home. Hotel-keepers and restaurateurs either failed (Italy) or refused (France) to speak English. These twin barriers excluded vast sections of the British populace from the Continent. Well, it's fruitless to lament the passing of those wonderful far-off days: they were too good to last.

For glider pilots, Abroad had more still to offer than Langoustines au facon du Chef and lightly-chilled Gewurtztraminer: it meant quite simply, thermals. Fatter, taller and more consistent thermals. Wally Kahn (not altogether poor and unmistakably an homme du monde, at ease in any international social gathering, and my role model in life) describes with relish in his book A Glider Pilot Bold *the frankly undignified scramble to bring his barograph trace back from France to the BGA's London offices and claim UK Gold C number 10 just one step ahead of Dr Brennig James in 1951. I was consumed with envy and admiration when I heard this story, and resolved to do likewise as soon as the Goddess of business fortune smiled upon me.*

Lederhosen und gamesmanship (1972)

The hills are alive to the sound of horse-flies and splintering plywood ...

This summer, mit Lederhosen und eine sensible Segelflugzeug mit decent airbrakes, we carved a swathe through Tyrolean thermals, carved a swathe through Rotwein and Bier, carved a swathe through a meadow that looked like part of a set from "The Sound of Music" and nearly carved a swathe through a skein of mountaineers who leaned out too far from the North Wall of the Inn Valley.

Which is by way of saying we joined the growing band of idlers who spread the fame of British soaring by more or less taking over the Austrian soaring site of Zell-am-Zee each year.

Fluent French.

About the flying – maybe some other time. But I must tell you now about the gamesmanship at the launch point, which was unbelievable. It is all to do with the fact that

a) If the day is to be very, very good, then you must be launched very, very early; ie, before 10am.

b) Tows from an airfield height of 3,000ft to 7,000ft, which are essential, are very time-consuming, so it is no joke being at the back.

c) No one is supposed to form a startline grid until *they* give the word, though it is not at all obvious who *they* is at the crucial moment, nor what the word is, nor whereabouts or whenabouts it is supposed to be given.

Sometimes a privately-started grid gathers momentum and becomes accepted as the *de facto* rule, at other times the private initiative is too blatant, like that of the lone British pilot who started the grid at 6am; his grid was not recognised and for all the good it did him he could have stayed in bed. Serves him right for being hearty as well as unsubtle. Finesse coupled with brass cheek was more the thing. It worked like this:

One moment all the gliders would be patiently sitting behind the perimeter track looking as though they weren't going anywhere special; then you would turn your back or blow your nose and when you looked again the whole lot had miraculously formed up into a competition-style grid – except that your glider would be the last of about 30.

If you got wise to this you might improve your position in the next day's line-up by casually strolling off, studying the sky intently or looking for somewhere to relieve yourself – then, as the opposition relax and put their heads inside their cockpits and make fettling sounds, you pounce, seize the K-6e by the snout and whisk it as fast as it is possible to whisk a glider through ankle-deep mud to a spot which by this very act of defiant skulduggery is now consecrated as the number one position for the starting grid that day. Phew!

At least, that's what you think. It's now 10.30; you have been rigged four hours and you are about to go. You know it's going to be an enjoyable day because the horseflies are ploughing into the hairs in your legs like Kestrels into fir trees, gouging great bleeding lumps out of the perspiring flesh. Under the canopy you gently baste at a Medium Rare Broil setting.

Never mind, you will be up and away into the high cool mountain peaks in a minute.

Heh! Heh! You can't suppress evil laughter. Some pundit in umpteen metres of glass-fibre has got sunk. Serves him right; he shouldn't have barged in at the front an hour ago.

Ye Gods! He is taking *your* tow, cool as a cucumber. You wave frantically, wondering in which of many tongues he will contrive not to understand you. Cheerily, he holds up five fingers, indicating that he is entitled to a second launch before your first because he is attempting five hundred kilometres.

You signal your opinion on the matter, with vigour.

He smiles broadly, delighted to know that you only plan to do *two* hundred kilometres...

Off to the prairie (1986)

I have given up mountain flying. My nerves won't stand it any more. Nor can I take the frustration and humiliation of being unable to get away from the nursery slopes on a mediocre day, while watching the typical Alpine pilot work his wingtip into every little lift-yielding crevice like a diner with a toothpick, to vanish on a 300km and reappear three hours later to dump a full load of water on the piste. That sort of thing giveth me to rend my soaring hat, pour dust on my head and vow to abandon the sport entirely.

Why not, you ask, fly with one of those magnificent instructors in a Janus and learn from them how it is done?

I've done that for as long as I could take it. They are indeed magnificent, and their local knowledge and skills are superb. The trouble is that

1) Every such instructor talks, without pause for breath, in very rapid, impatient French. Though that's a lot better than when they try rapid, impatient broken English. Now my French is not bad, and I can usually remember what a rudder-pedal or a flap or an incipient spin or a downdraught is, but it is less than instantaneous. It is not helped by the fact that the instructor is constantly on the radio to all his other little chickens, so a bellowing command from the back seat, "get closer to the rock face, silly boy!" may be intended for someone else, though if your wing is more than a few centimetres away from the mountain you can take it that he means you.

2) They all seem incapable of letting a pilot make any kind of mistake, but grab the controls immediately they feel that something short of perfection is being achieved. This makes sense when you are glued to the geology, so to speak, but the habit persists even when you are thousands of feet clear of anything hard, where the odd mistake would do no harm. I could only deal with this by promptly raising my hands over my head to show that I was not in charge and would not touch the stick until I was asked. This had no effect at all, so it seemed that half the time the aircraft was being flown by two people wrestling for supremacy and half the time was being flown by nobody at all, while the glider plummetted towards the snows and the chamois scampered nervously out of our steepening path.

To be fair to the French, the worst offender in this latter respect was a German. (That's right, alienate everyone. *ED.*)

So it's goodbye, beautiful and altogether-too-exciting mountains, hello lovely, flat and boring prairie. *Prairie is French for meadow-land and wide open country, and reminds us that the French possessed most of North America before the British mugged them and took it for themselves.*

My resolutions are flimsy things, even when made in public. I did in fact revisit the Alps in 1990, 1992 and 1997, and I have braved (though I wish there were a verb that suggested something less gung-ho) the vertiginous rock-faces of New Zealand and the turbulent mountains of Pennsylvania and California, though the last two are not very Alpine.

What – or who – brought about the change of heart? Two people, one British, one French. In 1990, after a spectacularly varied beautiful 500km flight in the ASH-25 from le Blanc via Roanne and the Rhone Valley to the Alps, Bill Malpas and I spent a week at Sisteron. There he helped me improve my knowledge about the area. Bill has thousands of hours of Alpine gliding, and lives in Angers, so he is an honorary Frenchman, while looking like Hollywood Central Casting's idea of an Englishman.

Then a professional course with the incomparable Jacques Noël of Aéro Club Alpin at Gap taught me to understand the hazards of mountain-flying. I learned thereby to contain fear. Well, up to a point: I found myself saying repeatedly to myself, "This-man-has-a-wife-and-kids-This-man-has-a-wife-and-kids" as we reversed 60-degree banks to stay in the lift that surged up hollowed-out vertical crags. No, not in the ASH-25, but in a Janus A – less performance but much better rate of roll. Not one of the unkind remarks I made in 1986 about Continental instructors applies to Jacques. He is a star. I must admit he has a disconcerting habit of indicating every hour or so that the spot we are over right now is where so-and-so killed himself through sheer folie, *but he has made his point. At least I now know precisely how and why so-and-so is sadly no longer with us, and the important lesson is digested.*

The rain in Spain sprays mainly on my plane (1993)

The speed with which one's mood can go from boredom to panic and then to exhilaration is one of the special appeals of gliding. Indeed it is what gliding is all about if you have any soul.

In May 1993 the European Soaring Club was ferrying our ASH-25 behind a Robin tow-plane, piloted by Brian Spreckley, from Monflorite to Soria in northern Spain, roughly 180km. (Soria is invitingly pronounced *Soar 'ere*. A misnomer, I would say, if the water-logged week that followed was any indication.) The other pilots and gliders came by road, so we were privileged. Platypus was in the front seat of the 25, Marion Barritt was P2. The journey would take about 75 minutes into a south-west wind, under a slate-grey sky, with rain threatening and no prospect of lift. The air got steadily rougher as we pushed across the high and increasingly unlandable ground, resembling the backside of the moon. I did begin vaguely to wonder whether it was rotor cloud kicking us around in the lee of a mountain that towered above us just south of our track. Wave isn't one of my strong suits – says he, implying that he has some strong suits but is too modest to mention them.

Then suddenly – without our having got out of position but with the cable alternately slackening and pulling taut – we heard a click and there were the rings on the end of the towrope briefly twinkling at us before they vanished into the distance.

My first action, once my voice had come back down a couple of octaves, was to ask on the radio for the GPS co-ordinates of the nearest usable airfield. The desolate Spanish moonscape looked horribly close. I could visualise Don Quixote and Sancho Panza plodding across it in search of windmills. Then a calm, small voice behind me (no, not my conscience) said, "Have you noticed we are going up at 800ft a minute?" I hadn't noticed, since I had switched the audio off early in the flight, not wishing to have it mewing at me for 75 minutes, and I was now preoccupied exclusively by navigational and getting-down-in-one-piece worries. I promptly lost the wave in my excitement, found it again and, pushing towards the mountain, worked it up to 14,000ft. With no oxygen, we reluctantly levelled out and sped over the top of our mountain along the 60km to Soria with hardly any loss of height, discovering that the wave must have been triggered by other ranges to the south-west. We cruised around Soria, scene of a famous and brutally successful siege by the Romans two millennia ago, until the tug and the trailers with the rest of the expedition arrived. As we landed the heavens opened up and stayed open for days. It just poured. That entirely unplanned wave flight turned out to be the only decent flight of the entire expedition. The other members of the group were oddly unwilling to listen to the exciting details of our story. I can't think why.

I hardly need to point the moral of this tale (apart from the practical one that if you have to use belly hooks on aerotow, they should have their back-releases immobilised for long distance tows or launches in rough mountain air). It is that the best flying often comes when you have not planned it – out of the blue, or in our case, out of the dirty grey.

Demented fellow-passengers (1992)

Gliding in Australia in January has many joys – chief among which is that one is not in Britain. I was flying around in the ASH-25 at Benalla with a visitor from London and he said, clearly unimpressed by the modest thermal we were in, "This is no better than July in England." "But it isn't July in England," I retorted, "It's bloody January!" He had no answer to that.

Australia in January does, however, have a few bugs. If you do not succeed in the immediate pre-take-off ritual of chasing out the flies with your hat before closing the canopy, then you have half a dozen absolutely demented fellow-passengers zooming around the cockpit for the next five hours. If you get up to 10,000ft the colder air makes them rather more docile, but if you are desperately trying to centre at 500ft over some featureless waste with not a habitation or a road in sight, that is for the flies the ideal moment to force you to land so that they can get out and walk home and tell all their friends about their nightmare journey. They

Zooming around in the cockpit.

suddenly feel thirsty and make for the only source of moisture, the sweat that, what with the heat and the pressing circumstances, is pouring down your cheeks. They acquire a keen curiosity about the interior geography of your nostrils and ears. They get wedged between your bifocals and the clip-on Polaroids and block your view of the airspeed indicator, vario and the ever-nearing featureless waste.

I have thought of fly-paper to trap them, a pot of honey to keep them happy, or a lethal blast from a flyspray to zap their central nervous systems, but with my robust airmanship every loose object in the cockpit except the flies would end up on the flypaper, and gobs of honey would get all over the canopy; and in the confines of a small cockpit I would worry about the effect of biochemical warfare on my own rather delicate central nervous system, whatever disclaimers they print on the can.

I have just this very second thought of a solution: a venturi device that is connected to the outside airflow with a hose, so that you can suck the little blighters up and squirt them out of the clear vision panel. Pure genius!

Damn! The wretched creatures have splattered themselves all over my leading edge. Featureless wastes, here I come. It'll be a long, lonely walk in 100 degrees F – but I'll have millions of flies for company …

End-of-tour traileritis (1993)

After thousands of miles of towing across many countries on the wrong side of the road, what bliss it is to unhitch the trailer and dump that long, dead weight back at the club! How exhilarating to zoom off on the open highway, free, free, no longer wondering whether the swaying monster behind you has just wrecked a market stall, ripped out a petrol pump or run over a gendarme's foot.

Talking about the *gendarmerie*, my worst moment with a trailer abroad was within sight of the white cliffs, at the Calais hoverport. An impatient employee of the hovercraft company was signalling energetically that I should turn right much more sharply than I wanted to, and would I hurry up, please monsieur? I obeyed. There was a series of rending metallic crashes of the kind that make one's heart sink. I looked in the wing mirror, aghast. The Cobra trailer wheels had demolished the aluminium folding doors of the customs shed, which were very tall, very new, very elaborate and certainly very expensive. They were folding all right, but not the way the manufacturer intended.

Immediately surrounded.

I was immediately surrounded by a dozen *flics* and *douaniers* and hauled into a tiny office to be interviewed at great length. I forgot that there are occasions when it pays to appear to be unable to speak any foreign language at all. Masses of forms and insurance claim documents were filled in. Mothers and grandmothers were pledged, and I braced myself, on returning home, for an avalanche of litigation.

I never heard a word about it again. I just hope they lost the paperwork. But I've never ventured near a hovercraft with a trailer since then. I'd sooner go on a big ferry that is used to handling articulated trucks. No, I don't intend to take my glider through the Channel Tunnel if it ever gets finished. I'm bound to get the trailer wedged across the hole at the French end, and then I'll see a strangely familiar bunch of cops and customs men bearing down on me with the glint of revenge in their eyes...

Hans-Werner Grosse on setting world records (1988)

Platypus flew with Hans-Werner Grosse in Hans's ASH-25 in Alice Springs just before Christmas 1987. No records were broken then, though the experience of flying at near to never-exceed speeds at 16,000 ft over a bright red and utterly uninhabited desert under a deep blue sky is something every glider pilot should experience at least once. As Plat departed for work in Sydney, Hans's wife Karin arrived, the weather suddenly boomed and several new world marks were set.

Platypus: What are the main ingredients in breaking world records?

Hans-Werner Grosse: First, of course, you need a good glider. Secondly, you need a lot of experience. Then you need to look over the globe for regions of good heating. Using the Met information of different countries you look for a "boundary" between tropical air and semi-arid regions. (Tropical air itself is useless; you don't want thunderstorms every afternoon.) Don't put all your faith in the official weather statistics, however: before making a costly expedition to a far continent with your own glider, you had better visit the region and find out about the local soaring weather for yourself.

For long triangles you need big plains rather than mixtures of high mountains and plains; discontinuities of surface features are only partially beneficial.

Plat: Many of us dream about crossing France by the Massif Central and flying on into the Alps.

HWG: You must arrive at the mountains at the correct time: it's difficult going from the plain to the mountains. You might have done records that way 30 years ago but not now. The exception is the Appalachian "tramlines" in the USA, but that is not for me. The only decision you have to make is whether you fly three metres or 15 metres over the trees. There's very little choice.

Plat: Haven't they run out of space in the Appalachians as the New Zealanders seem to have done? (Many world records, especially O/R distance, were achieved in New Zealand wave in the 1960s)

HWG: No. They could increase the triangular distance considerably. Five pilots did 1,360km triangles on one day, which shows that more is possible. One turnpoint has to be well away from the ridge, requiring a dash in ordinary thermals to and from the ridge.

The speed along the ridge can be increased by using massive amounts of water-ballast, since circling performance only matters for a short distance. However, one pilot has been killed flying overweight, trying to see how much he could carry.

— ooo —

Plat: What speeds are achievable with present-day gliders on tasks up to 500kms?

HWG: The current records are too low, since such small distances are only attempted on the second-best days. (Pilots confined to British soaring conditions are allowed to take a couple of minutes off while they bang their heads against the nearest wall or just cry quietly into their beer ...)

If you are prepared to waste a good day (I mean a day when you could have done 1,000kms or more) you might get 170 to 180km/h. On a really good day in this region there will be two or three hours in the middle when you can average more than 170km/h, which would take you round a 500km "sprint" for the world record.

Speeds achieved in flights in South Africa benefit from the high plains and consequent high cloudbases. Your True Airspeed increases relative to Indicated Airspeed by about 5% for every 1000m, and that is equivalent to extra ballast. Currently, however, taking everything into consideration Alice Springs is the best location as far as I am concerned.

Plat: What about wave?

HWG: We haven't seen really fast triangles in wave yet. Wave is best for O/Rs, and maybe for distance records – early morning and late evening, with thermals in the middle.

Plat: New Zealand ran out of land.

Daring final glides.

HWIG: The usable parts of American mountain ranges for wave may also be limited, because of the discontinuity between the airmasses north and south of the jetstream. That could limit the distances achieveable in pure wave flight.

Plat: Justin Wills says that the pure distance flight is not given the respect it deserves: it is seen as an easy downwind dash, whereas it requires a great deal of planning – as well as luck with the weather. He is thinking especially of the problems of organising a flight that starts in, say, Yorkshire, and takes you across the Channel with the opportunity to do a big distance on the other side.

HWG: I don't know whether it deserves respect as such, but it definitely is an enjoyable experience. Yes, he has there the special problem of crossing the Channel at the right time and with enough height, not just to reach the French coast but to be certain of penetrating the dead zone caused by the sea breeze (which as you know becomes worse as the day progresses) and reaching good soaring conditions.

Plat: And there are special UK airspace problems for a Channel dash, too. But looking at the question of good soaring conditions, how often do you get weather of the kind that enabled you to get 1,460km in 1972?

HWG: The flight in the ASW-12 from Lübeck to Biarritz was done in weather that I have never witnessed since that day – which explains why it is still the world record in spite of technical improvements in gliders and weather forecasting. Imagine a great "bubble" of cold air sweeping in from northern Sweden, ideal for soaring, that had passed over us in the night; I ran into the rear of it at exactly the right time in the morning over the Rhine, and ran out of the front of it south of Bordeaux late in the afternoon. With today's gliders in the same weather you'd exceed that distance, naturally.

Plat: But you'd run through the bubble quicker and maybe not go any further at the end of the day.

HWG: Yes, but you'd have a better chance of catching it from behind at the beginning of the day.

Plat: Are you saying that such an airmass is limited in size?

HWG: Yes, it always seems so – at least the most beneficial part of it is.

Plat: What sort of dimensions?

HWG: 800 to 1,000km is a goodsize airmass – and it's moving downwind quite fast, of course, which adds some hundreds of extra kilometres.

Plat: What about straight-out distance record possibilities in other parts of the world?

HWG: Some people in the USA describe flights of 2,000km, starting in wave, as possible.

Plat: Yes, starting very early in a high wave and doing a long downwind glide to reach the thermals just as they are starting. At the World Champs in 1965 at South Cerney I met one of the American support team, Brittingham, who told me of a heroic attempt which took them (I think it was a two-seater) about 300km from the top of a big wave with the help of a strong tailwind; only snag was, there weren't any thermals at the end of it, so they just ran into the ground before lunch time. The great wave day and the great thermal day don't necessarily plug into each other neatly – though Nick Goodhart got a (completely unplanned) wave to 10,000ft at the other end of the day on his goal flight to Portmoak in 1959, which still stands as a UK goal distance record .

HWG: Another problem is that the direction of the tailwind component is often inconsistent, because of the discrepancy between upper and lower level winds. In fact consistent winds over 2000km are unlikely. Obviously if the wind curves a lot you get less benefit from it in terms of free kilometres.

— ooo —

The Biarritz flight was a "gift from heaven." In southern Germany you couldn't have soared

Crossing frontiers.

at all – it was overcast. There was no special pilot skill involved.

Plat: But you showed me the weather maps for the period up to and including that day; you obviously expected good conditions.

HWG: You must prepare – you have to be ready and not be taken by surprise. The approaching airmass was quite easy to forecast.

You too could break records, if only you are prepared.

Plat: if you couldn't fly for some reason could you coach other people to break records?

HWG: Not everyone could be coached; you would have to be successful in competitions first. You have to be prepared to speculate and drive yourself forward. It's getting the balance between daredevilry and hesitation. You must be able to imagine the "energy-track" through the best air that will be your flight path. I think one could train people to be better. But what you can achieve that way is limited.

Plat: If you took the Top Ten from each Class in the World Championships and set up a competition at Alice Springs, could you get records out of such a meeting?

HWG: Yes! However, some competition pilots win just by their skill in gaggle flying and by more daring final glides. But the record-setter needs to sense where the invisible streets of lift are – without depending on other gliders to mark them. Ingo Renner, for instance, could definitely break all records here as soon as the right conditions came along. Some other top pilots might just kill themselves by misjudgment: landing out in this region can be fatal - it's simply not on.

Plat: What do you have to say about gadgetry and instruments?

HWG: The Biarritz flight was done without waterballast and with primitive instruments: the vario had a leaky total energy. Certainly good instruments make flights easier, but pilots have won competitions with elementary instruments.

I wouldn't like to fly now without my Schumann vario and Schumann box for total energy compensation. It's a mechanical vario and shows me a reliable picture of the value of thermals; it's American and the weaker US dollar makes it cheaper now, by the way.

Plat: Why isn't an electrical vario better?

Reach the French coast.

HWG: I don't know why, but the Schumann vario works. I use the electrical for the audio, for the computer and for final glides.

Plat: Have you ever flown gliders in England?

HWG: No, only Tiger Moths, when I came over to Southend and bought one after the war. (HWG subsequently told us how he came to be shot down in his Ju 88 torpedo-bomber in World War II, but that was in the Mediterranean.)

— ∞ —

Plat: Aren't you interested in championship flying any more?

HWG: Closed-circuit speed tasks, which is what championships consist of entirely these days, are a dead end. They are not meaningful tests of pilots, they only improve certain skills. Most of it is tactical point-snatching.

Sadly, free distance isn't practical nowadays – think of 3,000km retrieves! However, Maurie Bradney at Waikerie is testing a modern form of cat's cradle, which uses multiple TPs which the pilot does not have to declare in advance. Outlandings are avoided as much as possible but the ability to use the whole day is tested. This has real possibilities.

I quit competitions years ago and never regretted it. I lost interest when I found that my experience was not broadened, new insights not gained. The top pilots felt frustrated after Benalla. Yes, there were big distances flown at high speeds, but it became a treadmill.

There was no chance to show truly superior ability. Pilots should go to the briefings with an ability to understand weather, they should study those temperature traces and make their plans. It should be as in chess, where the superior brain has the superior chance of winning.

— ∞ —

Just as you can be too obsessed with the competition treadmill, you can also be too obsessed with breaking records. The experience is everything; the beauty of it – different scenery, flying over water. crossing frontiers, soaring from one country to another. Maybe I miss out from time to time on days when I could have had an enjoyable flight, but have not flown because it wasn't a record-breaking day. That's wrong.

Just fly cross-country, fly long distances whenever you can. It becomes a way of life.

A straight-out distance of over 1,500kms has been achieved in South America in their 1999/2000 season in a Stemme. Biarritz may now finally be beaten.

The rain in Spain sprays mainly on my plane – again (1998)

In May 1998 my second gliding trip to the Iberian peninsula contained one more hazard than the first one in May 1993 – a competition. It requires more airmanship and more common-sense than I possess to get through a contest unscathed in a country which has almost no aerodromes and in which ploughed fields are about the only resort in an emergency. All other fields in Spain seem to he full of little trees or irrigation pipes. Not a problem, of course, if the weather is benign and everyone stays up.

The weather was malign.

I'll skate quickly over the humiliating details and just admit that I did £3,000 worth of dings to wingtip and fuselage on Day Four of the British Overseas Championships. Lots of field landings were done by other pilots without comparable damage, so I offer no excuses. Disconsolate, we trailed the bits home through continuous down-pour from south of Madrid, through France – the entire country from Biarritz to Calais darkened in a veritable monsoon, the *péage* and the thundering *camions* barely visible even at mid-day – to the Dunstable workshop.

This set me thinking about field landings and the increasing undesirability of having to do them. In the 1950s and early 1960s nearly every cross-country ended in a field. This was exciting at the time, if only because we were young, but this necessity also conferred two advantages. First, because our gliders were expected by Fred Slingsby to have their noses rubbed violently into agricultural dirt after almost every flight, they were designed with monstrous great skids to do the work of stopping the aircraft and protecting the cockpit. Secondly the pilots got very expert at picking fields and landing in them, often doing 20 or more field landings a year.

Modern gliders, by contrast, have no protection forward of the wheel, and if the wheel sinks into soft, rock-strewn soil then stones can do a lot of damage. Pilots in modern gliders also do very few outlandings, and they can usually reach a proper airfield if the weather turns sour. It is now possible to go through entire seasons without ever being forced to land in a farm. So we aren't used to it – and when we do discover that this wonderful 60:1 craft really isn't going to stay up it is a nasty psychological jolt. We did not experience any such jolts in the days of wood: the question was not whether we would hit the spuds but where. Now we find we are approaching this unknown patch of terrain in a fast, slippery projectile that won't relish getting grit up its nose. All of a sudden we wish this was a Skylark 3.

Landing out, which was once the rule, is now the exception. There are now far fewer field landings per 100 miles of flying than 40 years ago, but the proportion that cause damage is probably higher, and as for the cost of repairs...

Comps directors and rule-makers can do a lot to minimise damage by clumsy oafs like me. I mean apart from banning us from comps entirely. There are a lot of us clumsy oafs, and we are an important constituency who need to he considered, almost as big as the leech constituency, with which there is of course a sizeable overlap. We usually prang in fields when we can't find somebody to leech off.

As a contest director and task-setter in the past – fear of lawyers now deters me, and I am not joking – I am guilty of having sent hundreds of people to certain outlandings. I used to he happy to get just one pilot back: that proved my task was feasible. Now task-setters want 70% or more back, and that's right. But it takes guts to scrub the task for safety reasons, especially after several days of bad weather.

Scrubbing after the entire field has been launched, or even announcing which of two or three pre-declared alternative tasks will be flown, is a good idea. Brian Spreckley, who ran the Spanish comp, did an airborne scrub of the little class on the day of my ding, and I'm sure he is right to want to make this a general rule. This way the director has an hour more in which to judge the weather. Sure it might waste an aero-tow, but the launch price is a small proportion of the total expense of a competition, even without counting the cost of the odd crash.

We need also to encourage people to land in safe places without sacrificing large numbers of points on those days when mass glide-outs under a dead sky are unavoidable. (Gosh, those used to be fun: "First one to open his brakes is chicken, yah, boo!") Mike Fairman's request in the last *S&G* letters pages, asking that contest pilots be credited with the furthest distance they have registered on the GPS-logger, so that they can turn back and land at a safe field, is already enacted in some competitions . It was agreed by the pilots in Spain and implemented by at least one pilot who was clever enough to find a real *aerodromo* to squelch down in. The new rule is called GNSS (I don't know what that means but, "Going Nowhere, $%*@ Scared" has been suggested) and seems to he an excellent innovation.

"Blimey, Plat, you'll be recommending engines next!"

Well, I won't be as abusive as I would once have been when that topic was raised. The notion that a usable engine gives competitors an unfair advantage is nonsense. The standard objection is that such people will venture over unlandable terrain and motor out of it if they don't get lift. In practice the wonderful unreliability of engines ensures that such people will fill the obituary pages rather than the lists of champions.

However the mere thought of Platypus and engines will make any mechanically-minded person shudder: all that can be said for it is that it has endless comic possibilities for this column.

The new supership for 2000 AD (1999)

If I were a Fleet Street hack, I would say "for the Millennium" except that am I one of the stubborn pedants who knows that the Millennium begins on Jan 1, 2001, and I hope the new project is not delayed till then. This limited-edition two-seat motorglider on order by Hans-Werner Grosse, Bruno Gantenbrinck and a handful of very keen span-druggies is rumoured to cost around a quarter of a million Pounds and will have 30.9 metres span, though it sounds more impressive if I say 101 ft. That is slightly more wingspan that the short-lived Austria[14] of 1930, in which Robert Kronfeld made history by being the first pilot to escape from a glider by parachute, after it broke up in cloud. Materials and structures have improved a lot in the past 70 years. In mid-May 1999 the test rig managed finally to break the wing at 9G. That is twice the G-loading at which Hans and his crew were starting to black out in Junkers 88 dive-bombing practice. So if you do manage to break the wing of the new ship, you probably won't hear it unless you are wearing a G-suit. With luck it will be flying in the spring of 2000.

---

[14] Kronfeld hoped that with the very low sinking speed and low flying speed of the Austria he should be able to gain sufficient height, by flying straight across a thermal, to get to the next thermal, and so on indefinitely. The Holy Grail of cross-country flight without this tedious circling business would thereby be achieved. The Austria never lasted long enough to test this proposition. However aerodynamicists who have examined the extremely cambered (high-lift, very high drag) wing-section of the Austria have deduced that its max glide was about that of Ka 8, say 27:1. With its limited speed range, and bearing in mind the sink between thermals, the Austria would have lost too much height before it reached the next source of lift to achieve the cross-country flight without circling.

The new supership is another matter. If you see it circling, it means either (a) the pilot's GPS has failed and he is lost, or (b) he is letting passenger take scenic photographs, or (c) soaring conditions are so terrible that everyone else might as well go back to bed.

Performance should be about 20% better than the 25-metre ASH-25, at least at lowish speeds that are appropriate to northern European weather: that is an L/D of around 68 to one. For those jaded with a mere 27-metres, it is the perfect fix, at least till the next one comes out, at, let me see...

(Are you calculating the span, the performance or the price? Ed.)

All of them. On the realistic basis that cost goes up as the cube of the span, and making a modest allowance of 3.5% annual UK inflation and another 2.0% annual slippage of the currently over-valued Pound against the D-Mark or Euro, then in 11 years' time, when I am the age that Hans-Werner Grosse is now, I should be able to get, wait for it –

33.2 metres (109ft), giving a max glide of about –

73:1 for –

One Million Pounds.

Monte Carlo, here I come!

Omarama nirvana (1998)

I return from New Zealand full of regret. Why hadn't I gone there 20 years earlier? Why do I only discover this wonderful place when I'm on the brink of collecting my old age pension? Well, there is no point in fretting about lost opportunities, Plat, just get yourself organised to go again every December from now on while you can still tell your port from your starboard.

I flew Justin Wills's ASW-17, one of the few Schleicher designs that I hadn't flown before, and a delightful machine it was, too. Justin flew his much-loved Libelle 301 – that's the flapped version – and I should have been out-flying him at every point with my 20 metres to his 15. Mysteriously this was hardly ever the case. In fact there is a consensus amongst the local pilots that we should get him a more modern machine – one with top-surface brakes only. That way we would be spared the humiliation, as we struggle to get to his altitude, of seeing his lower brakes sticking out while he waits for us to catch up. We could instead delude ourselves that we were truly gaining on him. While chasing Justin round the unfamiliar rockscape I would watch the Libelle gradually shrink in the distance until he heard on the radio a sound that must be familiar to the owner of 10,000 sheep – the bleating of a lost lamb, "Ju-u-usti-in, whe-e-e-ere a-a-are yo-ou?" – at which point he would throw a circle so I could see him. Since the ASW-17 outflew the Libelle in level flight in the wave, and is obviously the better straight-line performer, I can only conclude that Justin was getting more lift off the rocks than I was, and accordingly that he was flying much closer to them than I dared.

Day by day, however, this old and very unbold pilot acquired more confidence as he got lost less often, identified the best outlanding strips by eyeball, and applied the lessons learnt from Jacques Noël at Gap last spring, in particular: "Keep your speed up and always have your escape route in mind."

Soaring the face of Mount Cook, 100 kms north of Omarama, was the most enduring impression. The second most enduring

Get clean away in NZ skies (1998)

New Zealand air is clean. Not only is it free of bugs, it is free of dirt. Industrial filth does not pollute the leading edges, or the pilot's lungs, the way it does in England. The air that sweeps across the Tasman Sea or the Pacific has not touched land for thousands of miles. Take a little ride up in the wave, not very high, and you can see both oceans at the same time. The visibility is virgin vodka: on a 1,000 kilometre out and return the only thing that would stop you seeing both the start and the turn-point when half way down the first leg would be the curvature of the earth.

The South Island is about the same area as England and Wales, but with less than a fiftieth of the people. The mountainous west is truly unspoilt. It looks as the European Alps must have looked in the days before somebody decided that an Alp wasn't a proper Alp unless it sported a television mast or a funicular railway or a hotel or a ski-station or a massage-parlour or something ugly that made money. The sense of wildness and wilderness amongst the dazzling white New Zealand peaks is total: there are hardly any roads or even tracks down in the narrow green valleys; if there are I couldn't see them. And since there is nobody down there to watch television there are no masts. I wonder for how long?

impression was when I decided to take some pictures for *Sailplane & Gliding*, threw a lazy circle over the great tent-shaped peak, forgot that the westerly winds at 13,000 ft were 70kt, and plummetted 2,000 ft into the vicious lee-side downdraught in the cold, dark shadow of the mountain. Something to remember for next time. I made six trips to Mount Cook, and on every occasion the mountain looked different, sometimes wearing a teardrop-shaped cloudcap like a racing cyclist's helmet.

I may have just been lucky, but every day of the two weeks I was there I could have soared in wave, thermal, convergence or ridge-lift. The only reason for my choosing to stay on the ground for four days was for recuperation, especially after one eight-hour bout of polishing rock and pursing every variety of rising air.

Navigation in New Zealand is easy, so long as you can see the ground. Mountain ranges and distinctive lakes make GPS unnecessary for the experienced local. However it is a great comfort to the newcomer to have the GPS tell him that he is in easy gliding range of a scrap of ground that is occasionally used as a crop-dusting strip. I wouldn't have noticed the strips at all without the satellites calling out, "Look down now, stupid!" although some strips are said to have a telltale patch of white chemicals at the uphill end, towards which the busy Pawnee-driver, or the failed soaring pilot, points himself on the approach. GPS-linked glide computers are not idiot-proof, or at least not yet, and you do need to look at the terrain intelligently: the computers have not been trained to say, "You can reach this field, sir, but ONLY if you can drill through nine miles of solid rock. Would you mind if I suggested an alternative place to crash?" We'll have such gadgets soon, don't worry.

"Come on, what about the famous Kiwi wave?" you are asking. You know, I think that the damn wave has got the country typecast in the minds of the world gliding fraternity, like an actor that is only expected to play swashbuckling parts when he can do a hundred other more interesting characters. Thus visiting Australian pilots, and a lot of British too, come to Omarama solely for their height diamonds and head home the moment they have their badge. If a doctor said to me, "Your softening brain must never be taken above

12,000ft again except in an airliner," I would still want to glide in New Zealand as often as possible. Yes, some day I'd like to take some expert advice and try a really big distance flight that used the wave, but solely for the vast speed that it offers, not for altitude.

When you think of Kiwi gliding, don't think of height: think of beauty, variety, solitude and unlimited possibilities for exploration and adventure.

Up the Creek without a paddock (G Wills 1999)

If I said to you there's a top soaring pilot living in new Zealand by the name of Wills you'd think I was talking of Justin Wills, whose farm is near the foot of Mount Cook. But Gavin Wills, Justin's half-cousin, is a mountain soaring pilot of amazing skill. His flights in the New Zealand January 2000 Nationals left me, as hapless (and useless, except as undroppable ballast) passenger in his Duo Discus, quite staggered at the untamed beauty of the landscape, which I viewed at much closer quarters than I normally care to, and at his skill in extracting updraughts from every crevice. He wrote for the New Zealand magazine Gliding Kiwi *this account of a New Year's Eve adventure that I shall not forget. What is unique about this narrative is that Gavin was nowhere near the scene of the action at any time. From a few fragments of phone conversations and hearsay he has constructed a remarkably accurate picture of a near-disaster that was somehow averted.*

Platypus is a well known and respected correspondent for the English magazine *Sailplane & Gliding*. During a recent flying visit to New Zealand he left a message on my cell phone. It was obviously important but it was so full of unanswered questions that I thought it might be fun to share around.

He and Justin Wills were enjoying a glider flight from Lake Manapouri in the south of the South Island back to Omarama. Justin was flying his immaculate Libelle and the Platypus was pair-flying in Justin's ASW-17. They went via the scenic route (as Justin was wont to describe it) which meant 250 km of scraping along mountain ridges and over some of the

most inhospitable valleys of the Southern Alps.

The cell phone message went like this.....

"Hello Gavin, I've landed in a little meadow by the Lake at the bottom of Timaru Creek."

I'm thinking – Yikes, what are you doing there, mate? Timaru Creek is full of precipitous rock, forests and a long boulder-strewn valley floor. Glider pilots have spent many a drunken night debating how to deal with the awful consequences of getting low in Timaru Creek – does one land in the rocks, the lake or the trees?

"I'm fine..."

"What about the glider, then?"

"...and I'm drinking beer with the Lake Hawea fire brigade."

What? Not a good move; it's New Year's Eve and 30 km away from the glider! And anyway how did they get the Fire Engine up the track beside the lake and who the Hell called them out?

"Do you have Gillian's cell phone number?"

"No. But where is Justin?"

"Please let her know that I'm not with glider but I'm at the fire station."

"OK, but where's Justin?"

"Thanks a lot, see you later."

So I called Gillian at home but there was no reply and it was not until the next day that the story began to unfold.

The Platypus had lost radio contact with Justin, his pair-flying guide, at about the time they entered Timaru Creek. Whilst trying to establish radio contact and with Justin circling overhead, presumably with his head out the window trying to shout instructions, the Platypus descended inexorably into airspace hitherto unexplored by glider pilots – the terrifying canyon of Timaru Creek. The GPS trace subsequently showed that he was below about 500 feet above ground for 15 minutes before he exited the valley at 250 feet heading for Lake Hawea. Whilst he was preparing for a water landing, the "little meadow" apparently popped onto glide slope from amongst the trees and the Platypus gratefully ground-looped to a stop. He landed without damage.

And what about the Fire Brigade? Justin, ever mindful of his responsibilities, had called an emergency via the local gliding frequency and the Lake Hawea Fire Brigade took off up the lake. But what they are still puzzled about is how and why they were called to a crash site 15 minutes before it never happened!

The meadow is clearly an important place that should pass into local gliding legend. It should be known as the Platypus Patch, and because he solved the debate of what to do when one gets low in that inhospitable canyon, all South Island glider pilots should be forever grateful to the Man from Timaru Creek!

Gavin Wills

Platypus insists on having the last few hundred words: I'm bridling somewhat at the suggestion that I wilfully chose to abandon the glider and goof off to some party 30 kms away. Within minutes of my arrival the police, ambulance and fire brigade, in that order, all turned up on the unmetalled road that came reasonably near the clump of grass I'd landed on – meadow is far too grand a term. After I had photographed the ambulance ladies and the fire engine and all who sailed in her, the cop car whisked me away to the fire station to communicate with my friends at Omarama. Here the firemen insisted, against my

> ### The sport of cooks
> *National characteristics should never be crudely stereotyped. It's rude and wrong to assume that the English are cold, the Americans loud, the Germans boringly efficient, the Italians randy, etc. etc. I once landed at a farm near Vendome in France, where after hosing the cow-pats out of the tail parachute the farmer's two children kindly took me to the pond, in which the three of us began to fish with crude bamboo rods. In no time I hooked a sizeable perch which I swung joyously over my shoulder onto the grass. Knowing the French hunted solely for food and not, as the English, for the pleasure of inflicting terror and pain on dumb animals, I set about this fish with my rod and bashed its head in, yelling, "Look kids, supper!" in my best French. They burst into tears. "That's Alphonse", they cried, "we always throw him back!" I could have thrown myself into the pond in remorse.*
>
> *All the same, they recovered their sangfroid and not long after, Alphonse, sautéed in home-made butter, was as good to them as they formerly had been to him. Maybe the stereotypes have something to be said for them after all.*

protestations, that I was in shock from my ordeal and needed a stiff brandy or two. This diagnosis licensed an instant emergency raid on the medicine chest. Trauma is clearly contagious, because several of the off-duty volunteer firemen decided that they might be in shock, too. Since it was New Year's Eve, wives and girlfriends began to arrive and it became pretty gregarious.

After some hours waiting patiently by the phone, I eventually said that I better head back towards the glider since dusk was approaching and I had no idea where anyone was. A police car came and fetched me, and had gone about a kilometre when to my astonishment I saw Gillian and Justin Wills in their Holden station wagon, with trailer – and smiling! Apparently Justin had seen me hit the ground and knew exactly where I was, and soared home. A four-wheel drive vehicle and a large band of strong men supplemented the Wills team, and all had gone straight to the spot, found the glider quite unharmed (to general astonishment), and derigged it without any interference from me. Then the strong men headed back to Omarama to resume their interrupted New Year's Eve party on the site, and Gillian and Justin headed for the Lake Hawea town, where we joyously met.

I walked carefully and thoughtfully over that patch of ground two weeks later when on a motoring tour of the South Island. I would not accept £3,000 in hard currency to do that landing again, even after having the advantage of inspecting every hummock, hillock, gully, rabbit hole, tree and bush close up. Well, not if the other side of the bet was that I paid for any damage to the glider or myself.

Roar before you soar (1999)

One easy way to make enemies unnecessarily is to be the sort of person who will do anything to get a laugh, no matter at whose expense and no matter how unjust. That must be the only reason I have not got my knighthood by now – some cheap throwaway joke about the Royal Family, I seem to remember. The little grey men must have there with their notebooks.

Typical of this kind of cruelty to innocent bystanders was when, in a Soaring Society of America banquet speech in Seattle in 1993, I said that gliding cross-country with an engine in reserve was like making love with a condom: "The only time it gets exciting is when the bloody gadget fails!"

But now I may be changing my mind.

Before I am inundated with free samples and lavishly-illustrated 30-page user's manuals from the London Rubber Company, I should explain quickly that it is, of course engines in gliders about which I may be changing my mind. The SSA remark got a laugh at the expense of the motor-glider pilots but it was hardly fair, since at that time I had never flown in any glider with an engine.

More than a year went by before Marion Barritt and I visited Hans-Werner Grosse at the 1994 German Nationals at Neustadt-Glewe, in what had been East Germany. In the middle of the vast grass airfield, by the airport buildings, there were still the steel-wire cages erected by the old regime to corral the power planes so as to prevent unreliable elements escaping from the people's paradise to the West German border, only 50kms away. One felt the squalor and the chill of the Cold War as if it had not yet ended. In what had once been a beautiful area, the fields around Neustadt-Glewe were ripped up and stained by Soviet tanks, now long departed, their crews having poured used oil into the ground as a matter of habit.

I won't describe here the ordeal the previous day of driving at a snail's pace, Marion patiently at the wheel, with my un-motored ASH-25 in the trailer, across the Polish-German border with several thousand other vehicles after the British Overseas Nationals in Leszno, with no lavatories except the woods on either side: that revolting experience has been related elsewhere, and ruined many a reader's breakfast. However I now realise that if my ASH-25 had been equipped with an engine, I could have flown over the border on that damp and dreary afternoon, and taken my chances with the local customs and immigration wherever I landed. Anything would have been better than the hours in the queue at Frankfurt-am-Oder. Never again shall I take a glider by road into or out of Poland. No, it has not got better since 1994: I noticed from the aerial photographs taken near the border by Uli Schwenk, winner of the 1998 World Open Class Championships in Poland, that the Frankfurt-am-Oder queues are undiminished, and still stretch from horizon to horizon.

Hans-Werner Grosse has long been a convert to motor-gliding, and as one of Hans' fans

I ought to have been less skeptical about engines. Lübeck, where he normally flies, is a maritime town vulnerable to all the vile and variable weather that seaports are bound to suffer. In short, the air is very British. Even the biggest wings need help in such skies.

Hans flew his 27-metre ASH-25 from Luebeck to Neustadt-Glewe as a visitor, not as a contestant – Hans has some acid remarks to make about modern competitions: the unwillingness of pilots to take risks, and their preference for a day when all land out, or simply don't take off, over any risk that the other guy might get the smallest advantage . This glider, a Walter Binder modification, is soon about to be superseded by a 31-meter behemoth, but more of that later. Immense trouble had been taken to reduce weight. So the glider had no tow-hook, and only one instrument panel up front. That makes it a true motorglider, in that it cannot be launched at all except by its own power. However it was not too hard to see the key instruments from the rear seat. However that could just be because Hans is not a big pilot. The canopy was a single-piece affair, very much like a Schempp two-seater.

In case you think I am biased to Schleicher, I ought to mention that I fly a syndicated Janus C from Minden in Nevada, and love it. The Janus is the only tandem two-seater that – never having been an instructor and got used to back-seat driving – I am happy to fly from the back as pilot in charge; this I put down to the splendid view from the one-piece canopy. Sealing may be a problem with one-piece canopies (either from differential expansion due to heating or from airframe flexing) and I am terrified of damaging them when open on the ground, but on balance I prefer them.

I have flown with lots of friends in our Dunstable-based ASH-25, and those that have never flown in a big ship are always astonished. "It never seems to come down!" they all exclaim. After 11 seasons of flying an ASH-25 and being thoroughly spoilt, there is only one way for the blasé to recapture that sense of astonishment: that is to upgrade to a more powerful drug and add another two metres. The sense of floating through the clouds effortlessly in Hans-Werner's machine was evident even to a pampered old roué like me. On a somewhat soggy, overdeveloped day much like any English day, three hundred kilometres just drifted by in three hours without much circling.

However the real fun was at the beginning. After the uneventful but noisy climb to 500 metres not far from the airfield, the engine was supposed to retract. Instead it stuck in a part-retracted position, which was just about the worst thing it could do, since it caused massive drag but was unusable as propulsion. We probably could not glide back to the field and ought to prepare to land out. It was a less than ideal situation if we had to land on rough terrain in that state, I pondered as the individual with his head nearest to this big lump of inert metal. With all the calm of a battle-scarred Junkers 88 torpedo-bomber pilot, Hans fired up his mobile phone and called the designer of the engine at home. What plan B was if the inventor had not been at home, I never enquired.

As I tell the story to my cronies in the Dunstable bar, when we are vying for the honour of having had the most hair-raising experiences, the designer was in his bath, and he and Hans had a friendly chat about the state of their wives' health, as one does, before getting round to the fact that Hans and I were falling out of the sky and needed advice of a practical and immediate nature. This story is a gross (sorry) exaggeration since I have no grasp of conversational German and have only the most general idea of what was said. Certainly there seemed to be no sense of panic, and the essential information was obtained. Polite good-byes were exchanged, the mobile phone was stowed, the engine was stowed, and we soared away.

I have to admit, that *was* exciting .

French without tears (1999)

I am not joking when I say that if I had not been born British (I am I fact 45% English, 48% Scots, 12% Norwegian and 11% Irish – no, don't bother to write in) I would like to have been born American or French. The Americans I admire for their energy, enthusiasm and restless pursuit of perfection; the French I envy for their culture, sophistication and their confident assurance that they are already perfect. I am receiving from my good friend (well, he was until five minutes ago) Jean-Renaud Faliu a wonderful aviation magazine called *Volez!* It is

lively and good to look at. It is so attractive I am almost inclined to go back to France to glide after a lapse of several years. However the bureaucracy – and I am talking of the country that taught the world the meaning of bureaucracy – a British pilot now has to go through to be allowed to aviate in France is so tedious you begin to think they have mistaken the poor guy for a truck-load of condemned beef. Why French physicians have to probe every alien orifice to determine whether a visitor is a hazard to aerial navigation, and are not prepared to take the word of a British doctor, I don't know. No wonder French doctors of *Médecins sans Frontières* got a Nobel prize for boldly going where nobody else is prepare to venture.

But *Volez!* makes flying in France look enormous fun and I may decide it is worth the hassle. So I am reading it avidly not just to find out what exciting things are going on across the Channel – like mid-air collisions between gliders and airliners – but to acquire some vocabulary before a future visit. *Volez!* is written in a breezy style, a bit like Pete Harvey in a beret with a Gauloise stuck to his lip, very colloquial. Even my Distinction in School Certificate French in 1949 isn't up to capturing the nuances without a lot of help from a charming French-born female neighbour here in London. (And you can wipe that smirk off your face, too. These translating sessions are hard work.) Here are a few phrases that I found in *Volez!* that caught my eye.

What, for instance, is "trou bleu?" Since the context of the article indicates serious concern amongst the pilots involved in the world's first ever 500-km cross-country, this is clearly something worrisome. Should we pack all our trou bleus in our old kit bag and smile, smile, smile? No, a "trou bleu" is, of course, a blue hole. "Trous bleus" is therefore not the standard dress worn by generations of French farmers but a multiplicity of blue holes.

"Rues de cumulus" is so obvious I won't insult you by translating it. But I might mention that an Australian play called "Cloudstreets" is being highly acclaimed in London this month, and because of the title I am inclined to go along to see if they try to launch a glider into the auditorium in Act two. It's astonishing what stage effects they can get these days. I went to "les Miserables" some years ago and I could not remember a single tune, but came out whistling the scenery instead.

What is a "coque"? As Mrs Platypus found out years ago, after being asked by a Frenchman to hold it firmly as we de-rigged in a wheat field, that is merely the fuselage. As in monocoque construction.

"A deux doigts de vacher". That ought to mean it takes just two fingers to milk a cow. But I think it really means to be within an ace of landing out.

"Treuil bitambour" From the picture I can see that a treuil is a winch, but what is bitambour? Well I guess it is breaks down into bi-tambour – sounds like two tambourines. Two-drum winch, of course!

"Un bon vent dans le dos" could mean "I really had the breeze up" but no, it means "a good tail wind". Likewise to suffer from "prise au vent" does not mean those haricots in garlic butter you had at lunchtime are working overtime: it means Drag. (Sorry, Interested of Bedfordshire, dressing up in women's clothes is not "prise au vent". No I am not going to ask my French neighbour what it is either.)

I am sure that the punishment squad of the Académie Francaise will pounce on the Anglo-Saxon "logger" and drag the editor of Volez! to Devil's Island or to compulsory cultural re-education classes ("Devil's Island, any time!" shrieks the editor as we see his heels disappear through the doorway.) Yes, "logger" means logger. Soon the Académie will come up with a three-word, ten-syllable expression that means the same.

I bet "lancer au sandow" has you stumped. I knew by pure chance. I had tried for my height diamond over 20 years ago at Sisteron many times without success, and got to 20,000ft in my Nimbus 2 on the very last day of my third visit to that site. Kiki, later manager of several victorious French World Championship teams, produced an oxygen set and said he would secure it into the space behind my head with what he mysteriously called "sandows". These turned out to be bungies. But why sandow? Then I remembered that Eugene Sandow was a famous strong man a century ago, who was a whiz at self-promotion. He must have built his pectoral muscles with chest-expanders made of rubber shock cords, and marketed them on the "You too can have a body like mine" theme, so his name stuck. The usual chest-expanders one sees in sports gear shops use spiral steel springs, but they rip out the chest-hairs and pinch the nipples if you let go of them too suddenly, and whatever you might think to the contrary, that really is not my idea of a good time. Rubber is safer, though I still think you might catapult yourself out of the window if you are careless, so strenuous exercise should be restricted to the ground floor till Bronze C standard is gained. (What the heck has this to do with gliding? New Ed.) Sorry, all I meant to say was that "lancer au sandow" is to bungy-launch.

Now you have perfected your word-power, you are fully prepared for a soaring expedition to France. Well, apart for the medical, and how you practise for that is your business. ∎

Under western skies: gliding in the USA

It was either Oscar Wilde or George Bernard Shaw who said that America and Britain were two countries separated by a common language. Like most witty remarks that one is less than half true. If an Englishman wants to feel he is in a foreign country without the hassle of getting a passport he should board a bus in Newcastle-on-Tyne and try to figure out what the two Geordies in the seat in front are saying to each other.

Thanks to the happy chance that the earth rotates from west to east, you can board a plane in rainy London at breakfast-time, cross the Arctic Circle and arrive in California in time for lunch and a soaring flight over the Mojave Desert, where the dust devils spiral up to 18,000ft. The place is so near, the cost of getting there and the cost of living so low; I am astonished so few people come from Britain to the USA to glide. I can only put it down to lack of information.

Great snakes! (1991)

From the 1991 World Champs Newsletter, "Uvalde Express", Texas, edited by Marion Barritt

The best glider pilots are supposed to make a fresh decision every 30 seconds. This is believed to illustrate what massive intellectual pressures our champions are under as they battle with the elements. What it in fact means is that the greatest soaring brains in the world have the attention span of all of 30 seconds on a good day. A grasshopper could concentrate longer.

This was well demonstrated by the response to the excellent lecture by Dr Walt Cannon (one of the big guns in aviation medicine, as they say) in which he strove, against the collective will of the finest gliding minds in our globe, to get across the simple fact that the greatest danger to pilots flying in this neck of the woods was dehydration. Not snakes, nor alligators, nor the National Rifle Association, but plain lack of water. Dr Cannon's problem was that he addressed himself to the left-handed, or rational and cogitative, side of the audience's cerebellum (or cerebella, since glider pilots can never be said to be all of one mind).

"So you can see from all these graphs and tables that you must drink lots of wa..."

"What about cobras ... ?"

"There are no cobras. As I was saying, drink lots of ..."

"What about coral snakes?"

"Forget the coral snakes, it's thirst you should..."

A long argument ensues amongst the audience about whether snakes kill their victims with anti-coagulant or coagulant ... or by attacking the central nervous system.

"It doesn't matter, you won't die," explains a slightly impatient doctor.

"Not even from a rattlesnake sitting on your parachute?" asks an insistent pilot.

By now Dr Cannon is clearly wishing that his tormentors were all sitting on rattlesnakes.

I was tempted to bring up the report I'd heard during three minutes of television news – mixed in with 57 minutes of advertisements for haemorrhoid cures etc – that there were 200 swarms of killer bees loose in southern Texas. However that would have prevented me from raising the key issue: "What happens medically to people who have had nothing to eat since breakfast and have to wait till past 9pm listening to a load of irrelevant questions?"

But, being neither a pilot (admired and respected for being their country's chosen representatives) nor crew (cosseted, or at least tolerated, for their sacrifice and selfless labour) but an insignificant in-between, a back-seat, pass-the-pee-bags-don't-vomit-down-the-

great-man's-neck co-pilot, navigator and rear-gunner, I kept silent.

Dr Cannon deserves a medal. It's his audience who should be fired.

Noted in Uvalde

- A talking pickup truck: as we came out of a restaurant and walked between two parked vehicles, one of them boomed in a Robocop voice, "Get-away-from-this-vee-hicle! You-are-too-close!" It's the only time I've ever wished to vandalise an innocent pickup truck, partly out of curiosity as to what it might have to say on the subject.
- The heat. Pilots sat in air-conditioned cars until the last moment, then were escorted under umbrellas to their gliders. As soon as the pilots were launched the crews raced to the hotel pool, their radios close at hand.
- The domination of the automobile. I have seen no pedestrian crossings or "islands" half-way across those wide, wide roads. You just take your life in your hands and dash. Yes, Granny, that means you too. (So that's why the little old ladies all wear Olympic running shoes!)
- The perpetual sunshine. I could hardly believe the statistic that over 95% of days are good for cross-countries, but we are coming up to that ratio already since arriving here and no relief in sight. Nevertheless the yearning for a cool, wet English day is not strong: I recommend a spell here for Europeans who just yearn for the crowing of happy variometers for a change.

Ten gallon hat.

Texas is different (1991)

Coming home from abroad, you see your own country with new eyes. Texas skies are lovely, but the terrain is drab. In England it is the other way round. So green and undulating the land; so grey and flat the clouds.

After the rectangular fields, grid-plan towns and arrow-straight roads of America, I was vividly reminded, on the approach to Gatwick, that most fields in England are any shape but rectangular, towns are a disorderly muddle and no British-built road is straight. I once pointed this out to an Air Canada pilot sitting alongside me in the Caproni Calif: a real gentleman's conveyance, now sadly missed, apart from the annual rigging ordeal. (This was a year before I sold up and 18 months before the Caproni's starboard wing and tail fell off and the two pilots jumped to safety, but that is another story.)

He politely contradicted me: "Look, there's a straight road, from horizon to horizon." "That", I said, "was built by the Romans two thousand years ago, and since then someone has lost the piece of string."

- The speeds that little ships are doing are phenomenal. If I lived here I wouldn't bother with big wings. If you can do 140km/h in a Discus who needs 25 metres?
- "Andy Pybus flying a Discus from Australia at 138.5km/h…" announced Mark Huffstutler at briefing today. Sir Charles Kingsford-Smith would be proud of you, Andy. His historic flight in the other direction in a Fokker Tri-motor "Southern Cross" could not have been much faster.

— oOo —

I read a book of summaries of the OSTIV lectures on the way home, and despite the best efforts of the cleverest brains in the gliding movement to render their papers totally incomprehensible, I actually understood some of it, or I think I did.

By the number of papers, I guess that lots of theoretical work is going into the World Class glider of 13.4 metres, no flaps and a fixed wheel. I look out from my study and shudder at the 13.4 metres. To keep such a device airborne in northern Europe would not just require the combined talents of Heide and Holighaus at the drawing board but a pilot of world championships class at the controls. For Texas, yes, terrific! But in Texas wings are just ornaments. One of those ten-gallon hats would do the job.

With the benefit of hindsight, I can say that my doubts regarding a 13.4 metre sailplane in 1991 now seem fully justified.

Go west, middle-aged man! (1993)

July 1993 was a good choice of month to get away from the British rain and to cross the Arctic Circle to the land of snowy ridges – the Spanish for which is Sierra Nevada – to take part in the bonhomie and excitement of an American regional competition at Minden, Nevada. I rented a local DG-300: I knew from earlier visits that it had good instruments and functioning oxygen. In terms of upper surface wing finish it was about average for a rental glider that sits out in the open every day. The lower surface had been dragged over a pile of rocks on an away landing just a few days earlier – by another customer, not me. There had been no time to repair it before the competition and though the damage was not structural (I was told) it looked horrible, The DG handled beautifully and climbed OK, but if I tried to run with the privately-owned Discuses etc I fell away badly. (As neat an example of a bad workman blaming his tools as I've seen. Ed.)

The shortness of the contest period surprised me, only six days. But we got six contest days out of six, as was expected, and frankly that was quite enough in the heat. Tasks ranged from 250km to just short of 500km, though the Americans are resolutely un-metricated: every task is scored in miles and miles per hour.

We were flying for fun, and the atmosphere was relaxed and gentlemanly. After my two early field-landing disasters my maps were marked up by experts among the other competitorswith suggested routes through the mountains, and with their help I made fewer blunders. There were quite strong feelings about sportsmanship. When one pilot gave out fairly general information about the thermal he was enjoying, he was immediately rebuked for helping some contestants to have

an unfair advantage. No pair flying was evident and no codes, so far as I know. It's possible that, "May be landing in a field of spinach at X-ville" meant, "I've got a Popeye of a thermal at X," but so far as I could tell spinach meant spinach. It's very different in Europe – in which, as a good European, I include Britain – where all sorts of conspiracy and trickery are encouraged under the euphemism of "teamwork."

The first big mistake a British pilot can make about gliding in the western USA is thinking that it is going to be easy, because of the strong average rates of climb, the almost stratospheric cloudbases and unlimited visibility. A talent for working half-knot thermals with the cloudbase at 1,400ft over Middle Wallop or Lower Slaughter[15] is not to be despised, but it does not prepare you for the hot, mountainous terrain in the Sierras where, despite the sunshine, huge expanses of air are often just too tired to go up. The baleful influence of the big lakes many miles upwind of the contest area was such that slight shifts of wind could kill vast areas of lift. The place where the whole field was forced to land one day would the next day be yielding abundant thermals, and vice versa: yesterday's great thermal source would be today's sinkhole. By sink I mean *sink*: 15kts down or worse is common out west. I learnt the hard way by landing out twice in the first two days.

That's another thing different from England: in the Sierras great expanses of thousands of square miles can be unlandable. Local knowledge helps not just in finding lift but in having an unmapped airstrip or a small dry lake bed in mind when traversing what looks like the other side of the moon.

— ∞ —

After a landout on Day 1 I determined to follow the other pilots and learn from them on Day 2. This cowardly plan was working fine at first; I took no initiatives whatever. However conditions were turning out to be blue, stable and much poorer than forecast. All the more reason to cling grimly to the tails of the leaders. Then, while we were already half way down the first leg, I was thunderstruck to hear

---

[15] Foreign readers please note: these places really do exist.

a radio call announcing that the Contest Committee had decided to change the task. Worse still, instead of reducing the task length by lopping off the last turnpoint, the Committee made it a pilot-selected-turnpoint task, or POST. I had never done a POST before: I had naively assumed that if a POST were to be declared this would happen on the ground, and I would have enough time to sit and read the rulebook before launching. "Who are the Contest Committee?" I bleated. "We are!" came the reply from the other members of my gaggle, who immediately split off in different directions. Bereft of any ideas about where to go or whom to leech off, I alone stayed on the original track and headed for the foothills of Mt Patterson in California, where I had managed a brilliant escape from the rockface up to 15,000ft only the day before. However the whole point of gliding is that history can never be relied upon to repeat itself. I plummeted like a grand piano to the valley floor and enjoyed cold beers with Mrs Tammy Johnson and her family.

Before the contest I had nursed fears of outlandings, thinking not so much of rattlesnakes but of trigger-happy farmers protecting their property from varmints like glider pilots, and especially foreigners. In the event the hospitality was splendid. On the first retrieve the starving crew arrived just in time to find the pilot had been royally fed by Mrs Moreda and all the plates cleared away. The farmer's family had patiently waited long past their normal supper time, but one air mile was three road miles round those mountains and it was long past nightfall when the retrievers trundled in. Finding a small glider in one of several identical large alfalfa fields in the dark was just an extra challenge in the, "We'll all laugh about this in ten years' time" category.

After the next landout, the very next day, two carloads of helpers arrived from Minden airport, my reputation having spread. They came partly out of compassion and partly out of curiosity. Two outlandings in two days looks very much like recklessness. The farmer allowed only one vehicle to drive into the field, which was in effect fallow but had a light crop sown that was designed chiefly to bind the soil and prevent it blowing away. The trailer, carrying on its roof the half a dozen extra crew, was dragged towards the glider over a

> **Where to fly out west (1995)**
>
> *After two soggy and brutally expensive European trips in 1992 and 1993, I can recommend Minden. Food, beer, petrol and accommodation are cheap, the language is remarkably similar and the flying unbeatable. It is the World's best soaring site. People are very friendly, but as on most US airports with a soaring operation there isn't a club as we expect to find in England or France. To avoid loneliness, especially after the thermals stop, I suggest you a) go as a group from the UK, b) enter a competition or c) join a soaring safari.*
>
> *There are two gliding operations based at Minden Airport, Nevada, USA. These are: High Country Soaring and Soar Minden. Both rent gliders and provide aerotows, and there is an excellent glider repair shop on the airport.*

meandering track made of football-sized boulders, through a dense thicket and across a rickety bridge consisting entirely of loose planks, by a four-wheel drive truck that offered massive ground clearance.

The conventional saloon car (sedan) is almost a rarity in Nevada. Everyone seems to have some kind of four-wheel-drive all-terrain pickup truck, a camping van, an RV (recreational vehicle) or some other variant on the idea of having fun, going anywhere and looking rugged. It's the automotive equivalent of jeans, boots and a cowboy hat. But they are very practical too, if you make a habit of landing out in the Sierra Nevada.

At least these retrieves did not try to compete with those special delights of British outlandings – rain and mud. Everybody in Minden complained about the terrible weather, though the sun beat down relentlessly. "Where are the usual 20,000ft cloudbases?" they wanted to know. Nobody had done better than 15,000 so far.

Day 3 delivered the high bases, and I got the hang of it and came 3rd. It was like getting gloriously drunk in that I can't remember a thing about it.

On Day 4 I spiralled in a great crowd of sailplanes up to the mandatory ceiling of 17,500ft. (The organisers were meticulous about airspace. The legal limit is 18,000ft and the 500ft band ensures we have no excuse to infringe that limit "accidentally".) That was about 13,500ft above ground, and I set off confidently, not too concerned about the blue sky ahead nor about the fact that the other contestants were disappearing, most of them travelling quite a bit faster and flatter. But isn't it strange that when there is plenty of lift and good cumulus marking it the air is full of gliders, then when it goes all blue and difficult the others have vanished and you are suddenly on your own? It's like policemen: when you don't want them you see them everywhere, and when you need one badly there's not one to be found.

With the July noonday sun baking the stony Nevada wilderness, there should be bags of lift, or so you would imagine. Well, I tobogganed quietly down for 40 miles without a burble. (That's why 17,500ft is a necessity, not a luxury.) I had rounded the turnpoint, a grey and gloomy looking little mining town – the sort of place Clint Eastwood drifts into, blows apart and drifts out of three reels later – and ended up level with a stony wind-facing ridge about 1,500ft above the desert floor, bathed in sweat and self-pity. There was nothing to land on except a vast salt lake bed just within gliding range. I later learnt that the salt lake was fenced off in sections and was used as a Navy ammunition dump.

— ∞ —

From time to time little bits of thermal allowed me to gain the odd hundred feet and make a dash for another ridge a bit closer to the area of cumulus which I had left less than an hour earlier. This struggle seemed to take hours. It did take hours. The only consolation was to hear a whole gaggle of top pilots, including two with 1,000km diplomas achieved in Standard Class gliders, suffering for most of the afternoon on another ridge, debating their chances of ever getting away and comparing the merits of different alfalfa fields. They were obviously nearer to the greenery than I was, and nearer to the big lakes and the thermal-killing irrigation that made the fields green. I could see no green at all, just rocks. Thank Heavens it wasn't just me suffering, I thought.

Eventually patience was rewarded, and like a thirst-crazed desert explorer crawling on his belly towards a distant oasis I dragged myself into the cool shadow of a high, thin patch of cloud. In minutes I was back up at 17,500ft

and heading effortlessly for home. Champagne day! At $5 a bottle every day can be a champagne day.

— ∞ —

I was one of the only two to get back, and joyfully expected to reap hundreds of extra points to make up for the defeats of Days 1 and 2. Big mistake. Under the local US rules, large numbers of landouts devalue the day severely, whereas in Britain you can have a 1,000-point day even if nobody gets back – we frequently do in fact. I suppose it is a fair rule at Minden, since it has to be a freak day that keeps a lot of pilots from completing the task. So I remained doomed to be the bottom of the pile.

The next two days were similar race days, including a rendezvous with the World Hang Gliding Championships at Bishop in the White Mountains, which top 15,000ft. "Like flying through a swarm of gnats," said Gary Kemp, who won the contest in his Pegasus. The White Mountains are where I am going to try for my 1,000km Diploma before I get much older. Beautiful, spectacular, breathtaking – where's my book of clichés? All the clichés are true, though.

Incidentally Pete Harvey, later to become a formidable UK Nationals pilot, was taking part in those World Hang Gliding Championships, so we doubtless saw each other in our respective gaggles. It was quite perilous for the hang-gliders, with the turbulence close to the rock collapsing several contestants' wings. Three hang-glider pilots had to deploy their parachutes, and others extricated themselves from an inverted position. The heating in the western USA is so much greater than in the Alps that the risk of an upset even with a conventional glider is serious. Keep your speed up!

What do you do with a sunken pilot? (1994)

Imagine that you land on the shore of a lake in a desert landscape with no road in sight. It is late afternoon. A retrieve plane arrives promptly, but sinks up to its axles in mud and sand and is unable to tow you out. The tug eventually revs itself out of the mire and staggers back into the sky without you; it's getting dark and, as I've said, there's no obvious track by land from the airfield to the glider. What can you realistically look forward to now? You can expect to spend most of the next 24 hours with the glider, no doubt. With luck your hot and very disenchanted ground crew might find a way to you the next day – this place is vast and empty and roads of any kind are rare – while the burning sun climbs high overhead, and you might be out of there and back on the airfield just in time for tomorrow's cocktail hour. Or maybe the next day's.

Ah, but this is different. I mean unlike any gliding event anywhere on the globe. What happens is a helicopter comes buzzing in and whisks you back to the ranch in good time for a shower and join tonight's Happy Hour, not tomorrow's. The glider is left behind. It'll be taken care of. On the way back, a cameraman in the helicopter enterprisingly makes a continuous videotape movie of the only practical route from the landing spot to the nearest proper road with signposts. By proper, I don't mean an asphalt road, but a dirt road that four-wheel drives and horses are designed for. This videotape record is for the aid of the professional ground crew. They will venture out the next day with a four-wheel drive and a trailer and have a hell of a time extricating your glider, calling all sorts of blessings down on your name as they do so. You, however, following cocktails and a sumptuous dinner, have an excellent night's sleep in your air-conditioned mobile home.

After an early morning balloon flight, you try a spot of fishing for trout in the river or fat bass in the lakes, and maybe some skeet shooting. Then a monster breakfast – choice of steak, eggs, crispy bacon, ham, sausage, fries and umpteen kinds of fruit, fruit juice and cakes, buns, scones, toast and muffins, served by three devoted waitresses for whom nothing is too much trouble. There now has to

Through the scrub.

be a fly in life's otherwise perfect ointment, since you have no glider today, right? Wrong. Another sailplane is washed down by another professional crew, filled up with water, oxygen tanks topped up and wheeled out on to the airstrip for Sir to use today. Don't forget to take your delicious packed lunch and lots of ice-cold Coke, Gatorade and Calistoga Springs mineral water just in case you land out again.

As you thermal contentedly up to the cloud-base of 18,000ft (well, 20,000ft plus is attainable, but the Federal Law is the Federal Law) you might espy a little cloud of dust 13,000ft below on the desert floor. That is Tom Stowers and his team hacking their way through the scrub towards your first glider. Gosh, I'd nearly forgotten that little ship, sitting on the lake shore under the baking sun. But this new one is really nice. Gosh, I haven't circled for at least 160km. You know, I could get used to this...

Well, don't get used to it. It happens once only. This is soaring heaven, and the next time you find yourself experiencing anything remotely like it you are probably not in this world; you've probably just stepped under a bus.

To be one of the Barron Hilton award-winning pilots is strictly a once-in-a-lifetime privilege. If you achieve the best flight by the Hilton Cup rules in your Class and region in any two-year period, you are eligible to go to the Flying-M Ranch and have ten of the most astonishing soaring holidays that it is possible to envisage. Then your name is added to the list of names on the honour roll of medal winners, and you make way for other aspirants in subsequent years. Now you have something to tell your grandchildren about.

It is truly a vacation, too, not a competition or even a task week. The medals are awarded at the beginning, not the end of the proceedings. This trip is pure fun, but among pilots so skilled and eminent that naturally everyone tries to make the best of the conditions, declaring records or 1,000km attempts almost every day.

Plat, there's just one question. Ed.

What?

If this is for eminent pilots, with the greatest respect, what the Hell were you doing there? Ed.

I'm glad you asked that question, even if it could have been put more politely –

Oh, and another thing – was it you who landed by that lake to the immense inconvenience of all concerned? Ed.

I thought you said just one question. No, it wasn't me. I landed on a small dry lake earlier the very same day. That little story is told later. As to the second question: each award-winning pilot is allowed to bring along one friend. John Good of New Hampshire, the US Eastern Division winner, sent me a fax out of the blue – we'd never met before – while I was in Poland at the British Overseas Nationals in spring 1994, inviting Platypus to go as his guest. This was purely on the strength of my little column in *Sailplane & Gliding*. Literature has some rewards, I am amazed to learn.

At first I nearly didn't accept, since John's fax used a four-letter word. It mentioned my role as Crew. Not knowing anything about the Barron Hilton biennial gathering, I came over all faint at the idea of being Crew, and nearly said No Thanks, until my better-informed Nevada friends said I must be crazy. Hired staff with white gloves did everything on the flight line, they said with only slight exaggeration, and work (another four letter word which can give me a nasty scare) was not expected of award-winning pilots or their hangers-on. No, I would not be Crew at all, it was just a turn of phrase. Having witnessed what the actual crew had to do when these star pilots landed out, I was right to feel faint at the idea.

Start the US competition season gently with Geezerglide (1995)

The best way for a mature pilot, which loosely describes me, to get into the swing of the US contest season is to enter the Seniors Championship in Florida in March. Florida is inexpensive to fly to and living there is cheap. Life is cheap too, if you believe the media, but the fact that 40 million tourists visit Florida every year puts the occasional murder in some perspective, assuming you aren't the murderee. I did indeed become the victim of a vicious crime in Orlando, playground of the world, but more of that later.

The Seniors is strictly for pilots over 55. Every year now for six years, around February or March, veteran competition fliers have trundled to Florida from the snows of Canada, the Midwest and wherever thermals are still hibernating, in their vast motor homes. These monsters whip along at a lithe five miles per gallon, with a glider trailer behind making an insignificant difference to the already dire handling or fuel consumption. Once at Seminole Lake gliderport, these mobile mansions become gin palaces and social centres. Another popular gathering point after flying is the veranda of the clubhouse, where a vast fridge dispenses continuous free beer, iced. At that time of year (the Ides of March) in Britain, beer served outdoors would also be iced, but it wouldn't need a fridge.

Last year I very publicly abandoned Europe from Spain to Poland as a soggy, windy dead loss. I arrived in Florida in a monsoon. I kept hearing, "You should have been here last year" from people who have not read what that does to my blood pressure. I think I am towing areas of damp behind me everywhere, and might make a modest living by entering contests all around the world and then being paid to stay away. Show me a silver lining and I will provide the cloud.

Florida skies in March 1995 seemed rather like English skies in June almost any year, offering much the same mix of bright sun quickly followed by good thermals, then followed by sudden spread-out. This spread-out was of course good news for the ASH-25,

Platypus gets his entry in early for Geezerglide.

which has no chance in a handicapped competition unless something horrible happens to all the little gliders. It may seem ungentlemanly for me to pray for my rivals to land out, but every season I ask the good Lord to consider my handicap and arrange for the opposition to land safely at a convenient airfield, or at a charming ducal estate where butlers pour the tea and pretty girls divert the dashing flier until the crew (his not very diverted wife, probably) arrives. There aren't many ducal estates in Florida, but the little ships made masses of safe landouts in pastures and small airports on the first two contest days, which cheered up this spiteful old geezer no end. Whatever happened, you ask, to the fine traditions of British sportsmanship – losing with a gracious smile and all that tosh?

I am sorry, but handicapping relieves one of any obligations of that sort.

A stroll around the launch-point produced some startling insights into what the older pilot can do with a catheter and loads of plastic tubing, which I won't go into. (Gee, thanks. Ed.) Certainly people were ready for any contingency. One pilot sat waiting for take-off with a whacking great hunting knife, not quite as broad as a Crocodile Dundee special, but about as long, strapped to his chest. This, he said, was for such emergencies as finding oneself hung up in a tree in one's parachute, though I thought it might be just right for fighting alligators and cutting rattlesnake poison out of one's leg. Stan Nelson, a former director of astronaut recovery systems for NASA at Cape Canaveral and another citizen who knows Florida well, always flew with a .45 hand gun in the cockpit. I didn't ask him what he had in mind, but I think he did not much like the big shadow that an ASH-25 kept throwing over his Ventus CM's canopy. A few holes in the intruder's structure would let more light through, and would also diminish its performance significantly, as if the 25's handicap was not severe enough already. However he managed to win the contest without resorting to lethal force.

Talking about rattlesnakes, a live one was found making itself a home in a trailer. The snake's captor came with it to briefing the next day, looking either stone dead or just remarkably relaxed (the snake, I mean) and did a howdunit on his exploit. Florida is full of

Old contest pilots never die, their tasks just get shorter and shorter (1995)

Senior pilots do not much like retrieves (and senior pilots' wives even less), so Charlie Spratt, perhaps the world's most famous contest director, set the tasks with a determination to get everybody back, making allowances for the mix of Standard and Open gliders in one Class of 26 machines. I can give you an idea of how unusually poor the weather was when I say the tasks were too short to merit even one pee-bag in my ASH-25, No. 13. (Just as primitive tribes – and pilots with large motor homes and little trailers – measure all journeys in days rather than miles, so I measure flight distance in pee-bags. A zero pee-bag flight is not much over 100km. I admit the usefulness of this measure is flawed by the fact that it varies from pilot to pilot. as well as shortening steadily as one gets older, and finally the number of bags per 100km must obviously vary with thermal strength, but what the heck, this is my column and like Humpty Dumpty, I can make these terms mean whatever I want them to mean.) Anyway the tasks were so brief, it seemed that barely had everyone taken off that the smug so-and-sos with big wings were back on the verandah drinking the free iced beer and listening to the outlanding reports. Heh-heh. Handicap, schmandicap, who cares if the weather is truly British?

Do not much like retrieves.

wildlife, and you are well advised not to make it any more wild by, for instance, treading on it.

After the competition I returned to London to do a bit of work, at which you might say I am a minimalist, so my partner flew his airliner full of tourists into Orlando and took over the ASH-25 for a few days. Suddenly he rang me from Orlando to announce bad news. Since he is the sanest and safest pilot around, I could not imagine what he was going to say next. Outside his hotel our entire tow-hitch plus ball had been stolen. The bit that attached directly to the Jeep was easily replaced, but there are no 50mm balls generally available in the USA, where two-inch balls prevail. The 50mm ones normally on sale in the UK do not have vertical pins for fitting into US tow-hitches. Frantic telephoning by me located the only 50mm ball with a US fitting pin in the whole of Britain. Watling Engineers delivered it within 24 hours. The only problem then was taking this odd-shaped hunk of metal through airport X-ray machines when I returned to the USA in April. The Heathrow security people said nothing. Doubtless they are so sophisticated they said, "Obviously not a bomb, just a 50mm steel European standard tow-ball on a 7/8in US standard pin," and gave it not a second's further thought. But US airport security pounced every time.

Now I have to take the hitch off and lock it in the car whenever it is not in use. All the same, if that is the worst loss the glider or I encounter during this season in the USA, I shall not complain one bit.

Just after we were all launched on Day 1, Contest Director Charlie Spratt was suddenly whisked away to a hospital 500 miles away in a plane belonging to Chicho Estrada, one of the contestants. Up till that day his amazingly active life since he developed kidney trouble had been organized around the demands of a mobile dialysis unit. It now looked as it he would today be liberated from that constraint. He left with the good wishes every pilot transmitted, one by one. It was a very emotional moment. Then the anti-climax. Three people were lined up for two kidneys from a young man killed in a car accident. Charlie lost. He flew back and was very matter of fact about it, but it was a blow, and we all felt it.

The pilots bought the fuel for the 1,000 mile round trip. However on the day he got back from the competition, March 22, another kidney, scoring six, near perfectly matched as can be expected from a donor who is not a close relation, turned up, and he was lucky this time. He is recovering well.

Seminole Lake Gliderport, Clermont, Florida has soarable conditions all year round, though July and August are rather tropical and unstable. Knut and Ingrid Kjensle will give you a warm welcome to one of the most attractive soaring sites that 1 have seen. It's only 20 minutes' drive to Disneyworld etc so the family don't have to sit around waiting for you to land.

The curse of Platypus strikes again (1995)

June 13, the first day of the 1995 US Open Class Championships in Nevada, was decidedly interesting. You know, when someone serves you a dish you can't eat and they ask you how you like it, all you can mutter with your mouth full of the godawful stuff is, "Er, ulp, interesting." The five pilots who got round the more or less unlandable mountains and desert in the teeth of a high wind, by polishing the ridges low down then surfing the wave to over 17,000ft, each deserve a medal. The other 18 failed to make it – a monstrous failure rate for Minden.

Plat showed his increasingly craven character, the product of old age compounded by avarice and sloth, in rejecting the prospect of 100 points at the price of a certain landout on an uncertain airstrip. Instead, after five hours of struggle covering nearly 250km, I clawed my way back home over snow-draped peaks and settled for zero points. Not having any crew at this competition was a sort of excuse for such behaviour, but in the glorious days of my youth, when two field landings in a day were the norm, the absence of crew would never have stood in my way. It would have been, "Damn the torpedoes, full speed ahead, and let the Devil organise the retrieve."

Then the next three days in a row were scrubbed. At Minden Competitions this is unprecedented. Pilots were in shock and I was regarded with dark looks. I know how Jonah felt shortly after he was introduced to the whale. My jovial offer on Day One to quit the competition (and indeed the site altogether) for a fee of $100 per head, that is $2,300 in total, came to be taken seriously, and at briefing on the third scrubbed day several hundred green ones had been collected, but not sufficient to meet what auctioneers call the reserve. I think a round $1,000 would just about have persuaded me to derig and move to a safe distance, like 500 miles.

— ∞ —

After that the gods decided the competitors had been tormented sufficiently and relented to give six successive days of weather that in England would have been greeted with ecstasy, but which in Minden were considered just barely acceptable. Normal thermal soaring conditions were resumed, so I shall not report on them since I have forgotten, if I ever knew, how to make normal competitions sound fun. One day is worth mentioning, however, because it was the fastest ever US Nationals contest day, with Jim Payne's winning speed in an ASH-25 of 183km/h or just a hair under 100kt. This wasn't one of those freak speeds resulting from starts in the stratosphere, by the way. Starts were limited to 5,000ft above ground or 9,700ft above sea level.

It was a three hour POST (pilot selected) task in which the key rule to remember in this instance is that you cannot just shuttle back and forth between two turnpoints. You must use three or more turnpoints in any repeated sequence, and the trick in this particular day's weather – forecast to be strong Sierra Nevada wave to the mandatory ceiling of 17,500ft – was to choose a flattened north-south triangle or quadrilateral for your racetrack, with Minden roughly in the middle, and then zoom round it without wasting your time in circling or S-turning till the three hours were up.

Another relevant constraint was the limit of ten turnpoint pictures: 12 in total including start and finish. This meant you could only do three or four circuits, so if you were going very fast you had to choose a racetrack large enough – say, 200km per circuit – to avoid running out of film before the three hours expired. It seems that the fastest pilots did not hunt about from the primary to the secondary wave, as I did, but managed to stick to one or the other. That accordingly meant they did not have to dash through heavy sink, which required one to slow up again when lift was reached to restore the height lost.

Panic at the thought of dropping below 15,000ft and missing the wave would alternate rapidly with panic at the prospect of being sucked at never-exceed speed through 18,000ft and being disqualified. (Remember that at that height 120kts indicated is over 150kts true airspeed, and it is the true airspeed that determines the safe upper limit.) It was only within a very narrow window that you could relax and admire the dazzling view. Since Minden was visible in gin-clear air the whole time, any spectator with a sufficiently high-powered telescope could in theory have watched this soaring Indianapolis throughout and placed bets on the riders. I have to say that after my own three circuits at a paltry 145km/h I was happy to land. It was like finishing three massive bowls of one's favourite sticky pudding. Thanks, but I've had enough.

I notice I have been using food analogies a lot here. This must be to do with the difficulty in the USA of escaping from huge amounts of very inexpensive food, most of it delicious, and only some of it "interesting." It's amazing that everyone in the land is not 300lbs, though quite a few are. Such people don't often glide, of course.

— ∞ —

Hardened cynics (that is, any glider pilots with a pile of dog-eared logbooks) will not be at all surprised to hear that the best weather of the month of June was the week immediately after the Nationals, when the competitors had folded up their mobile homes and quietly stolen away.

Some of the more luxurious travelling gin-palaces literally do fold up: they concertina, at the touch of a switch, from a capacious 12ft wide on the field to a handy 8ft wide on the road. It's a disturbing experience, it you've not seen it previously, to watch and hear a monster caravan, with much whirring and heaving, attempt to vanish up its own back door.

One grand flight (1996)

Mike Bird describes how in the last week of June 1995 he did two 1,000km flights in the skies of Nevada and California with just two days' rest between. He also explains why.

Something very much like carelessness was to blame for my having to do two flights of well over 1,000 kms to get one FAI Diploma. Yet if I had done the first flight correctly I would have rested on my laurels and not attempted the second flight so soon after – if ever – which would have been a pity.

Superficially the raw statistics of the two attempts look identical. The task was identical. Take-off and finish times were about 10 minutes different. There was less than two per cent difference in achieved speed. Maximum heights were very nearly the same. But everything else that really mattered – where the good and bad conditions were to be found – was different.

— ∞ —

It is not actually cheating to get your 1,000 km Diploma by bringing a 60:1 sailplane to Minden and lying patiently in wait for The Great Day, but it comes pretty close. All you have to is to haul the best glider in the world to the best soaring site in the world (3,000 miles by road from Jacksonville, the port of entry in Florida), get briefed by local 1,000 kms expert Pat Philbrick, have your maps and declaration form marked up ready with the Pat's yo-yo (Start Rawe Peak; TP1, Keeler; TP2 Basalt; TP Radar Station; Finish Minden: see diagram 1) then plague the forecasters on the phone every morning. This is a game for old pilots with time on their hands. The rest of you will have to rely on exceptional luck or exceptional talent, of which I have neither.

Whereas the Sierras are a high and unbroken range, the ranges to the east are mostly lower and have gaps which require real work early in the day until – yes, wait for it – you get to the White Mountains 200kms south-southeast of Minden. They are not called White because of snow – often there is none, though there was plenty in 1995 – but for the pale-coloured rock. This 11,000 to 14,000 ft ridge is,

> ## Conversation piece (1995)
> *A friend of mine in England once landed miles from base, and there was nobody at the club willing or able to retrieve him (it must have been a quiet week day, since he is a perfectly reasonable guy, who does not make enemies easily) so in desperation he rang one of his ex-girlfriends (let's stress that EX) at her home, and pleaded for her to come to the club, hitch up his trailer and come out to get him. He must be one of the violin players of all time, for she eventually, if reluctantly, was persuaded to leave the comfort of her home late into the evening and retrieve him. I ought to offer readers a prize for the most convincing piece of dialogue between two former lovers as they meet in a ploughed field at midnight with the drizzle gently slanting down.*

when working, a glider pilot's paradise. Even hardened world champions go moist around the eyes when you mention the Whites. Pat's yo-yo is designed to enable an early start, and, after 200 kms of what may be struggle, to make use of four runs, each of 150 km, along the Whites during the best part of the day. If you are lucky, therefore, you get 600 km of your 1,000 km diploma in breathtaking conditions.

Talking about breath, reliable oxygen is mandatory, since you will be working between 10,000 and 15,000ft on a moderate day and between 13,000 and 18,000ft (the airspace limit) on a good day.

For those of you who aren't going to ferry a glider to the USA, I should mention that while some of the rental gliders might have idiosyncratic instruments, questionable total energy

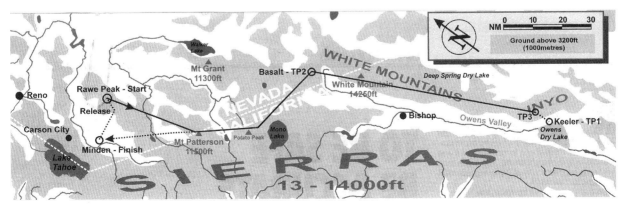

Steve Longland's map of the area.

plumbing and the odd dent in the sun-scorched glassfibre, they all have oxygen systems that work. When officialdom opens the wave "window", people take rented ships, following the rule that the best glider to take to great heights is somebody else's, to 35,000 ft plus. Can't have the paying customers passing out at altitude, it's bad for business. So you should feel pretty confident about renting a Minden glider from that point of view.

The idea is to be launched by one of Tony Sabino's Soar Minden tugs before the valley thermals have started: this entails releasing close to 11 am at 7,900 feet over the Pine Nuts mountain range (3,200ft above Minden) using a suntrap which Pat Philbrick swears will always work, where the dirt roads snake through a pass in the lowest part of the range. (Getting back to Minden Airport if the suntrap doesn't work would depend on there being no sink, and would certainly concentrate the mind if you were in a standard class glider. There are a couple of dirt strips *en route* that barely might suffice, however.)

Having released, found lift and crawled up out of the pass to a more reassuring height you then make your way north to Rawe peak a few miles south of Dayton County airport (which is fine for any 15-metre glider to land at but not for 25.4 metres, since there are rather tall runway lights roughly 20 metres apart), snap your Remote Start picture of a bunch of huts & aerials at the extreme north end of the Pine Nuts, and you are on your way. That means you have to soar about 16 km further than the 1,015 km of the task itself, but because the area starts working so early it is worth the extra distance.

It was now a matter of waiting for the right day. It soon came, though to the frustration of the many and the delight of just a few. The week immediately after the Open Class Nationals at Minden, with its very mixed weather including three consecutive days scrubbed, was the possibly the best week in 1995. (It was ever thus.) Indeed I believe that anybody with enough stamina, and a willingness to work around the overdeveloped areas on the days when I stayed on the ground, could have done five 1,000 km flights in a week.

— ∞ —

The first attempt was made on June 24th. Only later did I remember that this was exactly two years after my 758km Diploma flight in England. The Pine Nuts were working only moderately well, and indeed on the 200km journey down to the Whites I averaged only about 90kph, well under the 120 kph that I regarded as essential if I was to get home before 8.30 pm. The long spine rising up from Topaz valley to Mount Patterson is often hard work, the steep slopes needing to be scratched and ridge-soared every inch, and the morning of 24th June was no different.

Finally I reached the fabled White Mountains, muttering to myself discontentedly about the pathetic speed achieved so far. And then it was just as Pat had prophesied. His yo-yo task is designed to give four runs along 150 km of more or less continuous lift. In that 600 km I stopped to circle on four occasions, and that was twice too often. I experimented first with dolphining, zooming from 110 knots to 40 then plummeting back again. Each zoom added a thousand feet or more; the subsequent plummet through the sink subtracted most of that but not all. I was relieved not to have a passenger with a delicate stomach to consider. The dolphining was exhilarating and worked well enough, since I steadily gained height in this way, averaging 70 to 80 knots over the ground. By way of a change, in the next tour over the same terrain (what you might call Yo-2 of the Yo-yo, as opposed to Yo-1) I tried flying at a steady 100 knots regardless of the vario. The GPS, however, indicated between 120 and 140 knots ground-speed (230 to 260 kph) depending on the wind component and the altitude. This time I gained no height overall but just devoured the ground.

The first time I had flown the length of the Whites, during the Barron Hilton week in 1994 I left the range with excessive optimism and insufficient height across a desert without cultivation or airstrips, and landed the LS-4 in a dry lake (well, on it rather than in it, thank heavens). This time I had a better glider but conditions were similar. I took all the height I could get and set off at a sceptical 60-70 knots toward Minden. The abruptness with which the day deteriorated justified my caution. Every cauliflower cumulus ran to seed as I approached. It was the morning's struggle in reverse. I clambered over Mt. Patterson's southern slopes, fell into Topaz valley and took everything that looked, smelt or felt like a thermal. Water was dumped, both of the drinkable and undrinkable variety.

But heck, it was almost the longest day of the year and it was just past seven pm and this was an ASH-25 with one pilot and no water, why was I fretting? The much-needed thermals, after teasing me a while, took pity and lifted me gently into the Carson Valley and to a joyous champagne reception. It was all over but for the mere routine of photographs, declarations and the other bits of paperwork. All over, did I say?

One grand flight (again) (1996)

Disaster struck. I had photographed Basalt itself (which is a ghastly mess of mine-workings so far as I can tell) and not the road junction nearby. The road junction was specified in the declaration co-ordinates, which I had written out and signed. The junction did in fact appear in the photos but at the wrong angle. This blunder was due not to simple stupidity, but to complex stupidity – a more intractable kind, and much more difficult to cure. The reason was that in the competition the week before (and in all US competitions) the *turn-point* and the *aiming-point for the camera* are two different places, about a kilometre apart. You pirouette directly over the *turn-point* and snap the *aiming-point*. So I drew all my sectors laboriously through the Basalt photographic aiming-point and not through the turn-point proper. If you are confused that's fine, don't worry, you know how I felt.

Three days later, after a much-needed rest and choosing not to launch into thundery, overdeveloped skies for two days, I started again, about 10 minutes earlier than before. I eventually finished about 20 minutes earlier than before, so you might think that the two flights were much the same. But that is the extraordinary thing about soaring. You can't do the same flight twice.

The trip from Rawe peak to the Whites was quite astonishing: five knots at Rawe Peak at 1105, seven knots at Segal 20 minutes later and eight to ten knots between Sweetwater and Potato Peak before noon, with none of the familiar struggles up the spine of Patterson. Obviously I was going to do a sensational

time. Obviously? This time the Whites did not behave as the Whites should: no wings-level dolphining was possible. Good thermals, but no continuous lift. By comparison with the previous attempt, this was the slow portion of the flight. There I was, grousing at the fact that I had to stop and circle in eight knots.

On the return from the Whites around six PM, the whole area from Patterson to Minden looked stone dead. Gaps in this part of the world are vast. So I made a long, slightly worried glide to a cu-nim over Walker Lake, 90 degrees off track and about 100 kms from home. This dark and occasionally rainy cloud finally wafted me up to 17,000 ft, but like a fool I fretted about making it back, in case there was headwind or sink. As I tiptoed at 55kts due west directly into the setting sun – a time of day and a direction of flight that always make it very difficult to see anything on the ground at all – the flat, shiny object in the far distance baffled me for a long time

Minden: the other diamond mine (1995)

I should explain a few basic facts about Minden. It is 4,700 ft above sea level, lying between the Sierra Nevada and the Pine Nuts, a big range and a parallel small range running roughly NNW-SSE. Nevada means Snowy, by the way, and this really applied in 1995, when snows were especially heavy. Although the Sierras are spectacularly beautiful and are a renowned wave source, they are rarely used in thermal flights. The ranges to the east face the sun and the prevailing westerlies, and are the preferred terrain for summer distance attempts and competition tasks. They also have broad valley floors that are sort of landable. Where you can land on the west side of the Sierras the Lord alone knows. The only fellow who ever won a contest day going down the Sierras (using their western slopes, picking his way through lakes and trees that cover a very high rugged plateau) instead of the ranges to the east was a foreigner who didn't know any better. For some reason the east was washed out on that day, so he did the right thing by accident and got 2,000 points, since visitors' points are scaled relative to the best performance by a local US pilot. They still talk about it, many years later.

until I realised it was Lake Tahoe. Obviously if I could keep seeing the surface of Lake Tahoe, nearly 2,000 ft above Minden and 30 kms to the west of Minden, I did not have to be Euclid to work out that I had plenty of height. The nose went down. The champagne corks popped again and this time the sectors and all the other paperwork were OK. With the rather complicated start procedure in the morning and the detour in the evening, I had flown something over 1,100 kms.

An hour later, when it was very dark indeed and while I was telling everybody about my having come back just in time, Tom Kreyche appeared out of the shadows from the same direction in his Discus. It seemed as if that big old cu-nim was not at its last gasp at all but had gone on stoking itself for nearly two hours. That was the good news. The next day the developing people, instead of heeding Tom's strict injunction to leave his film in a continuous strip, cut it up in the usual way. He had to do the task all over later in the season. Murphy's Law strikes again.

For the record, only three people beat 1,000 kms flying from Minden in the 1995 season: Rick Walters in the above-mentioned Discus; Rick's partner in the Discus, Tom Kreyche (who did it twice because of his photo-foul-up); and Platypus flying his ASH-25 (who also did it twice because of his photo-foul-up).

Now it can be told – up to a point (1995)

US immigration (1995)

I do wonder about the green form you have to fill in for US Immigration, putting you on your honour to assure them that you have never taken part in genocide or terrorism. That must stop the crazed killers in their tracks, I bet. When I first came to the USA the visa application form asked, "Is it your intention to overthrow the government of the USA by force?" and a chap I know wrote down, "Sole purpose of visit." He still got his visa, which proves how tolerant people are over there. "Are you here on business, pleasure or terrorism, sir?" "Well, I hope I can fit in a bit of all three." "Say, that's just great; enjoy your stay, take care and have a nice day now."

I'm back in Uvalde after four years, girding up my loins to take part in what the Texans modestly call the Texas Nationals (don't query that claim if you wish for a quiet life) and memories flood back. After the passage of those years, I think it's time this column discreetly revealed the fact that the fun and games in Uvalde in 1991 between visiting World Championships teams and ladies of the Lone Star State were not confined to the French, though one member of the French *équipe* did earn his Green Card in the nicest possible way, and is now happily assimilated into Texas society.

One of the younger non-flying members of the British team is said to have had a torrid romance with a Uvaldean and was all set to go back over Christmas 1991 to pick up where he had left off, so to speak. A friend met him in the new year and asked how the trip went. "Nothing doing," was the glum reply, "her husband came back!" Very tricky that kind of thing in Texas: anywhere south of the Mason-Dixon line jurors are apt to take a very lenient attitude towards husbands who perforate their wives' boyfriends with anything from a Saturday night special to an AK-47. (Mason and Dixon were a couple of British surveyors, by the way, who knew where to draw the line, which is more than can be said for the British team members in 1991.)

It must have been the heat: age was certainly no barrier to Cupid's laser beam. Thus the most senior and distinguished gentleman in our entourage was snapped up by a Texas lady who specialises in collecting fine old English antiques. Well, she's got an elegant specimen there to be sure, and very hard wearing, too. A yearly rubdown with linseed oil and wire wool and he should last more or less indefinitely. An absolute bargain.

(What about you, Plat? Ed.)

Well, er – Good Heavens, we seem to have run out of space...

A fax From Minden

This issue's "Tail Feathers" comes to readers of *S&G* from Minden, Nevada, where I've been alternating landscape photography on the ground with gliding along the Sierras in the company of a distinguished former chairman of the BGA. In this climate, and at my age, and

with the lust for records, badges and diplomas already satisfied on previous trips, I'm happy to fly just every second day. The DFCBGA and I look off the day before yesterday in the Grob 103, rented from Tony Sabino, owner of the Soar Minden. Distinguished former chairman had not flown for nine years, having taken up croquet and photography instead (either a sad sign of senility or the beginnings of wisdom, depending on your own point of view) and I was eager to demonstrate both the excellence of the Sierra wave and the excellence of my skill in exploiting it.

Such eagerness and pride must inevitably lead to a fall – or in this case a plummet. I unerringly released in the trough of the wave at 2,500ft above the valley floor and descended at 700ft a minute, landing seconds after the tug, to be greeted by a chorus of, "Whaddya you two doing back here?" etc. The next time, better luck – and better communication with the tug – led to a rough but positive ascent into steadily smoother air and a swift ride to 18,000ft, the usual ceiling for gliders. Distinguished former chairman was much impressed and took lots of photos. These pictures will come in handy as postcards of the "Wish you were here" variety, designed solely to provoke furious envy in the recipient.

Talking about wilful provocation of envy – two years ago an Australian pilot dropped in at Minden and, being without a passenger, I took him up in the ASH-25. We did a brisk 500kms local-soaring the Sierras. I do literally mean local-soaring– we did 125 kms to the south and back, then 125kms to the north and back again, always within gliding range of Minden from 18,000 ft. In the back seat he would frequently focus his video recorder on the instrument panel while crowing into the microphone, "Eatcha heart out, Bruce: look, 120kts at 18,000ft!" Apparently he regularly

swapped tapes with a gliding friend and this particular tape was going to turn Bruce quite green. The thought obviously gave my passenger even more pleasure than the flying itself. The urge to make one's friends sick with jealousy is an innocent desire which I can entirely understand, and to which I myself give way whenever I get the chance.

Back to the DFCBGA – after 250kms wandering up and down the range we heard that a legal wave "window" was now open to 25,000ft. At 22,000ft, however, 20 wrinkled old toes were getting frozen and we were running out of oxygen, so we pulled out the brakes and dived back to Minden. (You mean you fumbled the wave and made a virtue out of a necessity? Ed Well, yes. Plat.) This was a case of an ill wind blowing some good: a young pilot who sorely needed his height Diamond gratefully seized the 103 and took it straight to 25,000ft. Our chilled extremities – and our fumble – did him a favour. Back on the ground I met another young pilot who last year got his height Diamond – wait for it – the same day that he went solo. Eatcha – no, stop eating your hearts out and buy an air ticket.

I tell my American friends that it is simply not true that English glider pilots like drinking warm beer. It is just that they start crying into their beer when they read about conditions in the USA.

— ooo —

A word of warning. This is a land of extremes. It can go quickly from being too easy to horribly difficult. Today, for instance, was gin-clear with 8 and 9kt thermals and wave. Trouble is, one gets nervous below 15,000ft because there are vast spaces which are unlandable – not to mention heavy sink. Glider pilots locally did once think of banding together to clear a strip of desert scrub near Lake Mono in California to cater for the possible outlanding in the middle of a vast area of nothing. A splendid idea? Not in the opinion of the Federal anti-drug squad who feared that such a strip would be used by armed narcotics smugglers flying from Mexico. Indeed it is suggested that if in trouble in a lonely area you should not land next to a light plane in the hope of getting help. You just might get shot instead.

— ooo —

Much concern is being felt by American glider pilots at the threat to ban all types of gliders from the great national parks – in which the DFCBGA and I have recently spent much time with tripods (a sure index of a serious photographer) and black and white film with orange filters (an even surer sign of a serious photographer, causing ordinary tourists with their point-and-click cameras to step back respectfully). Without wanting to say, "I told you so," I do remember writing about this threat in *S&G* some years ago after encountering scores of hang gliders, paragliders and conventional gliders swarming around every crag in the French Alps. At what point, I asked, do these stop being an occasional and attractive enhancement to the scenery and start becoming an eyesore? Conventional gliders usually fly higher, though some pilots can't resist the sadistic thrill of making low passes at 150kts over hikers. The irony is that ground-borne visitors are the ones that inflict the physical damage and pollution with millions of boots and car exhausts.

However, lovers of nature and the environment, splendid folks that they are at heart, are not in the Kasparov or IBM Deep Blue league when it comes to relentless logic and consistency. In Germany an environmental group has tried to stop a gliding club's operations because the gliders on the approach might disturb some rare species of fauna. If the glider pilots were grounded, it does not occur to the extreme environmentalists that the frustrated soarers might pollute the atmosphere by having to drive many miles further to find a site, or that they might take up power flying, or take four-wheel-drive vehicles across vulnerable terrain, to get their kicks. If they prevent a young chap doing something potentially

unfriendly to the flora or fauna, do they expect him to stay in bed all day, or simply drop dead? Maybe that's what they do expect: it is said that the only time we are perfectly integrated with our environment is when we are buried.

In France a glider pilot bought a farmhouse near the field where he flew; not long afterwards he was complaining bitterly about the noise of tugs. In Britain, airline pilots retire to country cottages next to long established gliding clubs, then – you guessed it.

Since I wrote that piece, I found on a 1997 summertime trip to the USA that all roads into Yosemite National Park in California were closed to visitors. Reason? Not snow, or rockfalls or forest fires, but just too many cars and too many people.

The Jeep from Hell (1987)

In a small town that I will not name, somewhere in the western USA, there's a man bowling happily along in a spotless Jeep with about 150,000 miles on the clock. My friends know the garage where he has it serviced; there's no doubt that he is a contented owner of a fine set of wheels. And so he should be. That Jeep he bought was like George Washington's axe, which, as the museum owner said, is the original apart from the new head and new handle. I should know, because I sold the Jeep to him, converting his cheque into sterling and skipping the country. There are parts of the USA where they don't use lawyers, and instead of getting mad they get a licence to take a rifle into public places like restaurants, lavatories and glider hangars.

In 1995 I was planning a trip with an ASH-25 around the USA. At my request Marion Barritt bought a used Jeep, Plat being sure that four-wheel-drive was essential. Having sampled in previous years an alfalfa field, a set-aside meadow and a dry lake bed, I felt sure I would land out in some inaccessible place in 1995. An old Ford or General Motors car would not do.

When the glider was unloaded from the RO-RO-RO (known in the seagoing trade as Roll On, Roll Off and Roll Over) at Jacksonville docks, the first thing Marion found was that if

she towed at more than 40mph, the normally well-behaved ASH-25 trailer, veteran of all of Europe, Australia, and the USA in the World Championships in 1991, wanted to force the Jeep to sniff the flowers, first at one side of the road then the other. As soon as I arrived in Florida I tried it, and simply couldn't keep it straight. "Ah," said the nice man who sold tires in Orlando, "those tires are the wrong spec. The guy you bought the Jeep from economised by putting skinny little tires on when the previous lot wore out." A pity, since the skinny tires were fairly new. When the improvement with the big, chunky new tires proved to be barely detectable, the even nicer man who sold steering components said we needed new steering components; there was far too much play in the old ones. At 50mph the Jeep and trailer were now tolerable so long as there were no side winds, bends in the road or trucks going by. Of the 12,000 miles of driving we did with that trailer, I doubt if I did a thousand. Marion did all the rest.

When in May we got to Tom Knauff's airfield in Pennsylvania to fly the amazing Appalachian ridges, home of Karl Striedieck and cradle of hundreds of Thousands, I asked Tom if the Jeep's engine really ought to clatter like that. We had weaved and clattered through six states without any serious symptoms apart from the clattering getting more strident.

"No, it shouldn't at all! That engine is finished," he said. He was right. So in the nearest town we found a lovely guy who sold as-new engines. His team made heroic efforts to install a new engine (well, when I say *new* I mean it had survived a wreck in a pretty new vehicle) in time for our trek westwards across the USA.

However, in Ohio late the next day, when I asked a garage-hand what might be causing the rear windscreen to film over with thousands of tiny oil droplets, he said he only sold gasoline but he was sure it was bad news.

He was right, too. He knew a splendid man who would fix it. It turned out that in the wreck from which our engine had been rescued, the cover that goes over the tappets and valves and other bits had been cracked, and oil was spewing everywhere. Total seizure of Jeep (and Platypus) was imminent. You can tell that I know nothing about cars; so could they, by my glazed look and a reflex move towards my credit card. This dire news entailed another heroic 24-hour engineering effort. After that the engine itself gave no trouble, barring a couple of incidents. During the crossing of Missouri, Kansas and Colorado the Jeep behaved itself. However, in the middle of the Utah desert, on a long, slow gradient, the engine boiled over and the temperature soared into the red. We just waited for an age, put in fresh water and gently pressed on. For some arbitrary reason, the engine behaved itself till we reached Nevada, despite steeper mountains and more pitiless sun.

Then, like squabbling children, the other bits of the Jeep felt it was their turn to clamour for attention. I won't list them all, except for one special favourite in the memories of all involved.

The electric window winding and door-locking mechanism had died and had been replaced, to all appearances satisfactorily. In July my friends Robin, Paul and Pete from Dunstable came out, pining for long distance soaring in the ASH-25. The conditions did not suit closed-circuits, so a brilliant straight distance record flight was made by Robin and Paul, 900kms eastwards towards Grand Teton. That's the mountain you see at the beginning of a Columbia Pictures movie. On the long drive through Idaho, Pete got out of the Jeep at 2.30am while the engine was running. He needed to get water from the containers in the back of the jeep. The engine was using vast quantities of water again, even at night. While he was walking round, the Jeep promptly locked all four doors and tailgate. He carried no spare key.

It is a good thing Pete is not given to hysteria. Walking back towards civilization along this deserted road, Pete eventually met a policewoman, who drove him back to the Jeep. She was very helpful, and kindly offered to shoot the lock off. An alternative but slower solution was to let the car run out of gas in a few hours' time, then maybe the electrics would allow him ingress. Or they could stuff something up the exhaust and stop the engine, with whatever side-effects that might have. The best solution of all manifested itself when at 3.30am a locksmith came out for a fraction of what they charge in England and got into the Jeep. After that, none of us ever got out of that vehicle without clutching the key tightly in one's fist.

I ought to say, in fairness to this much-abused (verbally abused, that is: physically it was treated like the Crown Jewels) Jeep, that although the essential items like engine, doors, windows, wheels and steering failed, the luxury items behaved well, if in that climate you call the continuous and refreshing blast of cold air from the air-conditioning a luxury. And for three thousand miles the car radio never faltered, riveting us with non-stop reports of the O J Simpson murder trial.

Then while we drove across the Nevada deserts in the dark, seeing maybe one other vehicle every 15 minutes, the local radio stations solemnly fed us, by way of a change, terrifying eye-witness tales of extra-terrestrials – in collusion with uniformed members of the US military and the United Nations – stopping cars, then kidnapping, experimenting upon and physically abusing citizens and aliens (foreign nationals, I mean) from the very road we were on, known as The Loneliest Road in the West. Your wallet could tell it was The Loneliest Road in the West as gasoline prices, in the few tiny towns distributed at hundred-mile intervals along our trail, rocketed up from a sixth of British prices to a quarter of British prices. The Jeep's faultless cassette-player entertained us with unabridged novels on tape, marketed to long-distance drivers who can't stand talk-radio. Talk-radio is for people who can't stand Country & Western singers.

Naturally you are curious to know, after all that agony, did we ever use the four-wheel-drive during 1995, that having been the sole reason for buying the Jeep rather than a big old Chevy station-wagon at half the price? No. Did we ever use the Jeep for any retrieve at all in a whole year's flying? Not once. But Fate lays perverse traps for the unprepared; if I had not had an all-terrain vehicle, who knows where I would have ended up? In 1998 I'll drive a Ford Bronco, a steady towcar with a monster 4.6 litre V8 engine. Marion bought this one too, from a pillar of society, just like the man who sold us the Jeep. My brow is unclouded by worry.

(Can I commission you to write "The Ford Bronco from Hell" in 12 months' time? Ed. Just watch this space. Plat.)

The Ford Bronco is doing fine and tows trailers without complaint or shimmy. Unlike the Jeep it boils not, neither does it spin.

As to the policewoman's proffered pistol, imagine the phone conversation we might have had afterwards. "Plat, I'm sorry but the Jeep's shot." "Well, it was getting pretty tired." "No, I mean it has two .38-calibre police slugs in it!" That would have silenced even me.

When ignorance is bliss, 'tis folly to be wise (1995)

Despite my uncanny ability, with trailer in tow, to end droughts and make deserts bloom, it takes a lot more of a curse than I and my ship can muster to spoil the 1995 Texas Nationals in Uvalde. Cloudbases were certainly lower than in the 1991 World Championships (6,000 to 7,000ft rather than 8,000 to 10,000ft-plus) and average thermal strengths correspondingly less powerful (5 to 6kt rather than 8kt) but for sheer consistency it is difficult to beat Texas. Texas is where I would head if I were coming to the USA to soar cross-country for ten days or less – and if I had access to a privately owned high performance glider, since renting good machines in Texas is difficult. The mountains of Nevada are more spectacular, the climate more pleasant and glass gliders are readily available for hire – but you should budget for more than ten days, since there can be occasional holes in what are usually the world's finest soaring conditions.

I did win just one day in the Open Class in Uvalde, so naturally I shall write about that and skip the rest; there's no silly nonsense about fairness and objectivity in this column.

Coming first is its own reward.

The first task of the contest was a 500km triangle with the last turnpoint at Laredo, way down south on the Rio Grande, which is the US/Mexican border. All the local experts told me afterwards that nobody starts a 500km task before 2.30pm in a big ship. Not knowing the conventional wisdom, I set off at 1pm with Duncan Cumming, an ex-Briton now a naturalised Californian (an ancestor of his was knifed to death by Robert the Bruce in a church, if you are interested) in the back seat of the ASH-25. Deciding never to circle so long as we had at least 4,000ft above ground, we found splendid stretches of as much as 100km that could be covered by pure dolphining, wings level. "This is the life!" we crowed. The absolute joy of soaring, and no mistake.

Then far to the south we saw streaks of high cloud, early warnings of massed stratus and rain coming to meet us. If we had been making a movie this apparition would have been accompanied by a low, menacing rumble of bass fiddles, as in Jaws. A hurricane in the Gulf of Mexico, the pet name of which I have forgotten (as you know, hurricanes now alternate male and female names to placate the politically correct lobby) was spreading its baleful influence northwards, and its outliers soon fell across our track. So, back to good old English soaring technique – a slow 30km glide into wind from 7,000ft at the end of the cloud-street to the turn, then 40km back through dead air to capture the rapidly receding cumulus. But our troubles were over: more joyous dolphining merged effortlessly into a final glide to finish with a 128km/h average speed.

Naturally, being a coarse glider pilot and no gentleman (I can't speak for Duncan) I had a very satisfying cackle at the prospects for the experts who departed after 2pm, since the murk was spreading relentlessly over the whole southern part of the task area. Most of them suffered dreadfully and arrived back at Uvalde after the free beer and food had been consumed by you know who. However it was our only moment of glory: the weather never again took Charlie Spratt, the contest director, or the other pilots by surprise, and over the next six days I slid gently towards the bottom of the rankings where I belonged, as true soaring skill prevailed over luck.

I have enjoyed two-seater flying enormously. I have learned a huge amount flying with National champions, World champions and record holders like Robin May, Hans-Werner Grosse, Brian Spreckley and John Williamson, and in the Alps with Bill Malpas and John Good in the mountains in Pennsylvania, not to mention geniuses like John Jeffries and Jacques Noël. It is the best way of expanding one's horizons without scaring the daylights out of oneself or jeopardising the glider.

I also find no difficulty in getting people to help me rig the ASH-25 either in hopes of future flights or as a thank you for past flights. There are also marginal days when I would not bother to rig and fly a solo machine, but in the 25, because someone else is keen to fly with me or because I have promised them a cross-country and don't want to let them down, I have gone and had some amazing flying. So the utilisation is very high. At one time I calculated that the cost per achieved cross-country seat-mile for our ASH-25 was six times cheaper than for any other glider in the club.

Power corrupts... (1999)

As I surveyed the ugly terrain below, I realised there was nowhere to land. Instead there was a muddy lake with a scattering of rocks around its rim, then rough, undulating scrub, and then steep walls on every side, higher than I was. And I was descending at 300ft a minute whichever way I turned.

How had I got myself into this fix? Overconfidence, as usual.

Then I saw a wisp of cloud against the relentless blue. My forehead was furrowed, my mouth dry, my hands clammy, my stomach knotted, my –

(Please don't descend any further down your anatomy – this is a family paper and we get the general drift. Ed.)

Yes, I was worried. The wisp, a mile away, grew into a puff. Still sinking, I tried to hypnotise the tiny cloud into growing.

Finally I arrived under the burgeoning vapour, swung into a steep left bank at 58 knots and ten degrees of flap. The rate of climb indicator slowly moved to zero sink, then to an increasingly confident ascent, settling at six knots up all round the circle. I was not going to become a vulture's lunch this time, after all.

But had I learned anything from yet another scare?

Indeed I had. Next time I went cross-country in the Sierras, I had better fly in something with more horsepower than a Cessna 152 – for that indeed was the aircraft I was piloting. Unless, of course, I relished a challenge that called upon every one of my 41 seasons of soaring experience. And I suppose I do relish such a challenge. That 300ft per minute descent over unlandable desert was in spite of the Cessna's throttle being pushed to the firewall. The lift in that part of the world is something I am always shouting about, but what goes up must come down, and when you are at 10,000 ft and the temperatures are high, little planes with little engines do literally need to be soared. I would never have got six knots climb at that height without assistance from thermal or wave. In this environment a gliding background is an essential accomplishment, not a luxury.

"What's this?" you splutter. "Plat's become a power pilot? A traitor to the Cause?" I apologise if any of you were eating soup at the moment you started to read this.

I don't know what came over me, but quite suddenly one day at Minden I thought, "Why don't I get my single-engine licence? It's cheap, the weather's wonderful and there are hardly any airspace problems." The opposite is the case in Britain, where it costs a fortune, the weather is murky and wet most of the time, and much of the air that isn't full of airliners is full of military hardware, with the fun-flyers all crammed dangerously into the little bit that's left. Sixteen days and 30 hours after that inspiration in Minden I took my test, passed it somehow, and glued an FAA certificate in my logbook.

There were one or two rational excuses for this move. I have a very good friend who is always inviting me to fly round exotic parts of the world in various light planes. What has up till now put me off accepting these kind invitations is my observation – when flying together in my glider – that this friend was born without nerves, or they were surgically removed at birth. Faced with any situation in which ordinary pilots would turn ghastly pale with fright, my friend goes, "Wheeee! Isn't this exciting?" We crashed my Caproni some years ago because my friend's expressions of delight drowned out the sound of my teeth chattering. The latter noise is Nature's way of reminding me that I am very near the ground, devoid of ideas, and am about to die unless I do something intelligent, by way of a change, very soon. The Good Lord implanted the instinct of Fear in most of us, with the odd exception of my friend, with a view to preserving the species. How my friend's ancestors got this far I can't imagine, but I suspect that the danger posed by hereditary fearlessness has been outweighed by an even stronger procreative drive, so that the breed has not become extinct. *Au contraire.*

Anyway, I now feel that I will now have some glimmering of what my friend is doing in the air, and that will somehow be reassuring. It could turn out to be the opposite of reassuring, of course, since I shall now know just enough to be seriously concerned. In that event, a lead-weighted sock in my pocket will be used to stage a swift in-flight mutiny. I'll deal with the court case later.

a lead-weighted sock...

Baiting the hook (1999)

To persuade speakers to leave the comfort of their homes and cross the Atlantic in winter time, a conference organiser must resort to every kind of bribe and inducement, so long as the budget can stand it. If the chosen speaker is a real bigwig, and is featured in a plenary session of all delegates (that is, not competing with two other guys in concurrent sessions) or is giving the after-dinner oration, then the organiser can offer a luxury hotel or even, it is rumoured, a transatlantic air ticket. I've had very fancy hotels on two occasions, but not the air ticket. Sorry – that sounds like a crude hint to would-be convention committees. It really is not. What follows, however, is most emphatically a hint to anybody who is listening.

At the Soaring Society of America Convention in Knoxville, Tennessee, in February 1999, the Chairman, François Pin, needed a star speaker for one of the concurrent sessions. So naturally he asked – Justin Wills. However, Justin couldn't make it. So, working down some list (I'd like to see that list) François eventually lit upon me. By now the budget was exhausted and the only thing he could offer was – wait for it – his own brand-new ASW-27, to be flown by me in Florida at the Seniors Championships, better known as Geezerglide, in early March.

That shows how desperate people can get when they are trying to fill a speaker-programme. One reason why François was willing to part with the ASW-27 for ten days was that he wished to fly another glider in Florida, namely his PW5. He would be flying hors concours, naturally, since he is far too young to qualify as a geezer. He wanted to get contest practice in the World-Class before the 1999 World-Class World Championships in Poland. So if it were not for the PW5, I would not have had the lovely ASW-27 to fly. For that reason alone, and for no other, I have a soft spot for the little 13.5 metre Polish ship. Thus it was that when I gave my talk at the SSA Convention "Sixty minutes wasted with Platypus" I told the audience that I felt unable

to make jokes about a) tiny gliders and b) Frenchmen.

However that moral obligation has long gone – it was only meant to last sixty minutes, and I am amazed at my restraint so far. Besides, so many jokes, mostly in appalling taste and some couched in dreadful verse, have been made in the USA about FP and the PW5 and The Bull, that I see no point in holding myself back while others let rip.

My impression as a spectator on the other side of the thermal was that the PW5 climbed splendidly, just like a Skylark 3. However it seems to descend just like a Skylark 3. Not bad at all, considering the difference in span of about 15 feet. Naturally the PW5 tends to land out more often than a modern 15-metre ship, even in the hands of top pilots, especially if the wind is unhelpful. (I am trying my damnedest to be tactful, you can see.)

Anyway, while the rest of us were drinking our evening beer on the verandah back at Seminole Lake, François landed in a Florida pasture, and carefully put a brown cover over the canopy. This presumably makes the front of a PW5 look like the back end of a cow. No, that is NOT my opinion, says he, looking nervously over his shoulder for libel lawyers, but it clearly was the opinion of a large, overamorous bull.

A quarter-century ago at the great annual French contest les *Huit Jours d'Angers*, loosely translated as the Eight Days of Danger, the formidable Director at the first briefing commanded us, "Go onto the field and mount your gliders!" (I think he meant us to rig them). I replied that we loved our gliders, but not that much. However the Florida bull did indeed love François's PW5, though the effect of his

mounting it was more likely to derig it. A great hoof went through the canopy. Then, like the US Cavalry, François's crew turned up and, having been brung up on a ranch, shooed the beast away with an fearless flick of the wrist. The bull either recognised an experienced no-nonsense cow-hand, or more probably decided the PW5 wasn't very good in bed, but in any event it clambered off and skulked away, muttering to itself.

Of course this story made many more column-inches in the local newspapers than the entire US Seniors competition. That's the media for you. And since S&G is part of the media, we dwell on it inordinately too. Much play was made of the fact that the French are experts in all aspects of love (a legend assiduously spread by the French, as you and I know) but that this encounter was something to astonish even a Frenchman. The next day, back at Seminole lake, where with glue and yards of scotch tape François patiently got the canopy ready for the day's task, I said that since the PW5 patently lacked penetration (otherwise it would not have landed in that field) the bull was kindly offering some. Other jokes were not fit for this journal. ■

The Mystery of Met (1999)

Frankly, I have never understood weather. Indeed that is the very reason why I love competitions: after a leisurely breakfast I am told by professionals, who have been up since five o' clock, exactly where to go and when I can start. Beautifully printed weather charts and task details are handed out to the pampered, spoonfed pilots. There's no agonising about meteorology. That's all been done for us. Add a bit of dedicated leeching and you can have a worry-free contest, with no serious challenge to the intellect once you're airborne, at least not until the crew calls up to say she has the peebags in her pocket and you have the car-keys in yours.

I only got my British 750km Diploma because Robin May had done the forecasts and planned the task while I was driving at Never-Exceed speed to the Club. Now I have started a Big Distance Group at Dunstable with much the same aim: get others to do the work.

If you are one of the lower echelons this approach to life is called bone-bloody-idleness and earns severe contempt. At my level of seniority it's called delegation and – in business at any rate – earns millions and invitations to Buckingham Palace.

Falling apart gracefully

Dr Alex Comfort, the author of a book we all read years ago called The Joy of Sex, *followed that best-seller many years later with* The Joy of Ageing. *No, I didn't read the second book, and neither did you. For some reason, age doesn't sell the way sex does.*

Yes, it is nice to have grand-children. It's like flying rental aircraft. After you get bored playing with them for a few hours you hand them back to their owners to be washed, refuelled and put to bed. All you have to do is find an armchair and a bottle of Glenfiddich in a room far removed from the noise of battle. You can enjoy Power without Responsibility, as Stanley Baldwin said in another context.

Physical and mental decline is no joke, however. Which is precisely why as I said in the chapter about Money, we can't help treating this solemn subject with coarse, ribald hilarity

---

Mentioning the unmentionable (1986)

This bit is for boys only. One of those splendidly witty women who write for S&G nowadays can describe their side of this problem, and I can't wait to see what they have to say. I refer to the dilemma–no, a dilemma is when there are just two unacceptable alternatives: this is a positive quandary, all the several answers being uncomfortable in every way–of how to have a pee in a glider. It never occurred to me before that there might be some advantages to hang-gliding other than cost, but now one advantage, of a sort, immediately leaps to mind. How high you have to be before you are free of any risk of prosecution for indecent exposure I don't know, though personally I'd worry more about frostbite, or buzzards, than the Law.

To return to the challenge as presented to the male pilot of the conventional sailplane: there seems no logic to it. Sometimes you can

If an official observer signs the bag it might become a novel TP confirmation.

fly nine hours and have no problems; sometimes it can get you after just 30 minutes, as happened to me in a Nationals on one of those epic flights round Wales and back to civilisation. (There go our three Welsh subscribers. Ed.) Seven and a half hours of discomfort rising relentlessly towards agony. No bags, bottles, tubes–total lack of *preparedness.* I began to regret, not for the first time, the gap in my education when I failed to make the grade in the Boy Scouts. When I eventually gave up the battle and landed at Bicester they couldn't understand why I steered the Nimbus right up to the far hedge and baled out over the side away from the control tower.

You mustn't risk dehydration, so you have to drink lots, and what goes in has to come out sooner or later. Well, to be accurate, a biologist told me that most of the fluid we take in comes out in *sweat,* believe it or not. (Anyone who has flown with me believes it.) We should be thankful for small mercies: we only have to find a home for about 40%.

The high-technology solution is a system of vessels and pipes leading to the outer air down near the tow-hook (preferably *aft* of the hook, if corrosion is something that bothers you, which it should). I won't go into the squalid details, but the chief snag about what looks like a very impressive piece of plumbing is that the pilot is supine–on his back, or very nearly so, with knees on a level with his chin, depending on the attitude of the aircraft–and therefore confronted with the difficulty of making water go uphill at the beginning of its journey into the void. Putting the glider into a steep dive to get the right angle of dangle is not a good idea for a number of obvious reasons. Try it by all means, but not if you are getting on in years, since the dive could be prolonged.

Then there are plastic bags stolen from the domestic freezer-cabinet: these must be pre-tested, please, in the time-honoured way, since you don't want to discover a tiny defect at 5,000ft, do you? You can either jettison the bag whole or empty it while delicately holding onto one corner. The first is an environmentally anti-social act. The bags doubtless arrive on the ground empty, but farmers don't like their animals eating plastic. You could always tie a knot in it (the neck of the bag, I mean) and drop it on the clubhouse roof at a rival site. If you could get an official observer to sign the bag before take-off it might become a novel form of turn-point confirmation. However this sort of thing might escalate dangerously, so let's discard the idea.

Holding onto corner of the bag is tricky. Best to wear ski-goggles while you try this, since you are liable to get a stinging eyeful as your reward for cherishing the environment.

How about just setting tiny tasks? A cure worse than the disease. We might as well stay in the bar all day and give up the sport.

Give us your thoughts. Any suggestion that is fit to print should be sent to S&G. The ones that aren't fit to print should also be sent here privately; after last summer we need a few laughs.

Careless rupture, or, Big is not always beautiful (1992)

One of life's many ironies is that the only people who can afford to fly huge gliders are those who are least capable of dealing with the damn things on the ground. It is only after three decades of clawing your way up the career ladder and nursing your capital from wood to metal to glass to carbon and Kevlar, that you might just be able to buy a slice of a supership. Most supership syndicates consist of empty-nesters who have paid off their mortgages and launched their children into the world.

"You mean, old farts?"

Well, yes. At this advanced age, however, the old far, er, senior pilot is beginning to find his discs slipping and his dorsals, metatarsals and abdominals not up to the job. The puffing and groaning around the big two-seaters at rigging time is so distressing to any sensitive person's ear that younger members tend to stay out of the way until it's all over, unless there is a serious prospect of getting a flight and being allowed to play with the GPS.

Someone will eventually make a pot of money selling a device for lifting the back end of an ASH-25. So far I have only seen crude diagrams and played with prototype levers and ramps that would have been despised by the chaps who thousands of years ago put up the great pillars of Stonehenge – a near approximation to the rear end of an ASH-25, by the way. Worse still, if your partner is a fanatic for ultimate performance he will have ballasted the fin with 50 pounds of lead, or its equivalent in batteries, to get the centre of gravity in the just right place for low-speed flight. "Gosh, that's adding insult to injury, Plat!" No, it just adds injury to injury.

If those brilliant young men from the German *Akafliegs* need a project for winter 1992-93, I suggest that instead of designing fancy wingtips for the 25, they should invent, for this great market of people with more money than muscle, a three-in-one combined rigging-aid, tail-lifter and Zimmer-frame.

And please hurry, before we all do ourselves permanent injury.

Despite my scorning of fancy wingtips for the ASH-25 I did of course buy them as soon as they became available in 1994. And I am still waiting for the tail-lifter.

At last, a subject on which we are all experts (1986)

You can bash away at your typewriter, or more recently the word-processor, for years, pontificating on every subject, lambasting all sorts of people, or nagging at respected institutions like the BGA Competitions Committee, and get what Lord George-Brown used to call a total ignoral. "Are glider pilots completely dozy except when the thermals pop?", one begins to ask. Well, some of them are pretty dozy even when the thermals *are* popping, but that has nothing to do with this piece. Now, however, I seem to have found a deep well of passionate interest in the bosoms, or maybe the lower parts, of the fraternity of glider pilots. And indeed in the sorority of soarers. I refer to the hot, or at least warm, topic of having a pee in a *planeur.* (I did that last bit for alliteration, but it occurs to me that we could widen this whole subject to take in the international scene, with contributions from Australia, where an outlanding in the outback has actually made at least one pilot resort to drinking his urine to avoid death by dehydration, or Alaska, where you could imagine the problem of having your pee-bag freeze between your knees and jam the rearward movement of the stick on the round-out.)

A truly gargantuan mailbag followed "Mentioning the Unmentionable" in an earlier issue. Well, eight letters and three free samples. Free samples of plastic gadgets, I mean, not fluid, silly.

The first sample comes from the Royal Air Force Gliding & Soaring Association at Dishforth in Yorkshire: this is a pretty simple and brutal looking piece of Service equipment (male only, designated 8465 99 137 6876 BAG CREW RELIEF ALEXANDER PLASTICS l985), best employed in smooth wave. "Effective use", says Paul Whitehead, "requires the pilot to 1) Undo seat straps 2) Undo Parachute straps and 3) Turn body through 90 degrees. The old problem of pushing water uphill otherwise applies".

As long as one does not get into the rotor at the *moment critique* this seems not a bad solution. However–and although I customarily throw howevers around like so much chaff this is a pretty solid however–if you were unlucky enough to hit turbulence or inadvertently jog the stick while rolling your torso through the requisite right angle, you would of course have no parachute as you left the aircraft. I only hope you would have the presence of mind to do up your flies on the way down, to spare the blushes of your next of kin.

Another male-only solution comes to me from another north country pilot who has connections with an old people's home, and is designed for constant use by those with bladder-control problems. The problem of incontinence is no joke, and any of us could reach that unhappy state in years to come, so there are strictly no laughs to be had here. However, the system looks like a combination of plumb-

Cobbled together similar looking devices.

ing (similar to ordinary instrument panel piping) and a device which looks like a modified condom. Its main advantage is that it would probably work in any attitude. Its only disadvantage is that it would take some effort to overcome initial squeamishness, and could well take your mind off aviating, not just for part of the flight, but the whole time. No doubt female versions exist, since sex is no bar to the disabilities of old age.

Lastly there is a commercially-available solution, both for men and women, by P&H Enterprises, for use in cars and vans when there is no opportunity to get out for relief. (If you are a security van driver you may not be allowed out of your vehicle for fear of robbers.) It is designed to be as elegant and unembarrassing as anything doing that job can be, and comes in a neat plastic bag that looks to the inexperienced eye as though it contains your overnight toothbrush and toiletries. The disposable bags come with self-tightening clips that close the neck of the bag after use, so the bags can be stowed rather than ditched on the countryside. Men can even get underpants that harness to the Carloo. This looks like the best all round answer.

While in some gliders with extremely reclining positions water will still have to be pushed uphill somewhat, so that some risk of getting a little damp may be unavoidable, pilots flying such machines will just have to reconcile themselves to not wearing their Sunday best while on long flights, and to dousing themselves in aftershave when greeting the farmer's daughter**. I'm glad for reasons of visibility, more that anything else, that ultra-supine gliders have gone out of fashion since the l960s.

That is enough of that topic for the moment: positively the last word in the next issue. In particular I'd like to cull extracts from the letters that say, "Whatever you do, don't mention my name."

** Though unless you douse all over she may wonder about the strange places that glider pilots shave ...

It only hurts when I laugh, or, the War of the T-shirts (1996)

Jill Burry, a heroic figure in women's gliding, very sadly (that is an understatement, let's try *tragically* instead) spent the last, spectacular UK soaring season flat on her back, not merely unable to fly but unable to move, because of a slipped disk. Her specialist said to her at the beginning of her four-month trauma, "This is only a wild guess, but you haven't been lifting the end of something heavy, have you?" and was baffled when his stricken patient went off into hoots of agonising mirth. Although hundreds of rigs and derigs over 20 years could all plead guilty to a cumulative responsibility for her losing the entire 1995 season, she suspects that the last straw (all two hundred kilos of it) was part of an ASH-25 – somebody else's. I suggest that the surgeon's remark could be incorporated into a T-shirt with a cartoon of puzzled doctor and immobilised patient, so that when Jill is wearing it people will forebear from asking her to hold anything heavier than a tailplane. Of course I greatly overrate the humanity and decency of Lasham glider pilots: they wouldn't forebear for one moment:

"Come on Jill, the medics have fixed your back to last for the next 20 years. Now cop a hold of this Nimbus root and stop whining."

Others would stand by and watch with hands in pockets, or take bets. "They say when Jill's back goes you can hear it in Basingstoke, so I want to be around when it happens." Yes, on mature reflection, there would be no mercy whatever.

A few years ago I arrived in a sunny foreign airfield, and in anticipation of great soaring in the coming week, promptly rigged my ASH-25 with the help of a single woman. (What has her marital status got to do with it? Ed. Thanks, I'll make the dumb jokes round

here. Plat.) The ground was rough, muddy and rutted, which made the task much worse than usual, but we did it. Then as we were resting, a syndicate of absolutely charming grey-haired geezers swept in with their ASH-25, all of them exhausted by the burden of years, much travel, and lunch. Moreover they all had bad backs. Truly terrible backs, to a

They all had bad backs.

man. Every back with an official certificate of orthopaedic unrigworthiness. Could we help a little? Well, Marion and I could not refuse, and we found ourselves going through the same sweaty routine again, with the odd bit of hindrance from Dad's Army. Pooped is not the word. Amazingly our two backs took the strain–though will we pay for it later?

The moral is, after having just rigged an ASH-25, don't hang around resting or chatting. Depending on the weather, rush your ship onto the aerotow queue and get airborne, or else hide away in the darkest recess of the bar. Or you can quickly don a Jill Burry T-shirt.

More ideas for 1996 to put off people who might approach you for a rig when you've just done yours, and you cannot bring yourself to say "No" bluntly:

Attack as the best method of defence, such as a T-shirt proclaiming: "Where were *you* when I was rigging *my* bloody glider?"

T-shirts with a price list stating pints/litres of beer charged per ton/tonne lifted.

Long-sleeved shirts and jeans printed to look as if your arm or leg or torso (that's the bit between the arm and the leg) is heavily bandaged or in plaster.

In hot weather, artistic tattoos or transfers that look like multiple sutures and hideous discoloration after a fairly recent compound fracture.

A well-deserved reputation for eager, good-natured clumsiness. You know, like a big stu-

---

pid dog. As Mrs Plat said 20 years ago, you can get lots of peace and quiet once you have dropped the odd wing.

— ooo —

You are already asking, "Aren't you giving ammunition to people who will refuse to help *you* when you need it? Aren't you shooting yourself in the foot, Plat?" You are so right, but I have thought about it:

Always have access to a two-seater, even if your main ship is a solo machine. Then you can bribe people with the promise of flights in the two-pew. Even an open-air flip in an old T-21 is fun, and very popular. But keep your promise, and soon.

Your T-shirt can say, "My other sailplane is an ASH-25 (or Nimbus 4D, or T-21, or whatever)." It is a good idea if these claims are true. T-shirt credibility should be maintained. Facetious T-shirts undermine the effectiveness of this important communication medium for those of us who are shy and tongue-tied. Downright silly T-shirts on the airfield might have to be policed.

Your T-shirt can carry your own Offer beer-per-tonne price list, which will naturally be less extravagant than the Bid beer-per-tonne price list that you wear when other people want a rig from you. What if other guy is wearing a Bid shirt? No problem: the two of you can now negotiate a brokered deal. The agreed exchange rate will depend on whether it's a 1,000km day or only marginally worth rigging at all.

Clearly you need at least two T-shirts or maybe a drawer full of them (like signal flags in the Navy) which I shall market through the British Gliding Association or RD Aviation. Bulk orders at special discounts, of course.

— ooo —

Lastly, if none of this gross, self-serving behaviour appeals to you, I suggest you turn away from it all and re-read the Bible. Memorise the Sermon on the Mount. And say thirty times before breakfast every day, "Rigging is its own reward". No glider pilot has yet been canonised, at which none of us should be at all astonished, but there's your big chance. You could become the very first saint in our movement.

If that's your inclination, I think I have got just the T-shirt for you.

A senior moment (1999)

It was bound to happen sooner or later. I came fizzing towards Seminole Lake Gliderport at red-line speed in François Pin's beautiful ASW27, wondering why I had heard no other "five-miles-out" final glide calls, though I had seen several sailplanes ahead of me at the previous turnpoint. At 140-kts-plus, 300 ft up, it is not a good idea to start fumbling under one's parachute or in side pockets looking for the task sheet.

"Plat, how can you lose things in that tiny space where there's barely room to breathe?"

"I dunno. It's just a talent I have. I should have been a conjuror; I could lose a dozen rabbits in here."

After a few low-level pilot-induced-oscillations I found the wretched piece of crumpled paper.

Oh dear.

You've guessed it: I had missed out the last turnpoint. I confessed my glitch publicly to Charlie Spratt on the finish line (and to 40 snickering rivals), pulled up and tried to thermal away, but it was too late. I had this feeling that the glider was bright red all over as I landed and taxied towards the motor-home where I had stored all my beer. At least some liquid consolation was in prospect. Every American motor-home has a vast fridge, and a friendly pilot had allowed me to use his, the rent being very reasonable, at one beer per dozen per day. Drat! He had amazingly managed to do even worse than me and had landed out. His crew and motor-home had trundled off on retrieve taking my beer with them.

Plat has a place for everything, but everything is in some other place.

It was the last day of the US Senior Championships, and I never saw them or the amber nectar again.

On the radio Charlie kindly said I'd had, "A senior moment". That's code for, "A senile moment" of course. I am typing this on my 65th birthday — tomorrow I get my free bus pass and become the terror of the London Passenger Transport Board, so maybe Charlie is right and these moments will increase in number. But I have decided that such absent-mindedness is not in fact proof of senility. If it is, I have been senile since the age of four, or at whatever age it is that one is expected to take some personal responsibility for one's actions.

No, I blame technology. Thanks to GPS and the Cambridge computer I had got entirely out of the habit of drawing lines on the map. This was the first competition in 40 seasons in which I had drawn no course on the map. "But", you say with incredulity, "surely the Cambridge computer told you there was another turnpoint to go round?"

Indeed it did, but I simply disbelieved it, the way airline pilots always ignore a 100-decibel klaxon and a 30-inch video monitor with flashing red letters saying, "There is a 15,000 ft mountain ahead of you and you are all going to die in one minute if you don't turn left NOW!" . Their last words are always something like, "Aw, shut up!" only ruder. As Ernest Gann said, once a pilot has an erroneous *idée fixe*, no amount of fact or logic will shift it.

"Plat, your resolution for the remainder of this season must be to draw the course on the map, and Scotch-tape the task sheet to the map. Then nothing can go wrong!"

Oh yes, it can with me. One of those damn rabbits will have eaten it.

Mad inventors line up here, please (1987)

I had vowed not to write any longer about the subject of having a pee in a glider, but I will make an exception, since it may help to prove, while I'm on this topic of varying cultures, that the further people are from London the more interesting (= weird) they get. At the BGA conference in Harrogate I was told this true story by a member of a famous northern

club. He wanted to overcome the classic problem of pushing water uphill, and he had the bright idea of *pulling* it uphill instead. So he built a device consisting of an assortment of plastic tubes with latex on the end, a car wind-screen-washer pump, and a 12 volt battery to extract the fluid by brute force.

"How did it work in flight'?", I asked.

Well, it never quite got to that stage, he said. He decided to test it out while lying on his back on the bathroom floor. His first mistake was to switch the thing on. When he did this he found it gave a violent and most disagreeable suck (I forgot to ask whether six volts would have given a more agreeable suck) which left painful marks. His second mistake was to have left the bathroom door open, so that when his wife–who as a gliding wife is more or less permanently braced for the unexpected–heard the strange noises coming from this Heath Robinson machine, shortly followed by even stranger noises coming from him, she dashed into the bathroom. There is no record of their subsequent conversation, which I leave to your imagination.

To us in the great soaring movement that narrative is absolutely credible. But I was wondering what the man in the street would have made of it all if he had read about it in the *News of the World,* which would certainly have reported the story if our inventive friend had used 24 volts and had required the immediate aid of the ambulance or police, or even the fire brigade. Knowing what Fleet Street journalists are like when they get their teeth into a bit of scandal, I simply shudder to think.

As a subplot for a bawdy novel I give this idea free (which is very generous of me, since the story wasn't mine in the first place) to Tom Sharpe, who could no doubt work it up into a masterpiece of bad taste.   ■

I have seen the future ... but I'm not sure it works

Ever since our sport began, people have been describing serious or fantastic scenarios of gliding as it might be in the future. We today can laugh patronisingly at the people who in the mid-1930's stated quite solemnly that Britain's major gliding clubs would in future have to be set up in the extreme western parts, because the prevailing winds were westerly and long cross-countries could only be achieved by flying downwind. The idea that sailplane performance and pilot skills would make wind direction irrelevant had never occurred to them

I wonder: what similarly foolish futures are today's experts predicting for gliding in the 21st century? Remember, should you wish to be regarded as a seer, the two important things about forecasting are:

1) If you are going to make precise predictions, such as the winner of the Soccer World Cup or the price of IBM shares, you must choose a date so far in the future that when if you get it wrong everyone else has forgotten. If you get it right you can of course remind them, with great fanfare.

2) If, however, you are bold enough to try to forecast the near future, make sure everything you utter is vague, hazy and capable of multiple interpretations after the event, like Nostradamus.

I should say that Nostradamus usually covered himself both ways, making very hazy predictions about the very distant future. That is why he is so hugely admired by the gullible, of whom there are many, and exploited by the crooked, who are not above tinkering with the text to make it fit after the event.

The first of these items, Almanac for 1990, totally disregards both of these criteria for the sagacious soothsayer. Tinkering with it to make it fit what actually happened in 1990 proved impossible.

Almanac for 1990 (1989)

January: Unusually mild weather; global warming blamed. Robin May and John Jeffries fly ASH-25 to Blarney and back in Limerick wave. Peebag inadvertently dropped on Mayor of Cork, causing serious Anglo-Irish diplomatic rift.

February: Unusually cold weather, global warming blamed. BGA Conference snowed in; Brennig James takes opportunity to tell life story to captive audience. Pete Saundby awarded the Mowbray Vale Insurance Brokers' medal for patenting new parachute that saves the glider and dumps the pilot.

Don't try to predict the future.

March: Cold snap continues unabated; so does Brennig. Frenzied mass breakout of middle-aged conference delegates across frozen Bristol Channel. All senior figures in UK movement lost beneath the ice. (Furious debate ensues in *S&G* re impact on future of British gliding: nil or positive?)

April: Unusually windy weather; global warming blamed. Platypus breaks 100km triangular speed record, but forgets to switch on barograph. Schempp-Hirth bring out 27 metre glider, announcing, "This is positively the limit on span."

May: Ralph Jones vows publicly to give up threatening pilots, tasksetters, editors and columnists. *Get Well Soon* letters pour in to Ralph. Platypus breaks 200km triangular speed record but one side of triangle is only 27.99% of total distance; disqualified under 28% rule.

June: Unusually calm weather; global warming blamed. Cloudbase goes to 8000ft. Platypus breaks 300km triangular speed record but flies wrong way round task. Schleichers bring out 29 metre glider, announcing, "This is absolutely the limit on span."

July: Unusually hot weather; global warming blamed. Cloudbase goes to 9,000ft; new airspace regulations bring ceiling down to 3,000ft over UK. Ninety-eight top pilots slammed in Wormwood Scrubs for infringements.

August: Cloudbases go to 10,000ft; global warming blamed. Frenzied mass breakout of the jailed 98, in gliders made from bedsteads and prison sheets, comes too late for Open Class Nationals, which has only two entrants. Platypus leads sole rival (16 year-old Silver badge pilot) by 7000 points, but incurs 7001 photo penalty points; comes bottom.

September: Platypus breaks 500km two seater triangular speed record but forgets to take passenger in back seat; disqualified. Schempp-Hirth bring out 31 metre glider, announcing, "We have positively no more territorial ambitions." UK National Ladder won by Dagling.

October: Season of mists and mellow fruitfulness; global warming blamed. Ralph Jones threatens Platypus after airmiss and latest column in *S&G*; *Get Well Soon* letters pour in to Platypus. P. vows publicly to give up writing for *S&G*.

November: Schleicher bring out 33 metre glider, announcing, "The Sailplane to end all Sailplanes," Schleicher factory strafed by squadrons of Venti, Nimbi and Jani; Henry Kissinger called in to arrange non-aggression treaty. Editor of *S&G* gets Club News from Dunstable: another record broken.

December: General astonishment that this month is somewhat colder than August; Tom Bradbury blamed. *S&G*'s Almanac for 1991 faxed from Alice Springs, under the mysterious pen name of Dingo; *S&G* readers complain all the seasons seem back to front.

In the January before this almanac was written, John Jeffries and Robin May in an ASH-25 (mine!), without any life-saving gear or flight plan, took off from Sleap in Shropshire and ventured upwind in wave to within easy reach of Dublin. The wave was from the Wicklow Hills and steadily improved as they approached Ireland. Discretion took over from valour when they were 17 miles from the Irish coast. They turned back and arrived over the Welsh coast at 7,000 ft.

A 31 metre glider is expected to fly in 2000, only ten years late. See "The new supership for 2000 AD" under Travel Broadens the Behind.

Platypus actually did achieve the British two-seat 500 km triangle record in December 1990 in Australia, and he did remember to take a passenger. He also set a 300 km Out-and-Return record. More predictions gone wrong!

Are glider pilots mad? (1981)

For Dr Brennig James, self-confessed hero of innumerable, but not untold, gliding escapades in many countries, including an abortive and ruinous expedition to the Himalayas (where the inscrutable local rulers rendered him every assistance short of actual help) to suggest that his fellow glider pilots may not have all the marbles that God gave them, verges, some would say, on *chutzpah.* The burden of Doc James's argument, in case you are interested, is that by flying a motor glider on a light throttle you can get 40: 1 and obviate the need for a £14,000 racing ship. A bit more power and you emulate the best the Open Class can throw at you.

Ye-es. The *reductio ad absurdum* of that logic is to pack all the Booker members into a 747 (or better still, a DC-10, suggests a Dunstable pilot) and fly the whole show round the world on a light throttle. The cost per passenger mile would be far cheaper than gliding. I'm sure there's a flaw there somewhere, but I'm not sure what it is.

Nevertheless the strange things that Brennig says usually have embedded in them some nugget of truth: in this case he is raising two valid questions: are we paying an unnecessarily high price for performance these days and what is the most cost-effective way of covering the ground in soaring flight?

An incomplete answer to the first question is that it doesn't cost any more in real terms than twenty years ago. But of course we could still be paying more than necessary because of the artificial constraints of contest flying, which may improve the breed, but only improve it from the point of view of contest pilots. The chief distorting factors are the entirely arbitrary 15 metre limit on the Standard and Racing Classes and the emphasis on speed-flying in the best part of the day. The best definition of cross-country cost-efficiency for the ordinary club pilot would be *the cost per closed-circuit mile across a whole year.* Clearly the glider that could soar cross-country before 1 pm and after 6pm not just in the summertime but in the early spring and late autumn or even the winter, daylight permit-

ting, would do well in the mileage stakes. Let us therefore encourage the National Ladder and any other scheme that puts a premium on maximum utilisation.

As to cost, I was impressed by the argument of Prof R. Eppler[16] that for the cost of a flapped 1 5 metre wing one can build a much more efficient unflapped wing of 18 metres, or more. A 1981 equivalent of the Dart 17 or SHK will not be built however, because there is no place for them in National and International contests. A pity, since it would almost certainly be the most efficient machine by the criteria I have suggested. I've just had a thought: why don't we persuade the owner of an ASW-20L to fly with tip extensions but with flaps fixed in one position (to simulate a 16.5 metre unflapped glider) against an ASW-20 without tips but having full use of all the flappery? My money would be on the unflapped version – except for landing in small fields where the flaps are superb. However that does not really affect the argument, since on a purpose-built unflapped glider a cheap but effective airbrake system is quite feasible. You see (If he says it again I swear I'll scream Ed.) – oh all right, out of respect for her feelings I'll say it under my breath: Th*r*'s n* s*bst*t*t* f*r sp*n

Now we have an 18-metre class and a wonderful unflapped 18-metre glider in the stretched LS8

Careless can mean carless (1988)

A fellow member at our club has just had his car stolen from a fairly remote launch point, not very accessible to the general public. Naturally the keys had been left in the ignition; we all do that in case we land out or in case, on

Unmarketable impediments.

our small and congested site, the car is causing an obstruction and needs to be moved.

Perhaps our friend paid the penalty of having a car that was far too tidy. The typical glider pilot's car is so full of junk, much of it heavy, bulky and utterly unmarketable impedimenta, that anyone wanting to steal the vehicle would be appalled by the problem of how to get rid of it without drawing attention to himself. Where do you hide, or how do you explain to the gendarmes if they stop you, the possession of (not to mention the purpose of), a seven-foot-long tubular steel device with a tow-hitch on the end, assorted dollies with red fibreglass mouldings, the front end of a bicycle, eighty feet of wing covers, six 10-gallon drums and a set of angle-iron tripods?

Much of this stuff is on the front seat. The reason most people driving to the launch point don't offer you a lift when they see you heading there on foot is not that they have no manners, but that by the time they had made space for you to sit down you could have walked there anyway. The reason someone doesn't offer you a lift on the way back from the launch point may be that he is stealing one of those very rare, tidy cars...

After I sent this item off to Sailplane & Gliding *I heard that Scottish police had very efficiently found the car quite unharmed a day or so later. I realised that I had probably met the perpetrator. I had found myself talking to an amiable Glasgow truck-driver who had strolled off the hill to express an interest in gliding. Spectators often do this, Dunstable being a natural amphitheatre. He said he had delivered a truck to in London and was now making his way home by hitch-hiking. I then busied myself with other things. About the time the car vanished, so did he. Let's amend* stolen *to* borrowed.

Gliding as mass entertainment: Chapter IV from the Centenary History of British Gliding, published 2029 AD (1982)

In 1999 the British National Gliding Championships achieved for the first time the distinction of the highest television rating of all sporting events. Motor racing's audience collapsed when the oil began to run out and petrol reached £75 a gallon, far beyond the reach of ordinary wage-earners on £1,000 a week. Silverstone was empty of spectators and TV viewers found little excitement in watching cars travelling at 25mph all day in the fuel-economy marathons which were the only form of competition the government permitted between internal combustion vehicles on land, sea or air.

The technical problems of conveying the thrills of gliding to the lay public were at first thought insuperable, but one magic ingredient quickly solved them – money. In the late 1980s advertisers, desperate to sponsor popular shows, offered the BGA ten million pounds on condition that an audience of ten million could be reached. The now Lord Rolfe of BGA-TV promptly hired a shy, retiring genius – of whom no proper record now exists, but whose name in some old manuscripts has been deciphered as P. Latipuss – to use all modern techniques to capture the masses for soaring. Ladbrokes soon matched that sum, the Grand National and the Derby having been abolished after the nationalisation of all horses by the Ministry of Transport. Betting money soon poured into the Totternhoe Tote.

A transcript of a 1999 TV broadcast conveys some of the flavour of those early attempts to bring soaring into the homes of ordinary gambling people:

"It's a beautiful day here at Dunstable Downs, viewers. You can see the giant double-skinned solar-heated launch balloons gently swelling in the noonday sun – and yes, there goes the Barclays Bank balloon and dangling beneath it the ASW-37 of Air Marshal Sir George Lee, five times World Champion and known as the Bjorn Borg of soaring. Because of his bold decision not to use water-ballast his glider is the first to leave the ground. Remember first back round the course is the winner, regardless of when he starts, so Sir George has quite an advantage – provided today's thermals stay weak! Look at the Tote board in the top left hand corner of your TV-wall. Odds against Barclays are whistling down from 5 to 1 to near evens. Any of you wishing to bet on a glider, just key in the contest number and your stake. It will all be placed instantaneously at the current odds and your winnings will be paid directly into your bank account the moment the race is over."

"Now there's general panic! Many contestants are leaking like mad as they jettison ballast, desperately trying to get away. Odds against white-haired veteran Ralph Jones are soaring – excuse the pun, punters – as he sits there, grimly holding onto his water as always. He's a rank 200 to one outsider. All the others are away and today's Dunstable-Paris-Brussels triangle is a pretty short task. But hold it! Just use the split-screen facility and you'll see the latest satellite pictures on the right half of your wall. Yes, it shows ground-heating two degrees above forecast and the strato-cu is breaking up into some pretty nice streets. Wily old Ralph must have installed a miniaturised satellite link in his cockpit; those weren't carborundum-fibre repairs he was doing last night after all. The Tote board is going crazy! Watch the odds tumble. Remember, you can bet any time till the first glider crosses the finish line."

"Lee has to make another big gamble soon. Should he release from his balloon now at 300 metres or should he wait till he's sure of contacting a thermal? He's got to drop 150 metres in a dead stall before he gets flying speed. There have been some nasty accidents with some of the eager types – especially when they forget about the Hill! If *that* happens today, viewers, we'll bring you action replays courtesy of Lloyds (remember the motto 'Disasters we deal with immediately. Catastrophes take a little longer') so stay tuned."

"No, he's hanging on, drifting away at about ten knots; he's got to come back over the steward's cameras to start or his flight is void. Someone's started! Dave 'Stubble' Watt, releasing at only 200 metres, plummets down the curve of the Bowl, pulls up into a chandelle then tiptoes at 250km/h along the ridge to Dagnall. Press the button for Channel 17 which

The deserted airport.

> ## Gliding as a spectator sport (1992)
> *Years ago I wrote a futuristic piece of nonsense about gliding as a spectator sport, in which the public could watch, and bet on, the progress of the contestants around the course. The heights and positions of the gliders would be seen as a three-dimensional holographic display, little points of coloured light representing each aircraft. That is just about feasible right now: I'm not quite sure how the hologram would work, but in principle the three-dimensional data can be transmitted, collected and displayed now. Will all the bookies interested please form an orderly queue?*
>
> *Oh, I nearly forgot the best thing of all: people who steal points from their rivals by sneakily climbing a few hundred feet – did I say hundreds? I've seen 'em take thousands – in prohibited airspace will be speedily brought to book and pilloried.*
>
> *Then what GPS will really come to stand for is God Punishes Sinners.*

will give you the view from his cockpit and a full readout of all Dave's instruments. Yes, his infra-red telescope is registering heat from a field just this side of the deserted airport at Luton. Just as well the other pilots aren't allowed to see each other's readouts, and of course crews cannot talk to their pilots – all available channels are used by the bookies and the entertainment media. The Lee and Jones crews are tearing their hair and pummelling the ground – with £100,000 in prize-money at stake who can blame them? Remember folks, for those stressful moments nothing calms the nerves better than (strains of Bach's Air on a G string) a Hamlet cigar..."

"Four o'clock and all's well, viewers. On the giant display board in the hangar you can see the update on each pilot. Fitchett has averaged 6.752km/h rate of climb and 213km/h ground speed and has arrived back at Folkestone first but at only 200 metres. There's £5 million in bets riding on the Spiller's cake-mix (It Doesn't Just Rise, It Soars!) glider and he won't be popular if he lands out now. Those reinforced cockpits aren't just for heavy landings – it's to keep out the disappointed punters till the cops arrive. If there is a lynching, viewers, watch for action replays by courtesy of your friendly local underwriters – our motto, *You Can't Take It With You, So Why Not Leave It All With Us?*"

"The special attraction this year is the huge three-dimensional holographic display which represents the whole of Northern Europe, or any chosen section of it enlarged. This occupies the new Joe Coral Geodesic Dome and projects the position of each glider as a spot of light, green if climbing, red if descending, suspended over the ground. The gaggles look like little revolving Christmas trees, while tiny red lights streak between one green cluster and the next. Talking about Christmas trees folks, remember there are only 152 shopping days left and if you press the keys for the electronic shop window..."

"They're neck and neck at seven o'clock, viewers. As they sweep past the Goodyear Solar blimp over Tower Bridge we all get a splendid view of the setting sun, and the vari-coloured plumes of ballast-water streaming from the quadruple vents – see the Green-Red-Yellow-Green for the Watney-Schempp Nimbus 9 – bringing cheers from the masses who dash from their sitting-rooms to see their heroes streak overhead. The odds on Lee are narrowing to 1.12677 to 1. And the winner is..."

At this point these spectacular images of vintage gliding at its best are suddenly replaced by a message to viewers about bad breath. When it comes to entertainment it seems that, then as now, there is no substitute for *being there*.

Not only were we able in 1999 to see what the contest pilot sees via the Internet in real time, but on-line shopping and betting were established and fast-growing businesses. The extinction of Luton airport remains a dream, however.

Bring back virginity (1991)

I told you in our last issue how I would literally go to the ends of the earth to avoid the after-dinner-speaking season. However I did not altogether succeed. The chairman of my club – where I have loyally stayed as a member for a third of a century through thick and thin, regardless of low launches in the 1950s, high fees in the 1960s, long queues in the

1970s and oceans of Somme-quality mud (they should have made puttees standard issue) in the 1980s – threw himself on my mercy. He had, he said, desperately searched for weeks across the whole country for a celebrity speaker, but had finally come to the right decision – he'd given up. Would I, *faute de mieux*, do the honours for the club's dinner? It was an historic occasion, remember.

I fought a stiff rearguard action. I pointed out that a retiring, though hardly shy, member of the club staff was embarking on a brilliant new career as a stand-up comic in the pubs and clubs, and was exceptionally funny. True, his material had absolutely nothing to do with gliding, but since half the people who come to annual dinners are friends and family of glider pilots and know little about the sport, this was a great advantage. Surely he was ideal? Yes, said the chairman, he had thought so, too. But when the chairman's wife, club censor and guardian of the club's morals, saw an advance copy of Bert's spiel, she scissored out all the words that were racist, and sexist, and blasphemous, and scatological, and obscene, so Bert's script ended up looking like a lace doily. Then there was also the embarrassing matter of a fee, now that he'd turned professional.

Platypus's material, by contrast, was believed to be more or less printable – relative to Bert's stuff, anyway – and more importantly was free in both senses of the word: available and gratis.

The chairman briefed me, "Don't go on too much about the glorious past of the club; people have had a bellyful of that this year, concentrate more on our glorious future." I suspected that was code for, "Don't talk about yourself, talk about me." That's all right, I'm not proud. I said to one of my partners the other day, "I'm just an old has-been," and he said, "Plat, that's rubbish – you never were anything!" That's what partners are for, to cut you down to size.

I had to tell the audience that frankly I wasn't looking forward all that much to the idea of gliding in the 21st century. Indeed I think that when the millennium arrives I shall sell my glider and take up wine, women and song – before my voice gives out. I'm always threatening to do that, of course, but something invariably crops up. This winter, for instance,

I was looking forward to getting away from gliding and broadening my cultural interests in London and Paris, when I get this phone call from a chap who says we can ship a two-seater in a container to Australia for the whole winter for almost nothing. So off to Australia we go. Bubbly, bimboes and Bizet in Paris will just have to wait.

My vision of the future of our sport is a pretty jaundiced one, as befits a person entering the curmudgeon phase of life. I am sure that by the time my successors are celebrating the club's centenary in 2030, the public lavatory on top of the hill will have expanded into Terminal Seven of London's fifth airport. Gliders will be able to go 20 miles from a thousand feet, which will be just dandy because nobody in England will be allowed to go above a thousand feet. Because everyone will have so much leisure time, when we host the National Championships it will consist of a solid month of polygons all packed into a tiny area around Bletchley; it will be so tedious that it will be compulsory, like jury duty.

In the Welsh mountains, however, there will be a legend amongst the shepherds that a great black sailplane, having shed all its gel-coat in 20 years of non-stop flight, is still piloted by an ancient aviator, permanently airborne and permanently lost, his beard streaming out of the clear-vision panel, living off rainwater and small birds and even the occasional unwary sheep, uttering his distinctive one-note cry, "There must be wa-aave here somewhere." At dusk villagers will hustle their pets indoors while pretending they don't believe a word of the story of the dreaded Jay-Jay-Bird. But those of us who are still around will know it to be true

Sometimes I look back enviously from this age of increasingly crowded airspace and cynical sophistication to that other age of freedom, innocence and simple faith. For instance, when you read the accounts of how the founders of this club operated, it is evident that they believe that as a special favour to them God had repealed the law of gravity. I'm amazed that they survived 12 months, 12 weeks even. Solo training is the most cock-eyed way to learn to fly – I started that way in the 1940s (and had to be completely retaught when I joined the club in the 1950s and they still haven't got me sorted out yet). At least we in the ATC had a high performance machine with crisp controls called the Kirby Cadet, and one or two of the instructors actually had a few dozen launches in their logbooks. But in the early 1930s the blind confidently catapulted the even blinder off the equivalent of the dome of St Paul's Cathedral, and on the way down totally inexperienced hands tried to grapple with primitive control circuits that had all the resilience of so much spent knicker-elastic. Oh, but the freshness and simple joy of it, nevertheless! In the greatest book on gliding ever written Philip Wills poignantly describes the pioneer members of our club, "We were young, virgin and ecstatic"

Now look at us...

But you know, even now I quite often feel like a virgin. I'd better rephrase that. I mean, I often feel as those pioneers did; there is so much in gliding that is still novel and exciting. It was only a couple of months ago that I flew to the Isle of Wight and back, and got just the merest taste of what Geoffrey Stephenson had experienced when in 1939 he launched from the Chilterns and crossed the Channel, in a glider of a quarter of the performance that I had. It was only two years ago that I explored the Brecon Hills for the first time, and I've not tried Scotland yet, or soared the South Downs, or used the sea breeze front over Lyme Bay. And I still want to do a cross-country in a Kite 1 or a T-21. Our club has given me – given hundreds of us – a way of life, lots of friends and always something new to look toward to, limited only by one's imagination. For that I shall forever be grateful to the instructors, to partners past and present, and above all to the people who all those years ago devoted their energies and risked their necks to get our club off the ground and into the air.

A matter of survival.

Try forecasting anything you like, but not the future (1985)

In New York the rainfall is vastly greater than in London; the difference is that in London it descends in a fairly continuous dribble whereas in the Big Apple the heavens open for a few minutes and drench everyone foolish enough to be out on foot. (Muggers being the other deterrent.) Driven to shelter in a bookshop for half an hour, I felt morally obliged to buy a book. The one I chose was called *The Experts Speak* which is a compendium of crass pronouncements uttered by able, intelligent and well-qualified authorities. The fact that some chap has a lifetime of creative achievement behind him does not mean his crystal ball is any less cloudy than the next man's. Here are a few about aviation:

"As it is not at all likely that any means of suspending the effect of air-resistance can ever be devised, a flying-machine must always be slow and cumbersome. . . . But as a means of amusement, the idea of aerial travel has great promise.... We shall fly for pleasure."

T. Baron Russell, A Hundred Years Hence, 1905.

"A popular fallacy is to expect enormous speed to be obtained. ... There is no hope of the airplane's competing for racing speed with either our locomotives or our automobiles."

William Henry Pickering, (American astronomer at Harvard College Observatory), Aeronautics, 1908.

"The aeroplane ... is not capable of unlimited magnification. It is not likely that it will ever carry more than five or seven passengers. High-speed monoplanes will carry even less."

Waldemar Kaempfert, (Managing Editor of Scientific American and author of The New Art of Flying.), "Aircraft and the Future," Outlook, June 28, 1913.

"Gliders . . . will be the freight trains of the air. We can visualise a locomotive plane leaving LaGuardia Field towing a train of six gliders in the very near future.

"By having the load thus divided it would be practical to unhitch the glider that must come down in Philadelphia as the train flies over that place – similarly unhitching the loaded gliders for Washington, for Richmond, for Charleston, for Jacksonville, as each city is passed."

Grover Loening, (Grumman Aircraft 1944 Corp.).

"It has been demonstrated by the fruitlessness of a thousand attempts that it is not possible for a machine, moving under its own power, to generate enough force to raise itself, or sustain itself, in the air."

M. de Marles, Les Cents Merveilles des Sciences et des Arts, 1847.

"Put these three indisputable facts together:

"1. There is a limit of weight, certainly not much beyond fifty pounds, beyond which it is impossible for an animal to fly.

2. The animal machine is far more effective than any we can make; therefore the weight of a flying machine cannot be more than fifty pounds.

3. The weight of any flying machine cannot be less than three hundred pounds. Is it not demonstrated that a true flying machine is impossible?"

Joseph Le Conte, (Professor of Natural History at the University of California), Popular Science Monthly, November 1888.

"Heavier-than-air flying machines are impossible."

Lord Kelvin, (British mathematician, physicist, and President of the British Royal Society), c. 1895.

"It is apparent to me that the possibilities of the aeroplane, which two or three years ago was thought to hold the solution to the flying machine problem, have been exhausted, and that we must turn elsewhere."

Thomas Alva Edison, (American scientist and inventor), quoted in the New York World, November 17, 1895.

Written by Christopher Cerf and Victor Navasky, Pantheon Books, New York.

Sleepless in South West Thirteen (1999)

I was delighted to find that the gentleman presiding over one of the interminable terminal enquiries – the usual public wrangle about whether London Heathrow should have a fifth terminal, or whether jets should be allowed to wake us at 4 a.m. – was a Mr Justice Glidewell.

There is one solitary Glidewell in the London residential phone directory, by the way. There are also two subscribers called Glide, two more called Sinker, and a least a dozen by the name Soar. I just thought you would like to know the useful ways in which I spend the winter months when I am not scaring myself silly in the New Zealand Alps.

Anyway, this lovely name made me think, always a dangerous activity. Why not make all the airliners glide, absolutely dead-stick, into Heathrow? After all, if the space shuttle can approach in total silence and touch down like a feather, a Boeing 747, with a lift/drag ratio many times better, can do so too.

There is a snag, of course. A single plane can do that easily, but in a stream of airliners all forced to follow the same three-degree path (roughly 17 to one) at prescribed intervals, many are going to have to use power to adjust their position on the glide-slope when they get a bit low or a bit slow.

Answer? Technology! Abolish all the current ground-based air traffic control systems. Every plane in Plat's brave new world will have collision-avoidance electronics (based on GPS or radar or something; don't hamper my racing brain with the details). They will all come in at whatever glide angle, at whatever speed and even from whatever direction suits them, as long as they are quiet. I suppose it would be nice if they agreed which runways to use, though even that may be unnecessary once we have ironed out the wrinkles, like how to get them off the runways fast enough to avoid the planes coming the other way. What I envisage is a high-tech version of the basic see-and-be-seen system, with minimal radio chat between pilots, at any busy British gliding site, or at a small American airport without a tower.

There would always be objections: nit-picking, unimaginative, pedantic gripes about one little problem or another. Like, if the engines get cold through being throttled right back you can't fire them up again quickly in an emergency, such as having to go round again. I delegate that small headache to the engine makers. Come on, you chaps, just redesign the darned engines, or it's the Gulag for the whole team. Well, we haven't got Siberia here in Britain, but we can create the equivalent: make them live indefinitely on airline food served in a tiny, cramped space in thin, unbreathable, recycled air, bombarded by

semi-audible movies on tiny screens, until they're screaming to be led back to the drawing-board. They'd come up with something.

The biggest difficulty, however, would not be technology, but people. The general public do not understand the principles of flight, and especially they do not understand the principles of motorless flight. The idea of hundreds of jetliners milling about in the dark over central London without power and without any ground-based air traffic control might unnerve them.

I would have achieved part of my great aim; the inhabitants of Battersea and Barnes (where I live) would no longer be woken up by airliners. However that would largely be because they would be too scared to go to sleep in the first place.

Motorgliding (1969)

The notoriously unreliable Tail Feathers News Team, just back from covering a motor glider jamboree on the Continent, report yet another sporting vignette of triumph and tragedy.

It appears that mountaineer Rudi Heidensieck has shinned up the North Face of the Eiger in world record time. When quizzed by our news-hound as to whether his performance had been aided in any way by the squadron of balloons and helicopters that dangled safety nets below him, the famed alpinist replied with scorn that he had never used the nets at any time, so how could they have helped him? Collapse of impertinent newsman.

However his doughty rival, Sir Fotheringay Tidworthy, so far from reaching the summit, actually failed to get on to the escarpment at all. Scorning all artificial aids in his bid to storm the Eiger, Sir Fotheringay insisted on walking and swimming the whole 500 miles from his home, stately Bucktooth Abbey, Wilts, to the foot of the dreaded mountain, whereupon our exhausted hero expired. As if in homage, the Pound Sterling dipped another couple of points on foreign exchange markets. His few remaining admirers subscribed for a plaque to mark the spot, engraved with the family motto, a fitting epitaph to a most British gentleman – Nice Guys Finish Last.

Getting worse.

Rain, rain go away, you're booked to come another day (1987)

I hate to admit it but weather forecasts are getting better. The weather itself is getting worse. But the glad tidings of yet another washed-out weekend are coming to us earlier and more accurately. For this privilege we can thank first the satellites and other data-gathering systems and secondly computerised forecasting models.

"What's the *&@$ use of that?" you ask gloomily as the 1987 definition of a Good Day slides from the five-knot-thermals-for-eight-hours dream to the long-enough-intervals-between-showers-to-derig-without-getting-soaked reality. Well, with better information we can squeeze better tasks out of the pathetic British climate. And again, if it's not going to be soarable at all, the sooner I know the happier I am, because I can arrange to do something else with my valuable time, like mangling Chopin's B flat minor Scherzo on the Yamaha (not the motor-bike, silly, the grand piano), tasting the contents of my cavernous cellar (the Bulgarian Red Infuriator in the toolshed), playing with the floppy in my Macintosh (steady on, family magazine and all that. Ed.) or even, as a last resort, writing something for this column ahead of the official deadline. (That'll be the day. Ed.)

In newspaper columns half-baked science hacks gleefully predict that man will soon be controlling the weather. That is just an appalling idea. We could no more control the weather than a drunk could control a juggernaut on black ice on a winding road in the pitch dark without lights at 80mph. We could

certainly *affect* the weather, but that's not the same thing at all.

Even now the Continentals blame us for all the filthy weather they get – jokingly, of course – but if they thought we were doing it on purpose they'd go to war with us, targeting three-inch hailstones on all our sporting events by way of a warning-shot. Then imagine an EEC Commission trying to decide how to allocate Europe's rain and sunshine. It would make the squabbles over the Common Agricultural Policy look like a triumph of harmonious statesmanship by comparison.

BUT – how different it would be if instead of trying to affect the weather we were simply able to forecast it a year ahead with perfect accuracy! Would that not be ideal? You would then have known that the first half of July 1987 was going to be delicious. So the BGA could have called the Bristol GC and said, "Sorry. lads, but we want July 4th to the 11th (eight glorious contest days, yummy, yummy!) for the Racing Class Nationals, and if there's any good weather left we need it for the Open Class and the Standard Class, so you provincials will just have to fight it out with the other Regional Competitions organisers for what falls off the rich man's table."

Picket the BGA.

"That's funny, the line's gone dead."

Furious deputations of Bristolians picket the BGA offices, demanding, "Give us back our eight days!", "We won't be second-class citizens!" etc, threatening they will secede from the movement and stage unofficial, pirate competitions in the best weather, and the BGA can do its damnedest.

Then you'd find all the air displays were booked into the best weekend days and we'd be warned off flying near any of them. With these events, not to mention Henley, Ascot and other grand occasions, all being scheduled in the few sunny days, every member of the Royal Family would be helicoptering frantically from one place to another to fulfil their engagements, so that Purple Airways would scythe through the serried cumulus, rendering vast areas of lift unusable. The Tower of London would be full of glider pilots whose sclf-rcstraint had cracked – after all, any system of radar, satellites and computers that can predict the weather perfectly would have no difficulty trapping and putting wing-clamps on errant soarers, would it? In the predicted good spells roads would be jammed, caterers, hoteliers and gliding clubs would have to charge treble prices to compensate for the dearth of bookings the rest of the year.

It's the Tower for Plat.

Soon people would have to draw lots to decide when they were allowed to go on holiday; clubs would spin a roulette-wheel to get their contest dates. Finally, to dampen the rage of the losers and lessen the risk of riot and civil commotion – not to mention a thriving black-market in sunshine, the gathering and publishing of such forecasts would be made a punishable offence. Then we'd be right back where we are now, not having the faintest idea what Mother Nature has in store for us when, full of renewed hopes that This Year Really Is Going To Be Different, we send off our deposits. Oh, bliss.

Idiot's guides needed, soon (1987)

The most useful motoring advice for the man who knows nothing about what goes on under the bonnet of his car (that is to say almost any man, if his male pride allows him to be honest) is to be found in women's magazines. No woman feels insulted if the writers assume she is automotively illiterate, so these magazines set out in simple Noddy-language the five basic things to do if, for instance, your car won't start of a morning. Her husband then takes a quick look at her copy of *Family Circle* – and, between sneers, actually learns something he didn't know before.

In the same way Tom Bradbury has cleverly addressed his splendid piece, "A Met Guide for Beginners", to the aspiring Silver C pilot, when in fact it ought to be read, studied and pinned to the wall of the briefing room by triple Diamond pilots. I have my full complement of gold-mounted rocks, but if I'd sat a written exam on the content of Tom's article before reading it this morning I'd have been lucky to have scraped a pass: more likely I'd have been sent off for a remedial course in soaring meteorology – probably in some very distinguished company:

"This piece of cardboard, gentlemen, represents a cumulus. No, Mr Platypus sir, hold yours fluffy side up, please. That's right, the *flat* bit goes underneath. All together now, after me, cuu-muu-luss, cuu-muuluss!" Disorganised chanting by 50,000 hours' worth of Open Class pilots, who only know to circle when their Cambridge computer tells them to.

"Cor Blimey, what a shower – pay attention at the back there, if you want those leg-irons removed before tea-time. Now, in this part of the world cyclones go anti-clockwise, and anti-cyclones go clockwise. Easy isn't it? What d'you mean, you don't know what clockwise is? I see, you're all using those nerdy digital watches. Well, this large round thing on the wall is a clock, and you'll see it's got a big hand and little hand . . . if you don't pass this part of the test you'll all have to fly Standard Class" – shrieks of abject terror – "and sit the Bronze C written examination."

Utter panic. One escapee is dragged back by a Doberman. Trusties (those who can tell Upwind from Downwind in the practical test, which consists of standing out on the field and waiting until their noses get colder than their bottoms, or conversely) manacle the victim to the wall. "Now, how to detect Signs of Decay: you lot should be pretty good at this. .."

Well, it'd be no worse than going to one of those fancy health farms – and a whole lot cheaper.

Tom Bradbury's "Meteorology and Flight" was published by A & C Black in 1991.

The seven deadly sins play: avarice (1989)

This playlet 2000 was written as the middle section of a dramatic trilogy with the titles 1999, 2000 and 2001, which in turn formed part of the great London Gliding Club Christmas Revue of 1989, where musical performances and comedy acts delighted an audience that was clearly several drinks ahead of the cast. The other two parts of the trilogy were considered seditious and obscene respectively.

2000

Open to almost deafening sounds of birdsong – obviously a beautiful soaring day. A sign on the club notice-board welcomes new members to the LGC: it is tastefully decorated with a picture which at first sight looks like an eagle soaring for joy but on closer inspection is in fact a vulture looking for lunch. At some point in the performance it should be arranged for another notice that is partially obscuring the welcome sign to drop off, revealing that LGC stands for

> **L**ift
> **G**enerates
> **C**ash

A pilot is seen impatiently struggling to get his parachute on, whilst staring ecstatically out of the window.

Pilot: This is *it* – the day of a lifetime – could be a thousand k's! Let's get launched! Where's the manager?

An opulently dressed figure – white suit, white shoes (or better still, spats), Panama hat, loads of chunky jewellery, giant Havana cigar – materialises at his side.

P: You the manager?

M: Well, manager, proprietor, owner what's in a name?
P: So you're the landlord?
M: Well, airlord, to be pedantic.

Pilot looks puzzled.

M: I own all the airspace over this site to the bottom of Amber One. And a real packet it cost me, I can tell you.
P: You're a lucky man. I've been looking forward to a day like this for years!
M: *(with heavy significance)* Me too.
P: Well, I must get airborne toot sweet. As it says in your *S&G* ad, "Standard Launch Price, £10 payable in advance." Here's my cheque for ten, so I'll...

Manager stares at the proffered cheque in obvious disbelief and disgust.

P: Nothing wrong with my cheque?
M: *(with brutal irony)* Nought wrong with it, nought wrong.
P: Well, that's all right then. I'll get going.
M: *(wearily)* I mean, there's a *nought* short.
P: A hundred quid?
M: That is correct, sunshine. The penny, or rather the pound coin, has finally dropped in your skull. You have grasped my message.
P: What about the Standard Launch Price? That's why I came here!
M: *(brandishes arm towards the sky)* And I suppose this is a Standard day? I seem to have just overheard you wittering on to yourself about *(mockingly)*, "the day of a lifetime!" A *much* above standard day, squire; accordingly, a *much* above standard price.
P: They told me at Booker they'd undercut any price of yours, after being bought by John Lewis Stores. "Never knowingly undersold" is their motto – and they're only 20 miles from here.
M: Look, John, now that the Tring Road is a six-lane turnpike it'll take four hours to get there.
P: Is the traffic that dense?
M: No, it's the unemployables that operate the twelve tollbooths between here and High Wycombe that are dense. Let's face it, it's my price or take up tiddlywinks.

P: I never thought it would be cheaper to stick to women, gambling and booze.

M: If you're serious I could fix you up in those departments: this is after all a fully-equipped leisure centre.

P: Yes, I've seen your commercial on BBC television, "Get rid of your complex at our complex!" No, thanks, I came here to fly, but a hundred quid!

M: I can arrange a substantial discount.

P: Oh?

M: Just sign this kidney vendor card which we took the liberty of printing up when we saw you coming – I mean, when you arrived at the office

P: You mean a donor card?

M: Nothing is *donated* round here any more, young man. Everything is for sale; that way we all benefit. You get a reduction of £15, all the spare parts clinics get your declaration form on the fax, and I get a commission.

P: What do they do with my declaration?

M: That depends on the state of their cold-store inventory and customer demand. They either just wait by the phone or they send out the refrigerated vans on spec, sort of thing, and listen in on decimal-one.

P: It sounds a bit macabre. But, what the Hell, if you're stone dead, who's to mind?

M: Hm, I wouldn't be too sure about *stone dead*. Some of the cowboys are a bit over-zealous. I wouldn't even doze off while waiting for the retrieve, that's my advice. Stay high, and if you do hit trouble, stuff it in properly. No broken ankles or concussion. But forget it, think about the flight! Where are you heading?

P: I thought I'd make for the Black Mountains in Wales, then –

M: Ah!

P: Ah?

M: A tiny problemette, squire. All the airspace from Talgarth up to Alpha Centauri belongs to a syndicate. *(Picture of John Jeffries with wadding in his cheeks projected on wall.)*

P: Like a gliding syndicate, all helping each other?

M: More like a Mafia syndicate, all knifing each other – same difference. Anyway it'll cost you the proverbial upper and lower limb to use the wave today.

P: They won't know I'm there if I'm at 17,000ft.

M: Want a bet? *(Holds up black box)* This new electronic wonder is a mandatory combined transponder and taximeter. Every time you enter a piece of airspace it starts counting time and height, and debits your account accordingly and credits *his* account. *(Nods towards picture of Godfather JJ.)* Any tampering is automatically detected, in which case my little remark about it costing you an arm and a leg ceases to be metaphorical.

P: How much will a Diamond cost me?

M: As the man said, if you have to ask, you can't afford it.

P: I might run out of money just at the last moment.

M: Then you'll hear this *(pushes button on black box). Alarm bell rings. Metallic female voice:* You have exceeded your credit ceiling! Your variometer has been disconnected! You have ten minutes in which to land safely or negotiate a second mortgage on your house; call 129-decimal-85! After ten minutes dive-brakes will be deployed automatically! *(Increasingly shrill.)* Come on, dozy, you have *nine* minutes –

P: I give up! Farewell, gliding! Goodbye, Dunstable! *(Sobs. Turns to leave.)*

M: Hold on, young fellow, if you have championship qualities they might even pay *you*. Turn professional! Join the multi-millionaires *(picture of Robin May)* now that soaring is the world's biggest TV spectator sport. Prize money, sponsorship from suppliers *(picture of John Delafield against background photo of giant RD Aviation warehouse),* fees for opening supermarkets, seats on the boards of companies...

P: What ever happened to Wimbledon?

M: Not for today's audiences. No blood. And you know how the viewers love tantrums; when they found glider pilots had manners that made John McEnroe look like John Gielgud, well ... *(Gets out pad and pencil.)* I'll put you down for next year's Open Class Nationals. Navigator all right?

P: Oh yes, that's great!

M: P2 in a multi-seater in the Open Class is the lowest form of human life, but you have to start somewhere. *(Licks pencil, fills in form, gets pilot to sign.)* And since I've taken a shine to you, I *will* let you fly for only ten quid today.

P: Brilliant! You're so kind.

M: Well, as your agent for 50% of all takings from next year onwards *(taps signed document)* I mustn't let you get rusty. *(Puts model glider into hands of bemused pilot and retreats into distance with reel of string.)* Now, all clear above and behind? Take up slack!

Fade Out. The music of Delius blends with the swelling birdsong.

Political correctness corrected (1992)

Just as the tyrannies of Eastern Europe collapse, a new tyranny replaces them over in the West. No, I am not referring to the use of the word *Compulsory* for gliding safety meetings, out of place though it is in a free sport. I refer to PC, or Political Correctness, in the written and spoken word, which started in the USA and is spreading here. Simple words are becoming taboo, and ridiculous circumlocutions are substituted. Thus *fat* is prohibited;

Countryfolk at close quarters.

alternative body image is recommended, do you believe. If you said, "That fat old girl is dead drunk," about the only word not calculated to set the Orwellian thought-police screaming after you is *is*. The fact that the sentence was true in every detail would only exacerbate the crime.

Now some officious woman in England has pronounced that we shouldn't use expressions like, "I am handicapped by not having a word-processor," because it somehow demeans disabled people. What that dumb broad (might as well be hanged for a sheep as a lamb) does not know was that the word *handicap* is, and has been for at least three hundred years, a sporting term.

The Oxford English Dictionary says it derives from hand-in-the cap, to do with forfeit-money being deposited in a cap when wagers were being made. It then came to

refer to a way of levelling the odds between competing horses. So we do not have to abandon this term to satisfy the busybodies. I imagine that this lady (can't say *lady* any more: that's offensively patronising. Ed.) er, this person would have a great time with the gliding term now in the BGA competitions handbook, *Windicapping* – she would no doubt intone that it cruelly mocked those suffering from chronically irregular bowels.

Of course this Political Correctness lark may still spread to our sport, the PC-ists' total lack of any sense of humour rendering them immune to ridicule. In a couple of years' time we will find that it will simply not do to suggest that any pilot or glider is inferior to any other. Consequently competition reports in *S&G* will become even more unreadable by those who did not take part. Slow pilots will tactfully be described as having taken the scenic route. Pilots who land out will be said to have chosen to commune with nature or to have expressed their intense interest in farming by meeting the peasantry (No! Ed) sorry, country-folk at close quarters. Pilots who get lost will get the JJ Pewter Pot for creative navigation. Pilots who crash will get a European Community Medal for giving employment to the craftsmen of Membury or Poppenhausen, depending on the severity of the accident – and the prang itself will be termed a High-Ticket Alternative Arrival Mode. Everyone will be a winner.

Best of all the National Ladder will be laid out horizontally so that I can't be at the bottom of it any more – though I might drop discreetly off the right-hand edge.

Positively the last straw (1992)

Talking about atmospheric haze, how do you feel about the recent and permanent ban on stubble-burning? A traditional feature of the late summer months has now been erased from the glider pilot's repertoire. Those billowing flames will slide into folk memory, in which the rates of climb and the dangers of being roasted alive will both be monstrously exaggerated to impress our grandchildren. I am in two minds about this deprivation, if that is what it is, so each of these minds has been allowed equal time to express in heroic couplets (ie doggerel. Ed) the emotions to which it gives rise:

To a departed friend
Farewell, O blazing fields of stubble!
You often rescued me from trouble;
we loved the scent of burning straw
as fifteen gliders – or a score –
swooped up in searing plumes of smoke
(no matter if we cough and choke.)
Lament! We've lost our heart's desire –
the English countryside on fire.

To a polluting pestilence
Good riddance to the man-made pall
that over hill and vale did fall!
I deplored the element of luck
that racers gained from acrid muck,
bursting through a low inversion
to make a contest a perversion.
Rejoice! Without the farmers' gift
we'll use our wits to find our lift.

Eat ya heart out, Will of Stratford. There's lots more where those gems came from. (To be published over the dead bodies of the *S&G* subscription renewals department.)   ■

Tailpiece

WHY DO WE DO IT?

Some years ago a woman writer, whom I've never met, before or since, sent me a letter asking me to contribute a short chapter on gliding to a book she was putting together about lots of different sports, to appeal to the ordinary reader, whoever that is. The book never appeared, which doesn't surprise me because people aren't interested in sport in general. We all tend to specialise: people who love sea-angling don't want to read about ice hockey.

Nevertheless I described for her a flight during what I believe was the only one-class contest ever flown in this country, the Dart Competition of 1968. It was a good day, and of course in my piece I threw in the usual descriptive purple passages about the joys and beauties of soaring. We whizzed round a 110km triangle in about 90 minutes, which was not bad for the old Dart. Having landed, all the pilots said, "That was fantastic, let's do it again straight away!" There's one great advantage, incidentally, that gliding has over sex. The second time round, however, the wind direction and cloudbase had changed, the thermals were working differently, the sun had moved round – as it does – and the rolling countryside began to look completely unfamiliar. Everything was so altered that I got totally lost, in spite of having done the identical task only an hour before. I got horribly low, and eventually struggled home, but with a very poor time. In those days you could pick your best time, so I discarded the second flight with a shudder. It was expunged from the contest statistics, though never from my memory.

The point I was making to her was that gliding is like Cleopatra, "full of infinite variety." The same day, the same aircraft, the same task, but two utterly different soaring experiences. A Greek philosopher once said, "You never step in the same river twice." Well, you never fly in the same air twice.

Faced with the usual question from non-aviators, "What is gliding like?" or "Why do you glide, why don't you fly power?" I find myself reciting this little anecdote because it really makes the point – for me anyway. There's no reason why two identical cross-countries in a power plane should not take exactly the same time and cover exactly the same ground: indeed, you might be rebuked by your instructor if they did not. But not even our world champions can make gliding uniform and predictable. And they wouldn't want to either.

Index

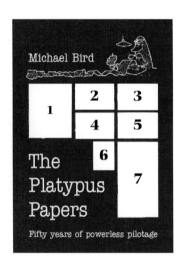

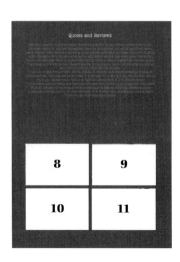

1. *With Robin May at the helm, Tony Hutchings actuates the radio-operated shutter on his Canon T90 to take one of gliding's most famous pictures. Number 13 is owned by Robin May (four times UK Open Class Champion in the same ASH-25), Steve Lynn and Platypus.*

2. *Mount Patterson, photographed by Marion Barritt from the ASH-25 en route to the White Mountains of California in 1995, the standard 1,000-kilometre milk run.*

3. *Joe Rise takes the starboard inner wing as Platypus pulls the pins, after an outlanding near Issoudun 1992. A party of French farmers, celebrating a friend's retirement at a vigorous age 60 (vive le Common Agricultural Policy!) lend enthusiastic assistance. Photo by Marion Barritt.*

4. *In Leszno, Poland, at the British 1994 Overseas Nationals, Plat celebrates his brand new winglets and a bit of extra span, for which there is no substitute. Natty soaring jacket is Plat's own design, consisting almost entirely of pockets. Photo by Marion Barritt.*

5. *A green valley in the South Island of New Zealand, photographed by Platypus from Justin Wills' ASW-17, 1999.*

6. *Veronica – Mrs Platypus – in 1977, the year she wrote "Advice to those about to marry gliding enthusiasts – DON'T!"*

7. *Platypus reflecting – in the wing of the syndicate Janus C, which ventured across Nevada, Utah and Arizona – on the 1998 High Country safari. In the background a Nimbus 3d also on the safari. Photo by Marion Barritt.*

8. *Platypus photographed with Marion Barritt at the 1995 "Geezerglide" – the Seniors Competition – at Seminole Lake Gliderport, Florida.*

9. *Platypus and his co-pilot in Janus C, Sam Whiteside, on Minden Safari in 1998. Photo taken at Ely, Nevada, by Marion Barritt.*

10. *Sunset in Monument Valley, Utah – the "Jeep from Hell" and Number 13 en route to Minden, Nevada, from the Texas Nationals, August 1995.*

11. *A curmudgeonly Platypus (the lowest form of mammalian life, according to experts), about to wade back into his natural element – water, not air!*